Sheffield Hallam University
Learning and IT Services
Collegiate Lea...
Collegiate Cres...
Sheffield   S...

D1625854

101 812 303 2

Sheffield Hallam University
Information Services
...m From Stock

ONE WEEK LOAN

1 5 JAN 2007   26 OCT 2009

-8 MAR 2007   1 4 DEC 2009

2 0 APR 2007

-2 MAY 2007

0 4 MAR 2008

-4 FEB 2009

MUSLIMS AND CRIME

For Ibrahim

Muslims and Crime
A Comparative Study

MUZAMMIL QURAISHI
University of Salford, UK

ASHGATE

© Muzammil Quraishi 2005

All rights reserved. No part of this publication may be reproduced, stored in a retrieval system or transmitted in any form or by any means, electronic, mechanical, photocopying, recording or otherwise without the prior permission of the publisher.

Muzammil Quraishi has asserted his right under the Copyright, Designs and Patents Act, 1988, to be identified as the author of this work.

Published by
Ashgate Publishing Limited
Gower House
Croft Road
Aldershot
Hampshire GU11 3HR
England

Ashgate Publishing Company
Suite 420
101 Cherry Street
Burlington, VT 05401-4405
USA

Ashgate website: http://www.ashgate.com

British Library Cataloguing in Publication Data
Quraishi, Muzammil
   Muslims and crime : a comparative study
   1.Crime - Religious aspects - Islam 2.Crime -
   Cross-cultural studies 3.Muslims - Crimes against -
   Cross-cultural studies 4.Muslims - Great Britain - Social
   conditions 5.South Asians - Great Britain - Social
   conditions 6.South Asians - Great Britain - Crimes against
   7.Pakistan - Social conditions
   I.Title
   364'.088297

Library of Congress Cataloging in Publication Data
Quraishi, Muzammil.
   Muslims and crime : a comparative study / by Muzammil Quraishi.
      p. cm.
   Includes bibliographical references and index.
   ISBN 0-7546-4233-X
   1. Crime and race--Great Britain. 2. Muslim criminals--Great Britain. 3. Muslim
criminals--Pakistan. 4. Muslims--Crimes against--Great Britain. 5. Muslims--Crimes
against--Pakistan. 6. Islamophobia--Great Britain. 7. Islamophobia--Pakistan. 8.
Crime--Religious aspects--Islam. 9. Criminal law (Islamic law) I. Title.

   HV6947.Q87 2005
   364.3'088'2970941--dc22
                                                                                                2005023192

   ISBN 0 7546 4233 X

Printed and bound by Athenaeum Press Ltd,
Gateshead, Tyne & Wear.

SHEFFIELD HALLAM UNIV
WL
364.088297
QU

Contents

Preface

This study represents the culmination of over four years of scholarship pursuant to evaluating the experiences of South Asian Muslims as both perpetrators and victims of crime and deviance. It is a comparative study of Britain and Pakistan and is framed by the following research objectives:

- to examine issues of offending and victimization amongst South Asian Muslim communities in Britain and Pakistan;
- to examine the ways Islamic criminal law (al-'uqūbāt) is understood and the impact of such understanding(s) on crime and social control among the sample;
- to explore the nature of Islamophobia and its impact on South Asian Muslims in Britain and Pakistan;
- to draw constructive policy-orientated conclusions in relation to offending and victimization experienced by South Asian Muslims.

The text constitutes a research monograph framed, but not restricted to, the objectives mentioned above. The data draws upon research undertaken in the UK and Pakistan between 1998 and 2002.

The impetus for undertaking the research was prompted, in part, by scarce British criminological sources in the field set against figures for a rapidly rising population of Muslims in prison (Wilson, 1999).

Terminology

Throughout the text reference is made to Arabic and Urdu words and abbreviations. Wherever deemed useful, footnotes have been included to provide immediate ease of comprehension. However, a complete list of such terms and expressions is contained in the Glossary.

The terms Asian, South Asian and Muslim are used interchangeably throughout the text. The reason for this stems partly from discrepancies in the way in which South Asian Muslims are classified in official statistics and existing academic literature. Whilst referring to studies about 'Asians' or 'Muslims', effort has been made to distinguish between South Asian Muslims from India, Pakistan and Bangladesh and other groups. The focus in this study is Muslims with ethnic origins in the Indian subcontinent, particularly Pakistan. This focus is important to within British contexts for a number of reasons. Not only do South Asians constitute the largest ethnic group of Muslims in Britain, but South Asian Islamic theology and culture has directly influenced how Britain has come to know Muslims (Ahmed, 2002).

By examining South Asian Muslim communities and crime it became plainly evident that use of certain terms to describe the people being studied was clearly problematic. That is to say, with the exception of prison statistics, official criminal statistics are more likely to record ethnicity and nationality rather than religion. Researchers are prompted to make the educated assumption that figures relating to offenders of Pakistani and Bangladeshi ethnic origin are most likely to be Muslim.

Particularly problematic is the use of the term 'race' and distinguishing it from the terms 'ethnic' and 'ethnicity' (Fenton, 1999). The cause of this problem is the frequently interchangeable use of these terms in popular, political and administrative discourses. However, there has been a positive movement amongst contemporary social scientists towards a qualified abandonment of the term 'race' in favour of 'ethnicity'. This argument is based upon a view that the term 'race' has traditionally been associated with a nineteenth and twentieth century 'white' Western Euro-American discourse which placed the 'whites', 'Europeans' or 'Caucasians' at the top of the evolutionary process within a 'science of races' (Fenton, 1999:4). Within such a science of 'races', 'race' was understood to control human capacities, culture and temperament in an essentially deterministic form.

It has become evident that some researchers firmly place the onus upon fellow scholars to begin a concerted effort to abandon the problematic use of the term 'race'. Scholars of ethnicity have expressed their discomfort with the uncritical way in which some researchers use terms such as 'mixed race', or 'slave-master' when researching this field (Small, 2004:81). Unless, however, use of the term 'race' disappears from community discourse, and in turn from legislative script, it remains an extremely hopeful if not entirely idealized quest. For example consider the 'Race Relations Act 1976', 'The Commission for Racial Equality' or the term inciting 'racial hatred' in the Crime and Disorder Act 1998.

What is perhaps less problematic is the use of the term 'ethnic', which has a greater claim to analytical usefulness within criminology because, according to Fenton (1999:4), it is 'not hampered by a history of connotations with discredited science and malevolent practice in the way the term race is'.

However, although the term 'ethnic' can be considered more favourably as an analytical term, it is not always clear what is understood by it. In this respect Richard Jenkins' 'basic anthropological model' serves to provide a useful guide. Jenkins believes ethnicity is about 'cultural' rather than biological differentiation; it is the outcome of 'social interaction'; it changes with 'the culture of which it is a component' and as a 'social identity is collective and individual' (Jenkins, 1997:18).

It is important to note, however, that an absolute rejection of the term 'race' is not advocated here but rather the use of it as an analytical term in criminological theory and conceptualisation. What prevents the complete abandonment of the term 'race', arguably, is the prevalence of a discourse where the idea of 'race' remains a powerful feature of commonsense thinking and of the ordering of social relations.

Comparative Criminology

An intrinsic aspect of this evaluation is its comparative nature. Awareness of the comparative dimension of crime is becoming increasingly more essential for criminologists (Nelken, 1997). Though the term comparative may apply to studies between two different regions within a country, it more commonly refers to studies between two countries, including those that are continents apart. As observed by Nelken (1997), there are clear strengths of comparative research when evaluating trans-national and cross-border crime including money laundering and tax evasion. Irrespective of the focus, comparative criminology can 'contribute to the theoretical development of criminology itself' (Nelken, 1997:472). It has also been argued that comparative work enables researchers to understand their own country better via an enquiry of how types of crime and crime control resonate with other aspects of a country's culture (Sztompka, 1990). Furthermore, comparative criminology can reveal the culture-bound quality of criminological work conducted within a particular nation, help overcome ethnocentrism, as well as injecting new life into a research area without resorting to stereotypes or denying differences between peoples and cultures (Nelken, 1997). A final justification for undertaking comparative research is not simply just to satisfy academic curiosity, but to help provide constructive policy initiatives drawing from jurisdictions where they have proved successful (Pakes, 2004).

However, undertaking comparative research prompts the consideration of significant cautions including questions of 'epistemology', 'different traditions of legal and criminological thought' and 'diverse international frames of reference' (van Swaaningen, 1997:14). The researcher must be clear as to what precisely is being compared and whether a particular study can be brought under the umbrella of a 'master theory' (Bierne, 1983). Bierne asserts that any comparative criminological study will encounter problems with comparative assessment, when the definitions and meanings of criminal behaviour may be different in each location or culture. This will apply whether the researcher adopts what Bierne (1983) refers to as the 'method of agreement' or the 'method of difference'. To address these issues Bierne suggests that the researcher concentrates upon the relationship between 'controllers' and the 'controlled' in different countries, rather than on the crimes themselves. Whilst there is inherent merit to this approach and it enables the observation of institutional practices, Nelken criticizes Bierne by arguing that surely one of the tasks of comparative criminology is to 'establish to what extent the meaning of crime in different countries is in fact comparable' (Nelken, 1997:473).

Further questions centre upon whether a comparative study should evaluate similarities or differences, and/or provide explanations or understanding. Also a pertinent issue is whether the researcher should examine culture as an explanation of crime, or crime and control as an explanation of culture? If the aim of the research is to discover similarities, the appropriate approach would be to explain the effects of similar factors in different situations, or to conduct a search for the 'functional equivalents' used in various societies to resolve common problems (Nelken, 1997). According to certain commentators, the adoption of the latter approach reduces comparative criminology to nothing more than an application of standardised sociological methods to new contexts, wherein culture is simply reduced to explanatory variables which can be used to explain why similar causes or problems lead to different outcomes in different societies (Sztompka, 1990).

If the goal, however, is to understand difference, where culture is understood as a highly complex process of meaning, greater attention would have to be paid to interpretative strategies. According to Nelken, in the latter case, comparative criminology becomes 'the hermeneutic exercise of trying to use evidence about crime and its control to resolve puzzles about culture' (Nelken, 1997:474).

A further useful framework is to consider comparative enquiry as an attempt to either widen or narrow the scope of the applicability of a concept. If the objective is to widen the scope, the work will attempt to seek commonalities and uniformities within cultural diversity. According to Sztompka, the consequence of such a strategy is that 'we know more, but we know less in the sense of detail, concreteness and specificity' (Sztompka, 1990:54). If the objective is to narrow the scope, the gain in 'informational content' (interpreting power) is paid by the loss of comprehensiveness (systemising power). In effect, we know more, but about less. Sztompka insists, virtually by definition, that these strategies are mutually inconsistent. However, he favours the second strategy of narrowing the scope. His justification is based upon the assertion that the so-called 'soft methodologies' of interpretation and hermeneutics are more appropriate than the search for positivist generalisations when it comes to unlocking the secrets of culture. Secondly, the increased opportunities for cultural contact and the (presumed) consequent growth in cultural uniformity mean that it is now the continued existence of cultural diversity that is worthy of investigation. We should, therefore, seek for divergences and uniqueness amongst uniformity, which should be understood as the results of past divergences and unique chains of historical traditions (Sztompka, 1990).

In overcoming the methodological obstacles discussed here, it was felt that a certain method that could go a considerable way towards narrowing the gap of mutual inconsistency between divergent and convergent enquiry, was a community study approach. The community study approach attempts to provide a more general context in the sense of providing a socio-economic profile of the social environment the respondents reside within. Some commentators, for example, may say it is nothing more than an attempt at shifting the conceptualised boundary of what 'society' or the social environment constitutes for a given group (Bierne, 1983).

However, in another sense a community study approach places the researcher within a manageable general framework. Although incapable of being representative of a society or societies as a whole, the 'wider than the individual' scope of a 'community' perspective provides an attractive venue from which to assess the wider applicability of concepts, such as 'Islamophobia'. Similarly, the dimension of direct contact with individual members of a chosen community allows the researcher to adopt 'soft' methodologies of interpretation towards the cataloguing and explanation of cultural diversity.

Outline of Chapters

Chapter 1 introduces the reader to the salient aspects of Islam, including Islamic history, theology and jurisprudence. Particular attention is given to Islamic criminal law. Pursuant to placing South Asian Muslims in context, Islamic movements in India (pre-and post-Independence 1947) are discussed in this chapter. The chapter concludes with an evaluation of the migration and demographic history of Muslims, and South Asian Muslims in particular, to Britain.

Chapter 2 presents a comprehensive evaluation of existing academic contributions to the field. A central theme to the present study is its interdisciplinary approach, and the literature reviewed demonstrates the diversity of secondary sources employed in defining the research field. The comparative nature of the study prompts an exploration of criminology in Pakistan. A picture emerges of scarce directly relevant criminological contributions to the research topic.

Chapter 3 develops the critical race theory (CRT)[1] perspective adopted by the study via an exploration of colonialism and the tracing of colonial practices into the post-colonial contemporary terrain. Further, the chapter evaluates the construction of the 'racialized criminal other' and discusses this with reference to colonial practices such as indentured labour and ethnographic showcases in addition to specific discriminatory legislative policies as demonstrated by the Criminal Tribes Act (Act XXVII of 1871). The concluding section of this chapter explores Islamophobia which is a phenomenon discussed throughout this study.

In order to comprehend the research findings it was necessary to compile a socio-demographic profile of each field location. Migration, settlement, social and political dimensions are explored with reference to the field locations in Lancashire and Karachi. Such information is deemed necessary in order to evaluate the research within local, national and international contexts. Due to comprehensive traditions of statistical data-gathering in Britain, the empirical information for Lancashire outweighs that for Karachi. However, again by adopting biographical and 'soft' methodologies, essential qualitative data ensures that the fieldwork locations have been given equal descriptive detail in Chapter 4 (Jupp, Davies and Francis, 2000).

Chapter 5 presents an analysis of the primary fieldwork conducted in Britain and Pakistan and may be considered as the core of the study. In making sense of extensive fieldwork, eight themes and priorities emerge from the study. These themes are: perceptions of crime; perceptions of policing; the festivals of 'Īd and their policing; 'no-go zones'; victimization; religion; offending and the 'racialized criminal other'.

Each theme is evaluated within British and Pakistani contexts. Differences and similarities are raised between the two field locations and relevant extracts from specific accounts of respondents are presented as part of the evaluation.

---

[1] Crenshaw et al., (1995) outline the history of the CRT perspective from its roots in the Black American civil rights movement of the 1960s. See Chapter 7 of 'Muslims and Crime'.

Taking each theme in turn, the work enabled a detailed examination of crimes that were of most concern to community residents in the respective sample locations. What emerges is the overwhelming nature of politically motivated crimes for the sample in Karachi and the threat of becoming a victim of racially motivated violence for residents in Lancashire. In both sample communities the study documents feelings of disenfranchisement and alienation from the respective police forces. In Karachi, political corruption and police brutality are commonly cited as points of serious concern for residents, whilst in Lancashire allegations of institutional racism and Islamophobia within the police and criminal justice agencies frame much of the discourse. In the UK, a case study of the celebration of the religious festivals of 'Īd by South Asian youth represents a bi-annual point of conflict between the police and the Muslim community.

The evaluation of Islamic criminal law, as comprehended by the samples in Pakistan and England reveal only superficial understanding of al-'uqūbāt, (Islamic criminal law) but almost universal acknowledgement of behaviour prohibited under the hūdūd[2] category. Although the study sought to examine incidents of offending in addition to accounts of victimization, it is accounts of victimization that appear to dominate the discourse generated.

The study also enabled meaningful consideration of the ways in which residents constructed the urban social reality as regards crime. In both locations residents spoke of 'no-go' zones, which were defined with reference to perceived likelihood of becoming a victim of crime in the identified locations. The work details how the construction of a 'no-go' zone is dependent on many variables including the personification of an urban space as occupied by the 'criminal other'. In the UK, a case study of the celebration of the religious festivals of 'Īd by South Asian youth represents a bi-annual point of conflict between the police and Muslim community.

The fieldwork data is essential to the formulation of theoretical propositions offered in Chapter 6. This chapter includes an evaluation of the relevance and applicability of the American Critical Race Theory (CRT) perspective to British and Pakistani contexts. The usefulness of the CRT perspective is discussed, in particular the examination of historical events to trace the construction of criminal and deviant groups through colonial practices (Mahmud, 1997).

The research findings are framed within an exploration of crime and deviance as experienced by South Asian Muslims within individual, community and global contexts. The inter-relatedness of each is explored before turning to policy-orientated suggestions stemming from the study in the Conclusion. This section also serves to summarize and highlight existing gaps in this relatively uncharted research field before suggesting directions for future research.

---

[2] Acts prohibited by God and punished by mandatory penalties see Chapter 1.

Acknowledgements

This text represents the culmination of research spanning over four years. During this period I have experienced the unique opportunity to meet and speak with innumerable people in Britain, Pakistan and America.

I am conscious that no amount of thanks stated here can precisely convey my gratitude for the important information, advice and support I have received over the years.

I would like to extend my heartfelt thanks to Dr Julia Wardhaugh at the Centre for Comparative Criminology and Criminal Justice, University of Wales, Bangor for her unwavering enthusiasm and invaluable advice during the whole research process. I am indebted to Claire Davis for all her help with administration relating to the research and to Laura Piacentini and Jenny Parry for their friendship and words of support. I am grateful for advice and guidance from Professor Roy King at the University of Wales, Bangor.

I am also grateful to the Area Study Centre for Europe, University of Karachi, for their hospitality and for providing me with a convenient research base for my work in Pakistan. In particular, I thank Dr Imdad Shah for his help.

I have also spent considerable time discussing the research with my former colleagues at the Centre for Ethnic Relations, University of Warwick and I thank them here for their words of advice. Thanks to Professor James Beckford; Professor Danièle Joly; Dr Christophe Bertossi; Dr Hideki Tarumoto; Professor Muhammad Anwar and Professor John Rex.

This study was only possible through the participation of respondents from the respective communities in Lancashire and Karachi and I thank them for their precious time and valuable thoughts. The research in Karachi was facilitated by the invaluable assistance of the following individuals who deserve specific mention: Shah Jahan Hameed, Abdul Rauf Hameed, Zahid Ali Jaffery, Shaukat Jahan Jaffery and Waqas Jaffery.

I am particularly indebted to Mr Mazhar Hussain for his wealth of knowledge about Haslingden and the Muslim community.

Finally, and most importantly, I would like to express my deepest gratitude to my family, in Britain and Pakistan, for their emotional and practical support, without which the research would not have been possible. I am indebted to my wife, Yasmine, for her words of encouragement and advice. I would like to acknowledge here the immeasurable love, respect and guidance given to me by my mother, Almass and my late father, *Mohammed Sayeed Quraishi* (1929-2004). May Allah (SWT) grant him peace in the hereafter.

There are many other people who have helped with my research and I extend my apologies for being unable to specifically mention them here.

Chapter 1

Islam and South Asian Muslims

دعنت داور/نا

The purpose of this chapter is to familiarize the reader with the salient aspects of Islam via an exploration of Islamic history, theology and jurisprudence (fiqh). The emphasis is on brevity, but whilst this necessarily involves exclusion of much material, matters are addressed as comprehensively as deemed essential to the understanding of the study.

This work cannot attempt to detail the richness and depth of Islam in a just manner. In essence, therefore, this chapter is a brief introduction to Islam in order to evaluate the significance of Islamic laws, culture and practices on the sample Muslim population for this study. It is not a sociology of Islam, nor a historical analysis of Islam, these matters are the subject of vibrant academic enquiry on a global scale by both Muslim and non-Muslim scholars[1].

The Qur'ān[2]

The origin of the 'five pillars' of Islam is the Qur'ān. The Qur'ān is considered by Muslim scholars to be a written record of the divine utterances made by the Prophet Muhammad (SAW)[3] in the course of his prophetic ministry starting around 610 CE and ending with his death in 632 CE (Cook, 2000).

The divine utterances of the Prophet Muhammad (SAW) have been distinguished in Islamic tradition from his normal speech and actions, which formed a second legal canon known as the hadīth (traditions). Following the death of the Prophet Muhammad (SAW) there were four Caliphs identified historically as being responsible for collating, maintaining and disseminating the text of the Qur'ān. There is general consensus amongst historians and traditionalists that the

---

[1] For an excellent text which evaluates historical and contemporary Islam see Ahmed, A. (2002) *Discovering Islam: making sense of Muslim history and society*. London, Routledge.
[2] The content and literary character of the Qur'ān defy brief categorization, and as a practicing Muslim I acknowledge a sense of injustice in being unable to convey the depth and richness of the text here. I must confine myself to a rudimentary and introductory position and hope readers will take their interests further by reading from the texts referenced.
[3] Arabic- Salallahu 'Alayhi wa Sallam-translates as-may the peace and blessings of Allah be upon him. Islamic etiquette when mentioning the Prophet.

official codex was adopted under the auspices of the third Caliph 'Uthmān[4] around 650 CE (Humphreys, 1991).

The Qur'ān is organized into 114 chapters or sūras. They are presented in order of length, with the longest near the beginning and the shortest at the end; this is with the exception of the Fātihā (opening). The Fātihā forms the first sūra and is an invocation repeated during the five daily prayers obligatory upon Muslims. The Qur'ān contains a fusion of prose and poetry and orthodox Muslims maintain that it is incapable of being satisfactorily translated from Arabic, although translations have been made in many languages, including the first in Latin in 1143 (Arberry, 1964).

The Qur'ān forms the first legal canon in Islam and reference to translated extracts from it shall be made throughout the course of this chapter. The Qur'ān defines what have popularly become known as the 'five pillars' of Islam. We shall consider each 'pillar' below.

The Five 'Pillars'

The Arabic word 'Islam' is a verbal noun literally meaning self-surrender to God as revealed through the message and life of his Prophet Muhammad (SAW) (Ruthven, 2000). The word 'Muslim' refers to one who so surrenders him or herself to God. Islam is the religion established among the Arabs by the Prophet Muhammad (SAW) in the early seventh century. The holy scripture of the Muslims is the Qur'ān, and according to Islamic tradition this was revealed to the Prophet Muhammad (SAW) through the agency of the angel Gabriel[5]. This took place partly in Makkah, the Prophet's hometown, in Saudi Arabia and partly in Medina, where he succeeded in creating a state in an otherwise stateless tribal society (Cook, 2000).

Islamic tradition records that although the revelation of the Qur'ān was complete before the death of the Prophet Muhammad (SAW) in 632 CE, he did not himself assemble the material into a definitive text. This was the responsibility of his successors, the Caliphs, who completed the task around 650 CE (Cook, 2000).

Islam spread from a small Arab community to a vast religious empire so that by 750 CE it 'threatened the frontiers of Latin Christendom in the Pyrenees and on the other stood astride the northern approaches to the Indian sub-continent' (Coulson, 1964:21). Islam had spread beyond the Arab peninsula into much of the 'civilized world, including Egypt, Palestine, Syria, Mesopotamia and the highlands of Persia' (Ruthven, 2000:28). Despite the historical and contemporary diversity of cultures encompassed by the Islamic empire, certain fundamental beliefs, practices and obligations, often known as the 'five pillars' of Islam, have come to represent the essential qualities of what being Muslim entails.

---

[4] In power 644-656 CE.

[5] In Arabic Jibreel, also known as Ruh al-Qudus (The Holy Spirit) and Ruh al-Amin (The Spirit of Truth).

The Declaration of Faith

Known in Arabic as the shahāda, the following constitutes the declaration of faith: 'There is no god but God; Muhammad is the Messenger of God'.

According to most of the classical authorities, virtually anyone could be considered Muslim as long as they proclaimed the shahāda, although historically the degree of conviction required of the believer became the subject of theological debate (Ruthven, 2000).

Salāh

Salāh is Arabic for prayer. Prayers are obligatory and should be performed five times daily. The prayers are timetabled as follows:

1. Fajr - dawn
2. Zhuhr - midday
3. ʿAsr - afternoon
4. Maghrib - sunset
5. ʿIshā' - night

There are no priests in Islam and no hierarchical authority[6]. As a consequence, congregational prayers are led by a learned person who knows the Qur'ān. He is chosen by the community and is known as an Imam. The five prayers contain verses from the Qur'ān and are recited in Arabic, but personal supplication can be offered in any language. In addition to these daily prayers, salāh is offered in congregation on Fridays. This is obligatory for men but not for women. Although the prayers are lead in Arabic, the 'sermon' or topics of discussion by the Imam are conducted in the language most commonly spoken by the congregation. Other congregational prayers are offered during the holy month of Ramadān (Tarāwīh), Muslim festivals of ʿĪd, and for funerals. Muslims must perform ablution before praying, this is known as wudū (partial wash), or ghusl (the washing or full bath).

Zakāt (Alms-giving or Compulsory Charity)

Zakāt is Arabic for 'purification' or 'growth'. Possessions are 'purified' by setting aside a proportion for those in need. Zakāt involves a payment of 2.5 per cent of ones net savings above a minimum, known as the nisāb, to be spent on the poor and needy. Zakāt implies that everything a person possesses belongs to God and therefore there is an obligation to share. In effect, the individual holds wealth in trust.

---

[6] Except in Shīʿte Islam.

Sawm (Fasting)

Fasting is obligatory upon Muslims for the duration of the month of Ramadān in the Islamic calendar. The conditions of the fast include abstaining from food, drink and sexual intercourse from sunrise to sunset. It is regarded as a means of self-purification also as self discipline and experiencing what the poor and hungry go through.

Hajj

Hajj is the annual pilgrimage to Makkah in Saudi Arabia. Makkah is where, according to Islamic tradition, God ordered Prophet Ibrahim (AS)[7] (Abraham) to settle his family and build the Ka'ba as the House of God. The Ka'ba is a cube-shaped structure at the centre of the sacred site at Makkah and it is towards the Ka'ba that all Muslims face when offering prayers. Hajj is only obligatory for those physically and financially able to perform it at least once in a lifetime. The Hajj itself takes place in the twelfth month of the Islamic year. Since the Islamic calendar is lunar both Hajj and the month of Ramadān can fall anytime in the British solar calendar. There is also a minor pilgrimage known as 'Umra, which can be undertaken at any time of the year.

Islamic Theology

Islam belongs to the Abrahamic family of faiths, which includes Judaism and Christianity. However, the cornerstone of Islam centres upon the concept of Tāwhīd. Tāwhīd literally means making one or unicity and it is the unicity of Allah[8] (SWT)[9] which challenges the Christian doctrine of divine incarnation (Ruthven, 2000).

The principal sources for the beliefs and practices of Muslims are the Qur'ān and hadīth, or traditions of the Prophet Muhammad (SAW). These will be discussed in this chapter in greater depth later. In simple terms, the Muslim believes in a single omnipotent God, creator and sustainer of the universe. The purpose for the creation of mankind is so that they may worship God. The following verse of the Qur'ān details how God created mankind:

> We created man of an extraction
> of clay,
> then We set him, a drop, in a receptacle
> secure,
> then We created of the drop a clot

---

[7] 'Alay salām - Peace be upon him.
[8] Allah literally means The God in Arabic.
[9] Subhana wa ta 'ala. One of the many ways of glorifying Allah. It translates as 'Glory be to Allah on High. Far removed is He from any imperfection.'

then We created of the clot a tissue
then We created of the tissue bones
then We garmented the bones in flesh
thereafter We produced him as another creature' (Qur'ān: 23:12-14 'The
Believers')[10].

Muslims believe in Adam (AS) as the first human created. Muslims also
believe in the existence of Satan ('Iblis) who was punished for failing to prostrate
before Adam (AS) (Qur'ān, 18:45). Adam (AS), as in the Bible, commits sin by
eating forbidden fruit, but in the Qur'ān he repents and is forgiven by God. Adam
(AS) is subsequently appointed as the first Prophet in a line of prophets ending
with Muhammad (SAW) (Ruthven, 2000). Therefore, as distinguished from
Christianity, mankind is created as innocent and there is no concept of 'original
sin' in Islam. All souls are created within the realm of God before they descend
into the foetus and are born into the world of humans as pure and innocent. The
soul is subconsciously aware of where it began its life and therefore struggles to
return to its creator.

This struggle marks the commencement of the 'test' for the Muslim. Life on
earth is considered a test for the eternal afterlife. Muslims are urged to use the
Qur'ān as their criterion (al-fūrqān) in distinguishing truth from falsehood. If they
live their life in accordance with the commands of God then they will pass into
paradise eternally. Paradise is the reward for conduct in accordance with God's
commands, and hell is the punishment for straying from these commands.

Since creation, the divine message for a Muslim has been sent to mankind
through prophets. The Qur'ān includes figures seen as prophets from the Judeo-
Christian tradition such as Noah, Abraham, Moses and Jesus.

Day of Creation, Day of Resurrection and Day of Judgement

For Muslims there are two extremities of human existence. First the meeting of
primordial souls at the dawn of existence for the 'original covenant', ritualized
during Hajj on the Plain of 'Arafāt where pilgrims stand, meditate and worship[11]
(Qur'ān 7:122). Second, the primordial end of time: the Day of Judgement[12]. The
first sūra[13] of the Qur'ān is known as the Fātiha or 'The Opening' and in it God is
described as 'Māliki Yawmi 'I-dīn' (Qur'ān 1:4), which literally translates as
'Master of the Day of Judgement'.

There are references to the Day of Judgement throughout the Qur'ān (for
example Qur'ān 4:40, and 20:100) and it is often mentioned together with the Day
of Resurrection (Qur'ān, 4:155) when all souls will be resurrected before being
called to account. Before these Days, life after death consists of paradise for the

---

[10] As translated in English: Arberry, A. (1955) *The Koran Interpreted.* Oxford.
[11] Day of 'Arafāt.
[12] Yāwm al-Ākhīr.
[13] Meaning chapter.

believer and doer of good deeds, and hell for the disbeliever and committer of sins. These periods of afterlife exist only until the Day of Judgement.

Festivals

In the Islamic calendar there are two major annual festivals, 'Īd al-Fīṭr and 'Īd al-Adhā, they are celebrated as traditional feast days. Each is celebrated by a congregational morning prayer, liturgically similar to Friday prayers (Peters, 1994). There is variation across Muslim countries as to how such festivals are celebrated due to cultural history and practices (Nigosian, 1987). In the UK, for some youths, the emphasis of the celebrations can be viewed as shifting from traditional family based occasions to public and communal activities[14].

'Īd al-Fitr[15]

This celebration marks the end of the Holy month of fasting in the Islamic calendar (Ramaḍān) and the first day of the Islamic month Shawwāl[16]. Although there is variation amongst different Muslim cultures as to how such festivals are celebrated, common practices include congregational prayers, families and friends meeting and the bestowing of gifts upon children.

'Īd al-Adhā

In the Bible Abraham's faith and devotion to God is tested and it is proven by his offer of sacrificing his son Isaac. In the Qur'ānic version Abraham (Ibrahim) offers his son Isma'il. This sacrifice is commemorated by Muslims globally at 'Īd al-Adhā (Feast of Sacrifice) and falls upon the conclusion of the Hajj. Sacrificed meat is shared out with the majority being distributed to the needy.

The festivals mentioned above represent those globally acknowledged by Muslims. However, there are also some festivals and memorial days which are celebrated amongst various sects and branches of Islam, but qualified or contested by others. These include, the Prophet's birthday (Mawlid an-Nabi); New Year Festival (Muharram) (specifically amongst Shī'ites) and the Night of Privilege (Lailat al-Bara'a) in remembrance of their dead.

Shī'a and Sunni Islam

The sample Muslim population for the present study consisted entirely of Sunni Muslims, hence only a cursory evaluation of Shī'ism is made here.

---

[14] See Chapter 5.
[15] Also often spelt Eid.
[16] Muslims also pay sadaqa al-fitr (welfare due) for the poor on this day.

Upon the death of the Prophet Muhammad (SAW) in 632 CE there emerged a crisis of authority regarding his successor, which arguably has never been resolved. Following Arab tribal custom, Abu Bakr (AS), the father of 'Aishah (RA)[17], wife of Prophet Muhammad (SAW), was elected leader in Medina. His appointment was opposed by the Prophet's cousin and son-in-law 'Alī (A.S), but his claims were bypassed on this and two subsequent occasions (Ruthven, 2000).

It was only upon the death of the caliph 'Uthmān that 'Alī (AS) inherited what he and his supporters considered to be his lawful inheritance. However, 'Alī's (AS) leadership was contested and he was unable to exert authority over the entire community. Although he gained the support of troops based troops based in Iraq, he met opposition in Syria under the command of Mu'āwiya. 'Alī (AS) attempted a compromise in the interests of unity but this collapsed. Some of 'Alī's (AS) supporters became so disillusioned that they left his camp and became known as the Khārijīs (Seceders) forming the first separate sect in Islam. One of them,'Ibn Muljam, subsequently assassinated 'Alī (AS).

'Alī's (AS) eldest son, Hasan (AS), compromised with Mu'āwiya and lived quietly in Medina. His younger brother Husseīn, on Mu'āwiya's death in 680, initiated a revolt but was defeated by Mu'āwīyā's son, Yāzīd, on the field of Karbala on the banks of the Euphrates (Ruthven, 2000). This moment is essential to the recurrent theme of sacrifice and martyrdom in Shī'ite tradition.

Shī'ism, therefore developed out of an allegiance to 'Alī (AS) and visible theological differences between Shī'ites and Sunni Muslims are demonstrated by each groups' interpretation and commentary of the Qur'ān, although originally the differences were based on disputes over leadership rather than doctrine.

By way of example, in the Qur'ān, sūra 3:110 begins: 'You are the best community (ummah) ever brought forth to men'. Shī'īte tradition has it that this should read: 'You are the best Imāms' (Cook, 2000). This essentially emphasizes the Shī'ite concentration upon the theme of 'Imamate' or leadership, and its necessity for salvation. Although there are Shī'ite branches that are similar to Sunnis as regards commentary on the Qur'ān, Shī'ism has developed its own theology and jurisprudence. In the sacred history of Shī'ism, during the administration of the 'Abassid caliphs, each Shī'a Imam was secretly murdered. The Twelfth Imam, Muhammad al Muntazār (the Awaited One), disappears altogether. He is considered the Messiah (al-Māhdī) and will return at the end of time to unify a divided world.

Most of the Muslims in the world would be considered Sunnis[18], however the Shī'ite followers of the Twelfth Imam[19] number approximately 80 million (Ruthven, 2000). The highest concentration of Shī'ites is found in Iran, where Shī'ism forms the state religion. However, significant populations also reside in Iraq, Afghanistan, Pakistan, Azerbaijan, Syria, Lebanon, Turkey and the Gulf.

Other branches of Shī'ites include Isma'ilis, followers of Isma'il (eldest son of Imam Ja'far). The descendants of the Isma'ilis include two prosperous modern

---

[17] Radi Allahu 'Anha/hi - May Allah be pleased with her/him.
[18] Followers of the practices of the Prophet Muhammad (SAW) - sunnah.
[19] Commonly known as Imāmīs or Ithnā 'asharīs (twelvers).

groups, the Musta'ian Bohras and the Nizari Isma'ilis. This latter group is the only Shī'ite group that claims allegiance to a living Imam, known as the Aga Khan. Often referred to as Aga Khanis, the Nizari Isma'ilis are found widely distributed in India, Pakistan, East Africa, Europe, North America, China and Central Asia (Ruthven, 2000). Significant numbers of Nizari Isma'ilis reside in Karachi, Pakistan, where they form an affluent community.

In Shī'ism Imams acquire a supernatural dimension and are considered bearers of the Divine Light of Truth. Amongst Shī'ites, such as the Twelvers, Imamate has reached a level of hierarchy comparable to the Christian priesthood.

There is some degree of overlap between Sufism (Islamic mysticism) and Shī'ism. Sufi masters are attributed with intercessionary powers attributed to 'God's friends' and according to the Shī'ite version of the declaration of faith 'There is no god but God, Muhammad (SAW) is the Messenger of God, 'Ali (AS) is the friend of God'.

Philosophical speculations have never been extinguished in the Shī'īte tradition. Mullahs exercise the right of ijtihād (independent interpretation of the sharī'ah), although they do not speak with one voice (Ruthven, 2000).

Sharī'ah[20]

The Qur'ān has been understood to contain the foundations for a Muslim society. It refers to general norms and values such as compassion for the weaker members of society, fairness and good faith in commercial dealings and in the administration of justice (Coulson, 1964).

According to some scholars the primary purpose of the Qur'ān is to regulate the relationship between an individual and God, rather than between an individual and others. So whilst the vast majority of the six hundred legal verses are concerned with religious duties, such as prayer and pilgrimage, only eighty verses deal with strictly legal topics (Coulson, 1964). However, some scholars assert the true number of verses dealing with legal topics is closer to five hundred (Kamali, 1991).

Nonetheless, the Qur'ān deals with a significant number of legal subjects, from female dress, division of the spoils of war, prohibition on consuming the flesh of swine and imposition of penalties for fornication. The Qur'ān also provides considerable depth as far as legal duties are concerned; for example the status of women, rules of marriage, divorce and inheritance (Doi, 1984).

In addition to the Qur'ān, scholars usually refer to three other sources or principles of Islamic laws. These are, the Sunnah[21], meaning the model behaviour of the Prophet Muhammad (SAW), the consensus of the Islamic jurists, and the methods of analogy (Schacht, 1950).

---

[20] Islamic Law.

[21] Strictly speaking the sunnah means the actual practice, whereas the hadīth refers to the documentation of the practice.

According to the late Joseph Schacht (in what has become known as the Schacht thesis), Islamic law as we know it did not exist during the lifetime of the Prophet Muhammad (SAW). Schacht maintained that although the Qur'ān laid down certain rules in family law, inheritance and ritual, the first generation of Muslims paid only perfunctory attention to these rules (Powers, 1986).

Schacht argued that the hadīth only came into existence at the end of the seventh century, as established by the qādīs[22] appointed by the Ummayad governors. As the group of legal specialists grew during the first decades of the eighth century there developed the ancient schools of law at Kufa, Basra, Medina, Makkah and Syria (Powers, 1986).

An important aspect of the Schacht Thesis is the 'back-projection' of legal doctrine to Prophet Muhammad (SAW) whereby there is an allegation against the Islamic legal scholars of effectively falsifying hadīth. Some critics of Schacht argue that whilst they agree with the general thesis they find it difficult to reconcile the discontinuity this thesis created between the Qur'ān and the formulation of Islamic law (Juynboll, 1983).

There has been a sustained evaluation of hadīth. In 1967 Nabia Abbot published an in depth examination of early papyri and concluded that hadīth has been transmitted both orally and in writing from the very beginning of Islamic history (Abbot, 1967). Reports about Prophet Muhammad (SAW) as transmitted by his followers were subject to rigorous scrutiny at each stage of transmission, and the 'phenomenal growth of the hadīth literature in the seventh and eighth centuries AD was the result of the progressive increase of parallel and multiple chains of transmission, not of fabrication of content' (Powers, 1986:5).

Further, the scholar Mohammed Azmi (1968) raises a number of important questions regarding the Schacht thesis; why would Muslim legal scholars of the seventh century confine themselves exclusively to discussions of rituals? Why would students project doctrine to weak authorities rather than to highly respected ones? Finally, how is it, if the bulk of hadīth were fabricated in the seventh and eighth centuries CE that we find traditions common in sense and form among the different schools of Islamic jurisprudence? (Azmi, 1968).

David Powers identifies two principal weaknesses in the Schacht thesis. Firstly that Schacht himself mentions that the Qur'ān contains many rules of Islamic law, such as family law and inheritance and that these were there 'from the very beginning'[23] but at the same time he argues that Islamic law did not begin to develop until 725 CE Secondly, Powers believes Schacht blurred the distinction between jurisprudence and positive law by claiming he was exploring the origins of Islamic jurisprudence and not positive law, yet continuing to write as though both only came into existence in 725 CE (Powers, 1986).

---

[22] Judges or legal specialists.
[23] See Schact, 1964:18.

Schools of Fiqh[24]

By the late Ummayad period (670 CE) sharī'ah had become controlled by the 'ulamā', a class of religious scholars whose authority was based on their knowledge of scripture but not spiritual power, and appointed judges (qādīs) who ensured the law was applied (Crone, 1987).

Many metaphors have been adopted by Muslim scholars to describe the diversity of doctrine in sharī'ah (ikhtilāf). All are seen as different but inseparable aspects of the same unity (Coulson, 1964). The earliest schools of thought were defined by geographical origin. Early legal schools were based in Iraq (Kūfa and Basra), Arabia (Makkah, Medina, the Yemen) and Syria. By the early ninth century the legal schools had evolved and formed what are now known as the classical schools of fiqh (Islamic jurisprudence). Of these schools eight survive today, four Sunni and four 'heretical' (Crone, 1987).

The four Sunni schools are named after their founding legal scholars: the Hanafī, Mālikī, Shāfi'ī, and Hanbalī. One Shī'ite school known as the Ja'farī, named after Imām Ja'far Sadiq, is also often acknowledged as a classical school alongside the Sunni schools. The Ja'farī school evaluates hadīth of 'Alī (AS) and the Imams alongside those of the Prophet Muhammad (SAW) (Ruthven, 2000).

In the early days of the development of the Sunni schools there was significant wrangling and tension. This arguably lessened in the late ninth century with the general acceptance of the basic scheme of the sources of law, gradually giving way to mutual tolerance and symbiosis demonstrated by the adoption of the doctrine of ijmā' (consensus of opinion) (Coulson, 1964).

The Hanafī School

This school was founded by Imam Abū Hanīfah (699-767 CE) in Kūfa in Iraq. Several legal doctrines and works have been ascribed to Imam Abū Hanīfah. Prominent disciples were Qādī Abū Yūsuf (d.798 CE) and Imam Muhammad bin al-Hasan al- Shaibānī (d.805 CE) (Doi, 1984).

The Hanafī school became the most influential of the Sunni schools. It was adopted by the 'Abassid caliphs and later by the Ottoman sultans. The Hanafīs, centred in Kūfa and then Baghdad, reflected the complex fluid society of lower Iraq with its mixed agrarian and mercantile economy, its ethnic variety and cosmopolitan culture (Humphreys, 1991).

In contemporary times this school is the most dominant in family and religious laws amongst the Muslims of the Balkans, Transcaucasia, Afghanistan, Pakistan, India, the Central Asian Republics, and China (Ruthven, 2000).

---

[24] Islamic Jurisprudence.

The Mālikī School

The Mālikī school was founded by Imam Mālik bin Anas al-Asbahi (713-795 CE) in Medina. The greatest contribution made by Imam Mālik was the codification of Medinan fiqh in his famous Muwatta. Some Muslim scholars assert this work is the most authentic compilation of hadīth (Doi, 1984). It is worth noting that some non-Muslim scholars have questioned the authenticity of the hadīth evaluated by Imam Mālik, asserting that he interpreted them in light of his own reasoning and the legal tradition of Medina (Coulson, 1964).

The Mālikīs were formed by the piety and the patriarchal, still quasi-tribal traditions of Medina, as reshaped by the Prophet Muhammad (SAW) and the early caliphs (Humphreys, 1991). The Mālikī school has been most influential in Morocco, Algeria, Tunisia and Libya (Ruthven, 2000).

The Shāfi'ī School

This school also emerged from Medina and was founded by Imam Muhammad Idris al-Shāfi'ī (767-820 CE). He belonged to the tribe of Quraish and thus was a descendant of the Prophet Muhammad (SAW). Imam Shāfi'ī was an expert on Hanafī and Mālikī schools (Doi, 1984). Amongst his famous works is a book on Islamic jurisprudence entitled 'Kitāb al-Risālah Fī-usūl al-Fiqh'. Perhaps his main work is the 'Umm'. This is a compilation of nine treatises put together by his pupils in Egypt (Crone, 1987).

Followers of this school are found mainly in the coastlands of Yemen, rural Egypt, Syria, Malaysia, Indonesia, East Africa and parts of India and Pakistan. It is less represented in the Middle East (Ruthven, 2000).

The Hanbalī School

The founder of this school was Imam Ahmad bin Muhammad bin Hanbal (780-855 CE). Although he was born in Baghdad the orientation of the school of thought is considered Medinese. His best known work is 'Al-Musnad'.

Imam Hanbal challenged the religious authorities of the Caliph Mu'tasim Billāh and was subjected to imprisonment and an inquisition. He rejected the concept of ijmā[25] and used reasoning by analogy only having exhausted the Qur'ān, hadīth, and legal rulings of the companions of the Prophet Muhammad (SAW). The Hanbalīs have been considered more as collectors of tradition rather than as lawyers proper (Coulson, 1964).

---

[25] Consensus.

Al-'uqūbāt[26] (Islamic Criminal Law)

Before discussing the Islamic classification of criminal offences it is worth noting that classical Islamic law books divide all human behaviour into the following five categories.

Wājib or Fard (Required or Obligatory)

Obligations deemed wājib or fard are divided into individual duties, such as prayers and almsgiving, and collective duties such as funeral prayers. Neglect of such obligations warrants punishment in this world and the afterlife, performance of such is met by rewards from God.

Harām (Proscribed or Prohibited)

Performance of harām activities warrants punishment in this world and the afterlife. Abstinence is rewarded in paradise. Harām behaviour includes a wide range of behaviour such as certain forms of theft, illicit sexual intercourse, and wine drinking. These offences are known as the hudūd[27] offences and specific penalties are prescribed in the Qur'ān.

Mandūb, Mustahab and Sunnah (Recommended)

These are acts which if followed are praise worthy but not required. Therefore, performance of the act is met with reward but its neglect does not result in punishment. They include supererogatory prayers, fasts and a variety of pious deeds.

Makrūh (Discouraged)

This is behaviour for which there is no punishment but for which there is reward for abstinence. Many contentious types of behaviour fall into this classification amongst the various schools of thought. Divorce is an example of what some scholars have deemed makrūh.

Jā'iz or Mubāh (Permitted)

This category refers to behaviour that is permitted and morally indifferent. That is to say, behaviour for which there is neither reward nor punishment.

Within al-'uqūbāt (Islamic criminal law) crime is divided into three categories: hudūd, qisās and ta'zīr (Khan, 1999).

---

[26] Islamic Criminal Law.

[27] Plural of Arabic hadd - which means prevention, restraint or prohibition, hudūd meaning punishment.

Hudūd

These offences are acts prohibited by God and punished by defined mandatory penalties, and such behaviour is deemed to violate a right protected by the Qur'ān. There is jurisprudential variation as to which behaviour firmly falls within this category. However, there is agreement that the following acts certainly falls within the hūdūd category: theft, adultery/fornication, and defamation (false accusation of adultery/fornication). A penalty imposed by virtue of being a divine right means that the proscription is deemed necessary for the protection of a fundamental public interest (Khan, 1999).

It is important to note that whilst there is often punishment for behaviour that violates the rights of another, for example failure to pay tax to the poor, breach of other divine limitations, such as missing prayers, is deemed a matter between the individual and God (Doi, 1984).

Qisās [28] *(Law of Equality)*

Qisās crimes include murder, maiming and battery (Khan, 1999). Although the offence and punishment are specified in the Qur'ān, the decision to punish rests with the closest of kin to the victim as 'avenger of blood' (Khan, 1999).

The closest of kin to the victim may decide to consent to the inflicting of the prescribed penalty, take compensation (diya) or pardon the offender. The ruler (State) may not pardon crimes incurring qisās penalties, however if the nearest of kin does grant a pardon, the ruler (State) may impose a ta'zīr punishment on the offender based on discretion.

Ta'zīr

Ta'zīr crimes are all those for which there are no specified penalties in the Qur'ān or sunnah. Therefore, this category permits the ruler (State) to determine what is deemed a crime and what penalties to impose in the public interest. This provides considerable freedom for the state to legislate against certain activities dependent upon changing social environments with the passage of time.

Al-'Uqūbāt in Pakistan

In 1947 Pakistan inherited significant pieces of its criminal legislation from the British colonial rule, namely the Penal Code of 1860 and Evidence Act of 1872. Together with a further piece of legislation, the Criminal Procedure Code of 1989, these acts form the statutory basis for the criminal law of Pakistan (Mehdi, 1994). In addition to this secular legislation, a system of Islamic law also operates in Pakistan.

---

[28] Derived from Arabic-qassā-meaning he cut or he followed his track in pursuit - therefore meaning law of equality or equitable retaliation.

We have observed that classical Islamic tradition and al-'uqūbāt classifies three forms of crime, but prominence has been given to hūdūd offences in Pakistan. In 1979 under the military dictatorship of General Zia ul-Haq, the Pakistan Penal Code was amended by what are collectively known as the Hūdūd Ordinances on 10th February 1979. The five laws promulgated are:

1. Offences Against Property (Enforcement of Hudud) Ordinance VI of 1979;
2. Offence of Zinah[29] (Enforcement of Hudud) Ordinance VII of 1979;
3. Offence of Qazf[30] (Enforcement of Hudud) Ordinance VIII of 1979;
4. Prohibition (Enforcement of Hudud) Order 4 of 1979;
5. Execution of The Punishment of Whipping Ordinance, IX of 1979.
   (Zahar-Ud-Din, 1997).

As part of General Zia ul-Haq's attempt to impose orthodox Islamic laws, Islamic education also became compulsory for students of higher education and a syllabus was prescribed by the University Grants Commission of Pakistan (Zafar, 1999).

It is not surprising therefore, that in Pakistan there is significant acknowledgement and awareness of hūdūd offences rather than the other classifications. However, the dynamics of criminal litigation, burdens of proof and legal procedure are not comprehended by most Pakistani citizens (Mehdi, 1994). Furthermore, the legal systems of India experienced a fusion of sharī'ah and British law. This was as a result of British or anglicised courts and personnel in India simply not possessing the legal expertise to apply sharī'ah and hence favouring English law (Coulson, 1964).

The application of English law in preference to any other was due to convenience rather than a determined proactive effort to overreach sharī'ah, according to some scholars (Coulson, 1964). Nonetheless, regardless of whether the superseding of sharī'ah by English law was intentional, the impact of the English legal system on the constitutional, criminal and civil legal systems of Pakistan remains plainly evident (Mehdi, 1994).

Islamic Movements in India (Pre-and Post-Independence 1947)

In the nineteenth century colonialism impacted dramatically upon all religious groups in India. For Muslims this contributed to the emergence of particular social and political movements, which emerged to defend the interests of the Muslim population. Such movements arrived in the UK with migrant Muslim populations originating from the Indian subcontinent, in turn transferring certain philosophies, practices and customs to the contemporary British Muslim Diaspora (Lewis, 1994). The principal socio-religious movements are briefly described here.

---

[29] Adultery.
[30] False accusation of adultery.

Deobandis

Founded in 1867 in Deoband[31] by Muhammad Ya'qūb Nanatawi (d.1888) and Muhammad Qāsīm Nanatawi (d.1887), this Islamic madrasah[32] re-emphasized traditional Hanafī jurisprudence (Metcalf, 1995). The Deobandis adopted a rejectionist philosophy that opposed non-Islamic influences, particularly from Hinduism and British rule. Whilst advocating traditionalism they simultaneously promoted and demonstrated a modernist stance in their adoption of Urdu (in addition to Arabic), rather than Persian, as their language of instruction and scholarship. Further, the Deobandis utilized modern technology to establish successful teaching institutions, structured timetables and syllabi, a postal donation system and an in-house printing press (Tayob, 1999).

One of the most important luminaries of the Deobandi madrasah was Maū'lanā Ashraf Ali Thanawi (d.1943) and his work highlighted the 'reformist Sufi' nature of the Deobandi tradition. Maū'lanā Thanwi was particularly opposed to the roles of Pirs[33] as intercessors between individuals and God (Lewis, 1994).

Most of the support of the Deobandis came from Muslim elites. Whilst their initial attempt at achieving relative unity amongst Muslims was not realized, the movement was essential to the formation of the revivalist movement known as the Tablighi Jama'at.

Tablighi Jama'at

This movement was formed by a graduate of Deoband, Maū'lanā Muhammad 'Ilyas (d.1944) (Ruthven, 2000). He was inspired by the Qur'ānic injunction of sūra 3:109 'You are the best nation ever brought forth to man, bidding to honour and forbidding dishonour, and believing in God' (Arberry, 1964:59). In order to fulfil the aim of building the 'best nation' Maū'lanā 'Ilyas adopted a firmly apolitical philosophy to encourage individual moral and spiritual well-being in accordance with the teachings of Islam. Essential to the programme and fulfilment of this goal was an emphasis on door-to-door revivalist activity (Lewis, 1994).

The Tablighi Jama'at has spread to more than ninety countries from Malaysia to Canada and is particularly active amongst settled British Muslim communities (Ruthven, 2000).

---

[31] Deoband is a village approximately 100 miles north of Delhi, Uttar Pradesh, India.

[32] Seminary.

[33] Pir - Persian for Elder, often also referred to in Arabic as shayk (elder) or Murshid (guide), considered to be able to lead devotees on the mystical path.

Barelwis

Originating from Bareilly, Uttar Pradesh, India, this movement was founded by Ahmad Raza Khan (d.1921). In sharp contrast to the Deobandi philosophy, Barelwis defend the concept of Pirs. According to Barelwi tradition, which stems from the Qadiri Sufi Order, Pirs act as intercessors between man and God. Barelwis therefore emphasize the importance of shrines for devotees to seek the benefit from the 'friends of God'. This view is so far removed from that of the Deobandis that each group had condemned the other as kafrs[34] (Lewis, 1994).

The Jama'at-I-Islami[35]

This movement was founded in 1941 by Abul A'la Maududi (d.1979), a journalist advocating the need for modern ijtihād[36] and a critic of the Sufi orders. He was also critical of religious scholars whom he considered to be keeping Islam in the Middle Ages, in addition to his critical thoughts on westernization in general, viewing it as a form of barbarism (Lewis, 1994).

His vision was to establish Muslims in positions of social and political leadership with the object of transforming Muslim countries into Islamic ideological states (Lewis, 1994).

Jama'at-I Islaami gained considerable support from the Mohajirs[37] in Karachi upon the partition of India in 1947. The majority of theoreticians, and intellectuals of the Jama'at-I Islaami political party, academics, lawyers and journalists come from this group (Lewis, 1994).

As a large urban-based political movement it has limited following amongst rural Pakistanis and, considering that the vast majority of Pakistani migrants to the UK are from rural locations, it therefore has limited support in the UK (Ruthven, 2000).

Having presented the essence of Islamic belief systems, legal frameworks and criminal law, we now turn to a discussion about the concept of migration in Islam, more specifically the migration and demographic history of Muslim populations in Britain. The impact of colonization of India by the British is briefly raised here and explored in greater detail in Chapter 2.

Muslims and Migration

Migration and displacement are firmly rooted historical experiences for Muslims. The Islamic calendar or 'Hijri'[38], which literally translates in Arabic as 'of

---

[34] Arabic for unbelievers.
[35] Popularly known as the 'preaching party' or the 'faith movement'.
[36] Arabic for scholarly effort.
[37] Arabic for migrants, refers to refugees from India to the newly formed Pakistan upon the Partition of India in 1947.
[38] Migration in Arabic is 'Hijrah'- see Glossary.

migration', originates from the migration of the Prophet Mohammed (SAW)[39] and his followers from Makkah to Medina on 16 July 622 CE (1 AH)[40]. Since the practices of the Prophet constitute part of the sources of law in Islamic jurisprudence, the concept of 'Hijrat' has always held an extremely significant position within Islamic theology.

It must be emphasized that the commonly understood interpretation of migration due to economic or geo-political factors, although applicable to Muslims, does not define the true meaning of hijrat for Muslims. One must acknowledge that the Prophet's Flight to Medina necessarily involved the establishment of the first Muslim proto-state (Lings, 1983).

The Flight has been interpreted by many Muslims to signify a:

> ... renouncing of territorial, tribal and even familial ties in order to establish a political community based on shared religious belief....because the purpose of the political order is to institutionalize the shared religious beliefs of the Muslims, the glue that binds the community is shared religion, rather than shared race, language, territory, culture or history (Mahmud, 1997:658).

The ideological renunciation of territory, language, culture, race or history is only possible for the Muslim by the creation of 'belonging' to the ummah. The ummah is the global community of people who practice Islam. Thus the State cannot have fixed territorial demarcations and therefore 'the borders of the Islamic State reside and move with the ummah' (Mahmud, 1997:659). It is important to keep such concepts in mind when discussing the experiences of migration and displacement for Muslims in the nineteenth, twentieth and twenty-first centuries, for it explains the duality of Muslim identities. The Muslim has been considered to hold two identities, 'one is immediate, social, spatially particular and the other is historical, ideological and global' (Mahmud, 1997:659). Furthermore, an account of Hijra serves to highlight the importance and theological significance of migration for Muslims globally.

However, the focus of this work is the particular migration of Muslims from the Indian subcontinent to the United Kingdom and this demands an exploration of colonialism. The impact of colonialism upon the contemporary socio-political canvas for Muslims is pervasive and inseparable from contemporary discussions of identity, marginalization, sovereignty, nationhood and State.

Definitions, experiences and reactions to crime and deviance, in the present context, can only be fully understood within a broader acknowledgement of historical fact, political constructions and the dynamics of colonialism.

The experiences of Muslims in India during the colonial period (1858-1935)[41] have, to some extent, been shared with other colonized communities

---

[39] Peace be upon him, these words acknowledge Islamic etiquette when addressing the Prophet - see Glossary.

[40] AH, i.e. The Year Of The Flight, Hijrah - see Glossary.

[41] In 1858 the Government of India Act was passed. This Act formally transferred the empire of the East India Company, which had been trading in India since 1600, to the

globally. However, specific colonial practices such as indentured labour contracts of Indians in Africa and the construction of criminalized Indian tribes by the British, make the Indian experience unique.

The deconstructing of the 'Muslim' stereotype as 'fanatic', 'fundamentalist', 'terrorist', 'book-burner', and 'wife-beater', is essential to our understanding of how Muslims are perceived as deviant, as well as accounting for Islamophobia and feelings of exclusion by Muslims in Britain (Runnymede, 1997). Through understanding the process of victimization light is shed upon some forms of criminal offending, particularly racially motivated attacks (Webster, 1994).

Muslims Migrating to the United Kingdom

The first known South Asian Muslim presence in Britain is directly related to the activities of the East India Company some three hundred years ago. Men from the Indian subcontinent were recruited into the merchant navy and were known by the British as 'lascars'[42] (Adams, 1987). These sailors were drawn mainly from Yemen, Gujarat, Sind, Assam and Bengal. A number of small communities of lascars developed in port towns and cities throughout Britain, particularly in and around London (Runnymede Trust, 1997). By the outbreak of the Second World War seamen from South Asia accounted for some twenty per cent of the merchant navy (Lewis, 1994).

During the nineteenth century the Muslim population increased and a number of businesses were established. By 1842 some three thousand lascars were visiting Britain annually. The opening of the Suez Canal in 1869 enabled sailors from Yemen to form small settlements in London, Cardiff, Liverpool, South Shields and Tyneside. The settlements contained 'zāwiyahs'[43] for the performance of ceremonies for births, marriages, circumcisions and funerals. Hence the Yemeni population constitutes probably the oldest permanent Muslim community in Britain, although presently they only number about 15,000 (Halliday, 1992).

At the turn of the twentieth century there emerged a group of Muslim intellectuals in Britain. They had a profound impact upon the development of Islamic institutions and raised awareness of the needs of the few Muslims in Britain at the time. One such figure was a lawyer from Liverpool, named William Henry Quilliam. He was a convert to Islam and founded 'The Crescent', a weekly journal in print between the years 1893 to 1908. Liverpool was also the location for the Islamic Institute, the Broughton Terrace Mosque, the Medina Orphans

---

British Crown following the 'War of Independence' or 'Great Mutiny' of 1857. In 1935 Britain finally declared that provincial governments should be chosen by Indian voters following the growth of Indian nationalism, which was initiated by the birth of the Indian National Congress in 1885. British rule in India ended in 1947, with the establishment of an independent Indian republic.

[42] Probably an Anglo-Indian interpretation of the Arabic word 'askari' meaning soldier.

[43] Small mosques or prayer rooms.

Home, the Muslim College and a Debating and Literary Society (Runnymede Trust, 1997).

The first mosque in Britain was opened in Woking, Surrey in 1889. The mosque was financed by Shah Jehan, ruler of Bhopal State in India. In 1910 a group of prominent British Muslims, including Lord Headley, established the London Mosque Fund to enable the construction of a mosque in the capital. By 1941 the East London Mosque Trust had purchased three buildings and converted them into London's first mosque.

King George VI donated land for the construction of a mosque in November 1944 in exchange for land in Cairo for a new Anglican Cathedral. After extensive fund-raising the mosque was finally completed in 1977. A large mosque had been open, however, in Bradford at Harris Street since 1959.

The first large-scale in migration of Muslims to the UK began in the 1950s. According to Ceri Peach, the probable Muslim population of Britain in the 1950s was about 23,000. By 1961 it had reached 82,000 and by 1971 it was about 369,000 (Peach, 1996).

This initial migration was overwhelmingly of men. They had been encouraged to arrive in Britain as guest workers to alleviate the labour shortages caused by the Second World War. There were particular shortages in the textile and steel industries of Yorkshire and Lancashire. These initial workers came primarily from the Mirpur District of Azad Kashmir, former West Pakistan, or from the North West Frontier Province (both in present day Pakistan) or from the Sylhet area of north-eastern Bangladesh, former East Pakistan (Runnymede Trust, 1997).

It is worth noting that in all the regions cited above, there was a longstanding tradition of men migrating for lengthy periods to other areas or countries to raise money for their families. Although the areas were predominantly rural in nature they were certainly not the most impoverished districts in the subcontinent, in fact most were prosperous well-irrigated farming regions (Lewis, 1994).

For the Mirpuris the extra push factor came in the form of the Mangla Dam project prompted by the signing of the Indus Waters Treaty in 1960. The building of the dam involved a colossal resettlement programme. Approximately two hundred and fifty villages were affected requiring the resettlement of about one hundred thousand people. Many of those affected received compensation for their resettlement and significant numbers used these funds to finance their journey to Britain (Runnymede Trust, 1997).

Significant migrants also arrived from India and approximately one sixth of those who came during the 1950s and 1960s were Muslim. As with migrants from the former East and West Pakistan the origin of migration for the majority was contained to a few areas of India. The majority of these Indians came from Gujarat and, in particular, from the three districts of Baroda, Surat and Bharuch (Peach, 1996). Gujarati-background Muslims are particularly influential in several northern towns in Britain where they have established Muslim schools, seminaries, and mosques. Significant numbers also came from Indian Punjab.

During the mid 1960s animosities developed under increasingly oppressive nationalistic regimes in East Africa. The intolerance of African rulers, such as Idi Amin, eventually led to the expulsion of one hundred and fifty thousand South Asians from Kenya and Uganda, some of whom settled in the UK. The South Asian presence in these two countries was a direct product of colonial indentured labour practices. Approximately fifteen per cent of those expelled were Muslim, including those of the Ismai'li sect of Islam (Lewis, 1994:14).

During the 1970s we also began to see the development of substantial communities in Britain of Muslims from Turkey, the Middle East and North Africa. The latest Muslim migrants to Britain are from Somalia, Iran, Iraq, Afghanistan, Kosovo and Bosnia. A considerable student population from Malaysia has also contributed to the cultural diversity of the contemporary British Muslim population, although this trend has been slowing recently due to the South-east Asian economic crisis (Runnymede Trust, 1997:14). In addition to those born into Islam, Britain is home to some five thousand converts[44], about half of whom are of Black-Caribbean origin (Nielsen, 1992).

Philip Lewis, in his work 'Islamic Britain' discusses the difficulties in accurately quantifying the Muslim population of Britain. Estimates place the Muslim population somewhere between three quarters of a million and two million (Lewis, 1994). The Runnymede Commission Report on British Muslims places the current figure between 1.2 and 1.4 million based upon the 1991 Census.

The cause for uncertainty stems from the traditional exclusion of questions regarding religious affiliation in the Census. Nonetheless, what is clear is that more than fifty per cent of Muslims in Britain claim their country of ethnic origin to be Pakistan (Runnymede Trust, 1997). If we include those Muslims from India and Bangladesh, eighty per cent of the total Muslim population of Britain claim ethnic origin from the Indian subcontinent (Peach, 1994). Therefore the significance of South Asian culture and practices of Islam become central to our understanding of Muslim life in Britain.

With regard to the settlement pattern and population distribution of Pakistanis and Bangladeshis, the two largest Muslim groups in Britain, we see most reside in urban localities. It should be stressed here that the terms Pakistanis and Bangladeshis refer to those born in the Indian subcontinent that have migrated to Britain, as well as those born in the UK of Pakistani or Bangladeshi ethnic origin. According to analysis of the 1991 Census by Muhammed Anwar, 14 per cent of all Pakistanis lived in Birmingham and 9.5 per cent in Bradford. The other main locations of settlement were Rochdale in Lancashire, Kirklees in West Yorkshire and Newham and Waltham Forest in East London. Most Bangladeshis appear to have settled in the Metropolitan constituencies of Bethnal Green and Bow, and Poplar and Canning Town (Anwar, 1996). These trends tend to be confirmed by the latest Census in 2001. Fifty four per cent of the Bangladeshi population resides in the London region, whilst the Pakistani population is more

---

[44] Muslims refer to converts as 'reverts' to acknowledge the philosophy that all individuals are born Muslim and embark upon a life journey of rediscovering their true faith, hence 'reverting' to Islam.

dispersed including significant representation in the North West of England and West Midlands (Home Office, 2005).

The location of Pakistani and Bangladeshi communities is a product of several factors, which have shaped the dynamics of chain migration from the Indian subcontinent since the 1950s. As mentioned previously, the demand for semi-skilled and unskilled labour in the textile industries of Lancashire and Yorkshire made settlement for Pakistanis, seeking employment during the guest worker stages, an obvious option. The manufacturing industries of the Midlands provided another location-specific pull factor.

After the initial settlers arrived cultural practices such as sponsoring kinsmen enabled chain migration to take place. Philip Lewis details how Pakistanis have experienced a four stage pattern of migration initiated by the pioneers, then 'chain migration' of unskilled male workers, followed by the migration of wives and children, and finally the emergence of a British-born generation (Lewis, 1994).

Chapter 2

Muslims and Crime: The Existing Picture

This chapter presents and evaluates the existing criminological contributions to the research field. An evaluation of the current academic contribution to our understanding of crime and deviance committed by and upon Muslims illustrates the present scarcity of meaningful criminological studies in this field. Such scarcity prompts the researcher to evaluate relevant sources attainable by adopting an interdisciplinary approach and briefly highlighting the usefulness of accounts from an anthropological, ethnographic or journalistic perspective. The final part of this chapter evaluates the current position and qualities of the discipline of criminology in Pakistan, emphasizing the strengths and limitations to the few studies available.

Principal Studies

Very few meaningful studies of offending by South Asians in Britain exist today. This applies to studies of all ethnic groups of South Asian racial origin. Therefore any criminologist preparing to investigate the dynamics of law, crime, deviance and victimization, pertaining to Muslims in particular, would be hard-pressed to locate valuable contributions.

The neglect of such important criminological enquiries could stem from the traditional under-representation of South Asians, and indeed Muslims, in criminal statistics. However, if a minority population has been perceived to have experienced prolonged periods of relative conformity, law-abiding behaviour and stability amidst social circumstances often cited as conducive to deviance, law breaking and instability, then surely this warrants detailed academic attention?

The prompt for further research in this field may come from the recent publication of figures for the Muslim inmate population for the UK that claim a doubling of Muslim prisoners from 1994 to 1999 (Home Office, 1999). The same report emphasized, however, that 'while a disproportionate number of Black people were behind bars compared with whites, the proportions for the Asian communities were not much different'[1].

Mawby and Batta conducted one of the earliest studies of South Asians and crime in 1980 (Mawby and Batta, 1980). Their work, 'The Bradford Experience', evaluated the Asian crime rate in Bradford, with its overwhelmingly Muslim minority population, for the period 1970 to 1979. The study evaluated official court and police records in addition to council and education department statistics. The

---

[1] (Guardian, 8/09/1999:12).

authors concluded that the Asian crime rate was 40 per cent of the non-Asian crime rate and that Asian juveniles in particular were under-represented in criminal statistics. Regarding offending patterns, there were proportionately higher levels of offences against the person (assault and sexual violence), whereas property offences were particularly under-represented and juvenile offences were overwhelmingly confined to shoplifting.

The sophistication of this early study is demonstrated by its inclusion of female offending. The authors observed that Asian females were least likely, of their sample, to be involved in offending. The research also claimed that violent offences tended to be intra-racial (Asian upon Asian). It must be stressed, once more, that their findings were based overwhelmingly on official statistics. The authors attempt to account for the patterns of offending by focusing upon Asian juvenile crime. It was noted that, during 1976 and 1977, Asian juveniles were heavily over-represented as receiving police cautions, were more likely to be fined and less likely to receive Care Orders or be sent to Detention Centres or Borstal than other groups.

Mawby and Batta attributed this to the fact that Asians were less likely to have previous convictions and more likely to come from stable family backgrounds than other groups. Furthermore, the authors observed, Asians were less likely to be involved in serious offences than other groups and this accounted for their high level of cautions, as opposed to other sanctions. The Bradford Experience concluded that despite the cultural and structural problems facing the Asian minority, crime rates for all age groups were lower than those for the non-Asian population of Bradford. Furthermore, crimes committed by Asians tended to be intra-racial and of a less serious nature according to Mawby and Batta.

The study, although commended for initiating criminological enquiry in this area, is victim to a number of limitations. The work evaluated court and police records exclusively at the expense of, arguably, more meaningful data attainable through victim and self-report surveys. The work was locality-specific focusing upon an Asian population predominantly of Mirpuri ethnic origin. One must note that the Bradford Experience is now quite outdated, demonstrated for example by its use of the term 'immigrant' to describe the sample. This brings into question how relevant the study is to our present day understanding of Asian criminality.

The authors looked towards strain theory for an explanation of low Asian crime rates. It was felt that Asians, in contrast to other disadvantaged groups like Black African and Black Caribbean youth, are less likely to respond in a criminal way to their failure to achieve goals by legitimate means. According to the authors, Asians are more likely than Black people to adopt alternative employment strategies such as self-employment.

Mawby and Batta suggested that relatively low Asian crime rates were due to informal control mechanisms exerted by the community and family upon youths and that this was likely to continue to second generation Asians, particularly those in large Asian communities. A pilot study that was undertaken shortly after the Bradford Experience, however, suggested that 'the closely-knit family structure which has often been held to account for low Asian involvement in crime may be beginning to breakdown' (Mair, 1986:155). Further, more recent commentators have suggested that whilst relative conformity may have been true in the past, it may not have been true for some Asian groups in the 1990s (Jones, 1993; Webster, 1997).

The contemporary view, regarding the Asian crime rate, is one predicting the emergence of higher levels of involvement in crime. This view rests upon the assumption that community and family informal control mechanisms are weakening, resulting in integration and assimilation to British norms by Asian youth. This view assumes gradual integration will equal higher crime for the Asians but denies the duality and complexities of culture-formation, which is not simply a one-way process.

A further factor, raised in support of the prediction of higher Asian crime rates, is that as pressures such as unemployment increase for a minority group we shall see a corresponding upturn in crime for that group. It is yet to be seen whether high Asian unemployment rates can be credibly linked to claims of increased crime rates for Asians. A recent article details the reports of the Labour Force Survey 1999 which claims that the unemployment rate for ethnic minority men is more than twice that for white men. Further, that the unemployment rate for Pakistani and Bangladeshi men is three times the rate for white men[2].

A further prediction of increases in the Asian crime rate rests purely upon a demographic analysis. Pakistanis and Bangladeshis have the most youthful demographic structure of any group in Britain. Following the observation that reported crime is largely a youth phenomenon, according to some researchers the number of crimes by Asians is predicted to rise (Jones, 1993).

However work by the Policy Studies Institute in 1993, which predicted higher crime rates for Asians, has been criticized as flawed and based on 'patchy and inconclusive' evidence. The claim by the PSI was 'based on assumptions that rates of offending among similar age groups in the Black community would translate straight across to young Pakistanis and Bangladeshis'[3]. Therefore, it appears that Mawby and Batta's view that informal control mechanisms were likely to continue to second generation Asians is proving, on the whole, to seem like a valid projection. However in the absence of any substantial studies exploring Asian crime, and the nature of these control mechanisms in particular, the relative conformity of Asians remains an observation that is based essentially upon statistics[4].

The next useful study was published almost ten years later with the work of Robert Waters (Waters, 1990). Waters' work, entitled 'Ethnic Minorities and the Criminal Justice System' did not specifically focus upon Muslim or Asian defendants but since it was based on a survey in Leicester where the Asian and Muslim population density is significant it is included here.

Waters' study represents of contributions to the race and crime debate and more specifically the results of a sample of social inquiry reports of ethnic minority

---

[2] (Guardian, 11/12/1999:21).

[3] (Guardian, 8/9/1999:12).

[4] Note the contribution by Ali Wardak (2000) later in this chapter regarding Asians and social control.

defendants in Leicester prepared by the Probation Service. This study sought to assess whether there was evidence of 'race bias', whether 'positive or negative'; whether the reports had a 'coherent framework for presenting race'; what changes were evident in practices of report writers regarding race; and whether more specific questions on race could be formulated for social inquiry report writing (Waters, 1990:98).

The study highlights inadequacies of the national classification system of ethnic minorities since Waters was prompted to devise one that attempted to reflect the demography of Leicester. Leicester's Asian population at the time of the study constituted 22.1 per cent of the total for the city. Waters' classification does not relate to British citizenship but instead adopts the cultures of the different ethnic groups as the main criteria. Therefore the Asian group was broken down into Gujarati, Punjabi, Muslim and Other Asian, and whether they were born in India, Britain or East Africa.

Waters' qualitative analysis enabled the development of a typology based on the individual styles and approaches to race, ethnicity and culture adopted by social inquiry report writers. Three types were evident according to Waters, these were 'culture conflict', 'racial marginality' and the 'alien offender' (Waters, 1990:115). The category of culture conflict was further broken down threefold to evidence of second generational culture conflict between British-born defendants and parents having emigrated to the UK; gender related culture conflict, such as with arranged marriages, and first generational culture conflict where 'the defendants were all the subject of primary immigration having well established lifestyles in their earlier country of origin' (Waters, 1990:115).

Waters' second typology, racial marginality, described those reports where 'the race of the defendant appears, from the confluence of the social inquiry report, the legal variables of offence and previous history and the sentencing outcome, to be either marginal or a secondary factor in explaining the outcome' (Waters, 1990:129). Waters claimed that the majority of cases in his sample fell into this category.

Waters' third typology, the 'alien offender', constituted the smallest in his sample. This classification is 'built up by combining legal and extra legal variables in such a way that the defendants appeared to be receiving sentences that had additional severity from them not belonging to this country, for offending against white values, or for having lifestyles that marked them out for different treatment' (Waters, 1990:144).

Waters concludes that this typology enabled representation of evidence of a coherent framework for addressing issues of ethnicity and race by social inquiry report writers, although this was implicit rather than explicit. Further, for Waters the study appears to demonstrate a tendency for a proactive and positive attitude rather than ambivalence or exclusion by the probation service towards ethnic minority defendants. However, Waters stresses further research is required to fully assess the practices of social inquiry report writing and racial bias. His study demonstrates a need for a repertoire to be employed by social inquiry report writers addressing questions of race and culture.

The impact of social inquiry reports on sentencing should not be underestimated and if defendants are assessed by probation personnel actively prejudiced or ignorant of cultural or religious norms and values, this only exacerbates perceptions of the criminal justice system as racially biased in absolute terms by ethnic minority defendants. Preliminary feedback from current research into the qualitative experiences of Muslim prisoners indicates significant dissatisfaction with, and perception of racial bias within the probation service by defendants (Quraishi, 2002a)[5].

Remarkably, the next significant study of Asian crime did not emerge until the mid 1990s with the publication of the Keighley Crime Survey (KCS) by Colin Webster in 1995. Although this work concentrated on victimization it contains a substantial contribution to the examination of Asian offending which warrants special consideration here. The KCS forms part of a longitudinal study funded by the Research and Planning Unit at the Home Office. The Survey primarily documents and evaluates the experiences of crime and racial harassment among young people in Keighley, West Yorkshire.

The Survey sought to evaluate the experiences from the viewpoint of both the perpetrator and victim of crime and racial harassment. A welcome theoretical framework adopted by Webster enabled the evaluation of offending and racial harassment on the same continuum. The author criticizes research that views the aforementioned as distinctly exclusive phenomena. Webster found that young people who were involved in racially motivated abuse also tended to be involved in more general anti-social behaviour (Webster, 1995).

Webster found high levels of racial victimization for both Asian and white youths in Keighley, and that each ethnic group used the same terms as the others to describe experiences of threat and exclusion (Webster, 1995). According to Webster, both white and Asian youths have learned to construct racism primarily as an experience of victimization rather than as an objective understanding of themselves as 'superior' if they are white and have resources, or 'inferior' if they are Asians and are denied these resources because of racial discrimination (Webster, 1995:7). Webster believes that the Survey has uncovered a form of racism that is understood primarily as that of being victimized for both white and Asian young people.

The Survey also examined economic and social conditions of young people in Keighley and revealed highly segregated patterns between white and Asian young people that can exacerbate racial tensions, according to the author. With regard to theoretical observations, Webster focuses on the 'usefulness' and 'predictive power' of control theory. He expresses an interest in whether youths' 'attachment' to social institutions predicts delinquency and anti-social behaviour, applied not only to offending but also to victimizing behaviour. This question was raised with specific reference to racially motivated crime (Webster, 1995:13).

The author also explores the concepts of offending and victimizing experiences in terms of location and a 'proprietorial relationship' to 'space' and

---

[5] Unpublished field notes by M. Quraishi for: *Muslims In Prison: A European Challenge*, Beckford and Joly, CRER, University of Warwick 2003.

'territory'. In particular, he questions whether racial harassment is primarily an experience of location (Webster, 1995:43). The main findings of the Survey provide data for analogous studies throughout the UK. The Survey supported previous public perceptions, conveyed via Bradford Safer Cities project, local schools and the police, of a youth crime problem in Keighley. Webster recommends that agencies need to deal with victimization of young people, as well as offending, through victim support.

In Keighley levels of victimization amongst both Asian and white groups were high. Over one third of the total Asian sample had been victims of some crime. This went to 37 per cent for personal violence and 40 per cent for vehicle damage. Many of these experiences of victimization had happened recently, that is, in the year before the Survey was conducted. Webster found that most of the racial violence against young Asians in Keighley occurred in the parks, town centre and at school (Webster, 1995:15). Webster attributes many aspects of this racism to territorial disputes and the conflict between areas within the town. Young people were viewed as being in the 'wrong area' at the 'wrong time' in relation to highly racialized perceptions of public space (Webster, 1995:15).

As previously mentioned the KCS primarily evaluated experiences of victimization but intelligently acknowledged that issues of offending are inevitably intertwined with such experiences. Indeed, Webster states that part of the study's objective was to measure the prevalence of offending among Asians. Webster believes that there is concern among the criminal justice agencies that offending by young Asians was increasing. Unfortunately, Webster does not expand upon the source of such concerns but does warn against the dangers of hypothesizing about the issues that could ignite a similar escalating spiral of police attention that constructed notions and discourses of the 'Black criminal' (Webster, 1995:39).

Webster expressly notes the lack of significant studies of Asians as offenders quoting the Bradford Experience as the only study he was aware of at the time that specifically dealt with the issue. The author also notes difficulties in comparing Asians with non-Asians, for example, young Asians are more likely to be males, working class, unemployed and living in poorer areas than young whites (Webster, 1995:39).

The KCS offers a unique evaluation of criminological issues pertaining to an under-researched and little known population. Whilst the work may be regarded as locality-specific, like the Bradford Experience, one cannot avoid acknowledging the theoretical and methodological merits of this significantly comprehensive study. By treating issues of offending and victimization as inter-related it provides a clear blueprint for any future research in this field.

The KCS could have greatly benefited, however, from an evaluation of the older Asian generations and their perceptions of offending and victimization. The inclusion of the latter appears more significant when one considers the dynamics of control theory and the exploration of the key agents of conformity within a Muslim community. Further, although perhaps not within the remit of the study, it would have been interesting to evaluate the influence of Islamic law, theology and culture upon the majority Muslim sample in Keighley.

However, it appears as if Webster goes some considerable way to address these issues in his subsequent paper entitled 'The Construction of British Asian Criminality 1997'. This paper details observations from a six year study of delinquency and victimization among Pakistani, Bangladeshi and white young people in the north of England. The work involved a multi-staged methodology comprising a four year quasi-longitudinal study of seventy victims and perpetrators of racial violence and offending, a self-report crime survey of 412 13-19 year old Asian and white young people, and an in-depth follow-up study of 65 young people.

According to Webster, there exists a recognizable public discourse about Asian masculine criminality informed by the local and national media. His principal argument is that a stereotypical image of 'law abiding' young Asian men has now shifted to labels of 'criminality, drugs violence and disorder'. Webster asserts that the origins of such 'racializing and criminalizing' discourses are not only found in the control culture (media, police, criminal justice system) but also among white and Asian young people on the street and among certain sections of the Asian parent culture (Webster, 1997).

An important observation by Webster is demonstrated by his emphasis upon deconstructing cultural attributes such as 'Muslim', 'Asian' or 'Black' in criminological discourse. According to Webster, use of such categories constructs stereotypes which 'deny the fluidity and variety of cultural identity and human behaviour' (Webster, 1997:66).

Webster observes that 'Asianess' is viewed within two extremes of discipline and disorder. The author critically evaluates Orientalist ideologies, and quotes Edward Said's observations that such ideologies are based upon a 'homogenizing and unchanging idealization of Asian family life and community structure' (Webster, 1997:66). The author's analysis of media discourse regarding Asians and crime prompts him to warn that the 'folk devil' as an Asian youth has arrived in Britain (Webster, 1997).

Within this discourse the parent culture is perceived as law abiding and respectable whilst the youths are perceived as out of control. Webster notes that whilst the police and popular discourse reflects reality to a degree, it also serves to:

> Amplify and exaggerate popular racism in the wider context of a demonization of Islam, accompanied by stories of Islamic fundamentalist youth groups like *Hizb ut-Tahrir*, of Asian inter-gang rivalries, vigilante groups, drug-crime, no-go areas and the like (Webster, 1997:67).

Webster predicts that where this has happened we can expect to see a corresponding change upwards in the police statistics of Asian arrests, delinquency and crime rates. The author believes that the police, in their public discourse, and with tacit support from the Asian community leaders and elders, have evolved a split between what is deemed a respectable parent culture and elements of a youth culture, which is constructed as being involved in drugs, crime and disorder.

Further, it is suggested, that such discourse is designed to elicit crime intelligence from the parent culture so as to reassert discipline and control over elements presumed to be out of control. Tacit police-community co-operation is designed to solve an alleged crime problem for the police whilst addressing cultural and religious control problems for elders and community leaders arising from conflicts within Asian Muslim communities.

According to the author, these conflicts are found between 'traditional and modernist versions of Islam, between Islamic and Muslim social identity and westernization, and tensions arising from very high levels of youth unemployment and low levels of educational achievement' (Webster, 1997:68).

Webster believes current control strategies will fail because Asians will come to feel racialized and criminalized by the police since the 'rough and respectable' split only succeeds in 'painting them with the same brush' (Webster, 1997:68). Such a strategy, according to the author, will eventually backfire on the police as the parent culture withdraws its support, as the police become increasingly perceived as 'picking on their youth'. Furthermore, Webster stresses that neither the police nor the parent culture are able to rationalize to Asian youth the cumulative and persistent 'failure to take up educational and employment opportunities against the background of decline in the demand for unskilled labour' (Webster, 1997:68).

Webster also details the representation of Asian juveniles in the official criminal statistics, noting that they have significantly lower rates than whites or Blacks who have very similar rates of offending. The author adds:

> Although there is certainly cause for concern about offending levels among *young people in general* involvement in offending is widespread within this group - at present there is little evidence to suggest that offending among Asian young people is any more worrying than offending among other groups, certainly not so as to support a growing moral panic about Asian crime (Webster, 1997:69, author's emphasis).

Webster notes that any increase in Asian crime could simply be a reflection of the demographic structure of the Asian population, with Asians having the most youthful population and its members falling within the peak-offending category of 14-20 years (Webster, 1997:70). As previously discussed, such predictions have yet to be actualized (Guardian 8/9/1999:12). However, if we focus on the Pakistani Male Muslim prison population, official statistics reveal an incarceration rate of 260 per 100,000 population, compared to 184 for whites, 74 for Bangladeshis and 93 for Indians (Home Office, 1999).

Webster reviews the work of Smith (1994), which indicates that although Asians are as much the victims of racism as are Black people, this is not manifested in high levels of criminality. Smith believes this refutes the idea that there is a generalized racist bias in the police and criminal justice system. Furthermore, Smith argues that Black people are subject to bias but that this is not necessarily racist and may be justified in so far as Blacks have a higher rate of offending. It is difficult to see how Smith could justify such bias on any account and Webster is critical of researchers such as Smith, who do not disaggregate specific offender groups.

Webster, by referring to the study of street crime in Lambeth by Burney in 1990, criticizes researchers, such as Smith, for failing to observe that a small group of Black recidivists 'sully the reputation of the majority of wholly law abiding young Black men' (Webster, 1997:72). Similarly with regard to Asians, following Webster's own research, a failure to acknowledge that a small hard core of Asian recidivists are not representative of the whole group will lead to problematic misrepresentations of Asian youth (Webster, 1997).

The author argues that Asians may be equally subjected to racial bias as Blacks but it is just that racism towards Asians takes different forms. Webster does not expand upon the forms such racism may take for Asians but not for Blacks. An important point raised by Webster is that 'Asian' like 'Black and White', has been deemed to imply a sociologically and culturally homogenous group, whereas the reality reveals widespread differences and variations within and between such communities. For example, Webster notes that although Muslim communities share common concerns they are also marked by enormous differences. Although he does not expand upon such differences, one assumes he is referring to the linguistic, cultural and racial differences exhibited between Pakistani, Bangladeshi and Indian Muslim communities. It is a complex matter however to comment on issues where these communities are united and where any differences may be problematic.

With regard to Islam, Webster makes the following statement:

> Islam as such cannot explain how Muslims behave, or how they might/ought to behave. Other factors outside of Islam must be invoked (Webster, 1997:79).

It is not precisely clear what Webster means by this statement. Any cursory evaluation of Islamic hadīth will provide, according to Muslims, the perfect role model for ideal behaviour, certainly at least how they *ought* to behave. Considering the majority of Webster's research population are Muslim, a detailed assessment of religious teachings, practice and influence upon youth conformity and community self-identity would substantially contribute towards deconstructing the Asian offending puzzle.

The only study directly relevant to the present work was published over the research period and is entitled: *Social Control and Deviance: A South Asian Community In Scotland* by Ali Wardak (Wardak, 2000).

Wardak's study represents qualitative research into the lives of a largely Pakistani Muslim community in Edinburgh, Scotland. Interestingly, in his introduction, Wardak outlines the lack of preceding research in this field commenting that the Scottish Pakistani population is often researched under the general categories of 'Asians', 'South Asians' or 'people from the Indian subcontinent' and it rarely specifically addresses issues of crime (Wardak, 2000:1).

The text is presented in two parts; the first evaluates the organization of the Pakistani community in Scotland and specifically how it is established as an agency of social control. The second part of the book addresses deviance amongst the Pakistani sample. Central issues addressed by Wardak include how experiences of exclusion and discrimination have impacted upon the Pakistani community in

Edinburgh as well as a theoretical assessment of community. The latter is understood at three levels, the national, the local and the kinship level. For Wardak, a central question is how social order is maintained by the Pakistani community and the

> Extent to which the community's social institutions promote order and regulate behaviour through the social bonding of members to its moral and social order (Wardak, 2000:3).

In order to assess this, Wardak focused on the institution of the family, biraderi (kinship and friendship networks), the mosque and the Pakistan Association, Edinburgh and the East of Scotland (PAEES). Wardak concluded that the family is the most important agency of social control in the community (Wardak, 2000). The study is situated within the context of comparatively low official crime rates amongst the Pakistani population of Scotland, despite significant levels of socio-economic deprivation amongst this group. The author argues that one explanation for this is that exclusion has meant a more self-reliant community opting for self-employment for stability and sustenance rather than engagement in deviance and crime. Processes of social bonding further maintain such stability expressed via institutions such as mosques, the family and the PAEES. According to the author, these institutions define what is 'right' and 'wrong', 'morality' and 'immorality', 'normality' and deviance', and 'rewards' and 'punishments'.

Wardak allows the sample to define what it understands as deviance. The study, therefore, merits from not restricting or pre-empting the discussion to simply an objective definition. Deviance is evaluated according to identified norms and Wardak developed a typology against which to assess his sample. This four-fold typology consisted of 'conformists, accommodationists, part-time conformists and rebels'. Wardak emphasized that the first two categories depicted 'non-deviants' whilst the latter two indicated 'deviants' (Wardak, 2000:5).

Wardak's study is unique in that his fieldwork included self-reporting of delinquency amongst the Muslim youths. However, Wardak chose not to include self-reported delinquency data in his text, instead focusing on what he terms the 'sociological category' of deviance. The exclusion of the self-reporting of delinquency appears a curious omission given the importance of how individuals construct their own sense of what is morally or legally wrong. An exploration of self-reported delinquency can only seek to illuminate the picture beyond mere statistical records for Muslim youth involvement in crime.

Wardak's theoretical framework rests upon the work of Travis Hirschi and his social control theory (Hirschi, 1979). Social control theory evaluates an individual's social bond to society based on the four essential elements of 'attachment', 'commitment', 'involvement' and 'belief'.

Wardak's study benefits from evaluating the Scottish Muslim population from within an historical framework providing a detailed exploration of how colonial practices lead to the exclusion and stereotyping of early migrants from the Indian subcontinent to Scotland. His conclusions include, inter alia, an assertion, based upon empirical findings that racism and prejudice experienced by the Scottish Pakistani population has increased over time and that this is true for Pakistani and Bangladeshi populations throughout the United Kingdom (Wardak, 2000:242).

Such prejudicial treatment has arguably contributed to a process of exclusion of Pakistanis and Bangladeshis from the spheres of employment, housing, sports, social, cultural and political institutional life of wider society (Wardak, 2000:242).

Wardak highlights Pakistani social, cultural and socio-political movements as evidence of counter-strategies to the experiences of exclusion, citing 'bhangra' discos, local campaigns for Muslim schools and the establishment of the Muslim Parliament of Great Britain by way of example. According to Wardak, all of these exclusionary factors have resulted in a more 'closed' Pakistani community in Edinburgh.

Wardak's study also evaluates concepts of identity in so far as identity contributes to exclusionary practices and differences between the 'Britishness' and 'Pakistaniness' of second generation British-born Pakistanis and that of their parents.

Wardak's work goes some considerable way towards assessing the multiple-layers of 'identity' and self-definition by Muslims in the UK, highlighting that whilst second generation British-born Pakistanis identify more strongly with their 'Pakistaniness' than their 'Britishness', they aspire to a concept of community that is based on modernist religious and cultural interpretations (Wardak, 2000:243).

The author concludes that the family, and in particular 'parental authority' operates as the most important mechanism of social control. Complementary to such control is that exerted by the mosque-school where an Islamic belief system further compounds 'parental authority'. A fundamental social phenomenon of kinship and friendship ties (biraderi) is given significant prominence in Wardak's work. He describes what is known as 'lina and dina'[6], or giving and taking, which creates interdependence and social cohesion amongst members of the community.

Closely related to this phenomenon is family honour ('izzat)[7] and Wardak explains that for his sample honour was related to high caste, a large number of males in the family, social or political influence in Britain or Pakistan, professional or educational qualifications, generosity, honesty, piety and wealth (Wardak, 2000). However, whether any individuals or families were considered honourable was down to subjective evaluation by members of the community itself and not necessarily according to an objective fulfillment of the qualities mentioned.

Reflecting on the function of the mosque classes, Wardak concludes that the congregational and collective prayers further operate to promote a common moral community.

The final significant agency of social control in the PAEES. and Wardak's study provides a clear example of the mobilization by marginalized communities to

---

[6] Lina (Urdu) - to take or receive, dina (Urdu) - to give or bestow - see Glossary.
[7] 'Izzat (Urdu) honour - see Glossary.

articulate and meet specific needs through institutionalization, all be it within a semi-formal framework.

Interestingly, the PAEES. includes dispute resolution within its remit, including domestic violence and feuds between community members. Although it is not discussed by the author, it is interesting to ask whether 'users' approach or are directed to the PAEES in addition to or instead of 'official' or outside agencies including the police? Do members of the community come firstly to the PAEES and is their referral based on low levels of trust with the police and courts?

Wardak's study provides essential building blocks for further criminological enquiry in this field. He has taken the suggestions of criminologists conducting earlier studies (see Mawby and Batta, 1980) that the answer for traditional low rates of deviance amongst Asians may lie with the institutions of the family and religion.

However, Wardak's study prompts further questions and wider evaluations. For example, whilst Wardak's study includes essential discussions about identity at an individual, community and national level, arguably an assessment of identity at a global level and how this impacts on feelings of exclusion and Islamophobia are increasingly more relevant to the British Muslim Diaspora (see Runnymede, 1997).

Further, by concentrating upon issues of social control, issues of strain are perhaps understated. To elaborate this point, Wardak concludes that the 'family' and 'parental authority' operate as the most important mechanisms of social control. Whilst this certainly may be the case for the sample evaluated, these very institutions are equally often the cause of strain and deviance for individual Muslims. This is particularly so where a disjuncture exists between the idealized goals of parental figures and the aspirations of their British-born children.

Similarly, the kinship or friendship structure could effectively operate to exclude who 'is' and who 'is not' deemed acceptable by those empowered within the community. Therefore, rather than promoting social cohesion, such informal institutions are also capable of perpetuating conflict, strain and marginalization.

These observations are prompted by Wardak's work and are therefore not retrospective critiques of his particular study. In fact, Biko Agozino, in the foreword to the text, accurately observes that Wardak's study serves as a pretext and prompt for further research perhaps in communities that are less peaceful than the Pakistani community of Edinburgh (Wardak, 2000:x).

The contributions of Mawby and Batta (1980), Webster (1994, 1997) and Wardak (2000), as we have seen, may be cited as the principal studies that have specifically evaluated Asians and crime. Any further work discussed here represents either analysis of Home Office data or contributions from the inter-related disciplines of race, education, anthropology and journalism. Indeed the relative scarcity of meaningful criminological contributions prompted enquiry into the diverse yet related disciplines mentioned.

One of the most recent comprehensive statistical evaluations of ethnic minorities in the British criminal justice system is offered by Marian FitzGerald in 1997. The author details the history of migration by ethnic minorities generally in addition to evaluating Home Office data on ethnic minority offending and victimization.

Regarding demographic information FitzGerald evaluates figures from the 1991 Census and confirms the increasingly acknowledged fact that Asians have the most youthful population structure in Britain (FitzGerald, 1997). FitzGerald notes important socio-economic differences among and within the minorities themselves. In terms of their economic status, the Indian population is not dissimilar to, and in some respects is more privileged than, the average for whites[8]. Blacks are much more disadvantaged than whites, and the Pakistanis and Bangladeshis, in some respects, 'face greater disadvantage' (FitzGerald, 1997:38).

A further valuable evaluation by FitzGerald involves her observation that the academic and political debates over race and crime in the UK have tended to focus on the Black groups as the cause for concern with regard to offending. This debate, however, has been conducted quite separately from the more recent, less academic and relatively politically consensual discussion about racial harassment. The author notes that the main focus in the latter debate has tended to be the Asian. Both debates, according to FitzGerald, about offending and victimization have been conducted in 'highly ethnicized terms' (FitzGerald, 1997:36).

FitzGerald outlines the phenomenon known as 'Paki-bashing' (racially motivated assaults on Asians) during the 1970s and early 1980s, and comments how remarkably little attention has been given in British criminology to issues of race and crime (FitzGerald, 1997). The author criticizes criminologists, such as the British New Left Realist School, for relying too heavily upon secondary sources, and argues that their attempts to explain the apparent differences between ethnic groups have come close to stereotyping.

FitzGerald's evaluation of the Home Office statistics is informative and succinct. She notes that ethnic monitoring of the British prison population began in 1983 and since 1985 has produced data on a comparable basis over time. FitzGerald acknowledges the main limitations of the prison data in that it is impossible to differentiate between British ethnic minorities and those normally resident abroad (although this was refined in 1992) and that they refer to a very small proportion of all offenders, the rest making up the hidden figure of unrecorded crime.

The analysis of the statistics prompts the author to state that little is known about actual rates of offending by different ethnic groups, as reported by themselves in self-report surveys. FitzGerald quotes one study, however, which suggests comparable rates for Black and white youths with low figures for Asians (Bowling, Graham and Ross, 1994). The author claims that there is little information regarding whether crimes committed by different ethnic groups are more or less likely to be reported. The author claims that there is some evidence that Black people are disproportionately brought into the system through proactive policing (Skogan, 1990).

---

[8] A recent article publicised the affluence of Indian Patels in Britain. The annual 'Rich List' compiled by Dr Philip Beresford claims that if your surname is Patel you are seven times more likely to be a multi-millionaire than if your name is Smith. Beresford claims there are 37 multi-millionaires named Patel and a further 500 Patel millionaires in Britain. Stuart, J. The Independent 27/06/2000, The Tuesday Review 'Meet Britain's Richest Family' page 7.

Overall ethnic minorities are five times more likely to be stopped by the police than whites (36 stops per 1,000 in the first year of recording compared to 6.8 stops per 1,000 for whites). There are variations in the level of overrepresentation both between and within forces (FitzGerald, 1997).

These show a starker overrepresentation of Black people in some areas, which is often masked in the aggregate data by average or lower than average rates for the Asian groups. FitzGerald notes, however, that this also suggests that part of the variation between areas may be explained by differences in their ethnic makeup. The situation may also become clearer, according to the author, in the future because police forces have been required from April 1996 to collect the figures broken down into: white, Black, Asian and other.

An important pattern suggested by the Commission for Racial Equality is that fewer Black people are likely to be cautioned than whites, rather than charged and prosecuted, whilst Asians are (if anything) more likely to be cautioned. The figures for Blacks, according to FitzGerald, appear to be largely explained by the lower likelihood that they are prepared to admit the charges brought against them. Further evaluation by FitzGerald supports previous research that has consistently shown that both Black and Asian defendants receive longer prison sentences than white people (Hood, 1992). However, FitzGerald notes that once allowance is made for all relevant factors the rate of imprisonment for Asians in Hood's sample was if anything, slightly lower than for comparable whites.

Regarding Black and Asian defendants, the author concludes that Blacks are disproportionately more likely to enter the criminal justice system and disproportionately less likely to be filtered out at each of the key stages, while the picture for Asians is much less clear but is rather in the opposite direction right up to the point of sentencing. This may no longer be the case (Spalek, 2004).

One commentator believes the difference between Asian and Black crime rates is 'not too difficult to explain'. According to Bob Roshier, the Asian community incorporates a substantial business and professional class, which, combined with the 'the relative cultural separation of the Asian community generally' provides avenues for 'conventional need fulfillment that are lacking in the West Indian community' (Roshier, 1989:109). Roshier also believes that differences in the controlling influence of the family relationships between the two communities are substantial, with Asian communities demonstrating the constraining influences of close family ties.

In terms of victimization, FitzGerald notes that while ethnic minority victims differ in the extent to which they said they thought the incident was racially motivated, Pakistanis are the most likely to perceive racial motivation. The author expresses her concern that while the UK data on ethnic minorities is more comprehensive than in other European countries it is still 'patchy and unreliable'. According to FitzGerald, this is principally because it has treated offending in isolation from victimization, ignored important commonalities among different ethnic groups and taken insufficient account of the limitation of official statistics (FitzGerald, 1997). The author suggests that some inferences can be drawn about the likely involvement of different groups in offending from their demographic and socio-economic profiles. She continues by explaining that Asians are a very diverse group, with Indians dominating numerically.

In 1991 19 per cent of whites were aged 0-15 years compared with 22 per cent of Blacks and 29 per cent of Indians. The figures for Pakistanis and Bangladeshis were 43 per cent and 47 per cent respectively. The author suggests that it is only because of socio-economic and demographic factors that we are facing an upsurge in criminal involvement in these groups; but that it will continue to be masked as long as it is subsumed within a generic Asian category (FitzGerald, 1997).

Whilst emphasising the need to evaluate demographic and socio-economic factors the author stresses the need to supplement this with an examination of the role of discrimination at every stage of the criminal justice process. She argues that Asians (particularly Pakistanis and Bangladeshis) are echoing the Blacks thirty to forty years ago by alleging police discrimination as during the Bradford riots of 1995. FitzGerald concludes by evaluating the role of international perspectives warning of: 'reading across uncritically of their results because of diversity of ethnic range, size, histories and interrelationships' (FitzGerald, 1997:58).

The author welcomes international parallels that provide an account of the 'social, political and organizational' processes at work rather than the inference about inherent characteristics of individual ethnic groups. The work of FitzGerald must be commended for an intelligent and succinct evaluation of the only empirical data available regarding Asians and crime in the UK. The author prudently warns all criminologists about drawing conclusions from official statistics and about the neglect of the true level of ethnic minority crime (FitzGerald, 1997:52). Perhaps what is being suggested is the adoption of more qualitative methodologies that can begin to address simultaneously the issues of offending and victimization.

Continuing our evaluation of secondary sources, a particularly unique text is offered by Cashmore and McLaughlin in 1991. This publication entitled *Out of Order* provides an evaluation of the relationship between the police and Black communities on a comparative basis between the UK and USA. In a similar way to many academic texts in this area the book provides contributions from experts in the field.

The text largely deals with issues pertaining to Black Caribbeans[9] and policing. Parallels and comparisons between Black Caribbeans and Asians are inevitable and indeed valuable, however, the specific evaluations of Asians and policing shall be explored here. The first mention of Asians in the text is in the introduction by the editors. The authors speak of police policy regarding issues of protection against racial attacks. They note the comments of the then Commissioner of the Metropolitan Police that racial attacks would be made a police priority. The authors further note that despite a significant publicity campaign launched in 1989 designed to increase the reportage of crimes of racial violence the 'Asian communities are still demanding more action from the police to deal with such crimes' (Cashmore and McLaughlin, 1991:7).

---

[9] The original text uses the now outdated term 'Afro-Caribbean'.

Tony Jefferson, in his contribution to the text entitled 'Discrimination, disadvantage and police work', comments on scarce secondary sources pertaining to Asians and crime. Jefferson notes the outcome of the work of Stevens and Willis (1979) and Walker et al. (1989), which indicated an under-representation of Asians in the overall arrest rate in London and Leeds. Jefferson states that the over-representation of Black Caribbean defendants can be, and in part has been, linked to social disadvantage. However, the author notes that Asians are also subject to a disproportionate level of disadvantage including an even greater likelihood (than Black Caribbeans) of being victims of racist attacks (Home Office, 1981). However Jefferson states the arrest rates do not match their disadvantage. With regard to Asians and crime the author notes:

> But finally we must confront the question of Asians … Though I have no space to explore this properly- and, in truth, little research exists to help here- it seems clear that we will need to look towards certain cultural factors (probably those to do with family and community structure and religion) (Jefferson, 1991:181).

Jefferson's contribution also involves an evaluation of attitudes, perceptions and experiences of ethnic minority populations in relation to policing. The author evaluates the research by the Home Office Policy Studies Institute, which found a:

> Dangerous lack of confidence in the police among substantial numbers of white people and a disastrous lack of confidence among young people of West Indian origin (Smith and Gray, 1983:332).

Furthermore Jefferson refers to his own findings in Leeds where, regarding attitudes towards police, Black Caribbeans had the highest (of all racial groups) overall 'disapproval score' and were less likely (when asked what they would do on witnessing various crimes) to co-operate with the police. Asians, however, according to the findings of the PSI were less critical of the police than Black Caribbeans in London (except with regard to racial attacks) though more so than whites (Reiner, 1985). In Leeds the author found that Asians held significantly less critical attitudes to the police than either Black-Caribbeans or whites (Walker et al., 1989).

The author suggests that one obvious way of explaining differences between Asians and Black-Caribbeans and whites would be in differences in experiences, and the possibility that the fact that Asians have fewer arrests and stops accounts for their more positive attitude. However, the author continues by stating the aforementioned is not necessarily the true picture since research by Smith found that people of West Indian origin who report no personal adversarial contact with the police are still more hostile than whites, who have not had contact with the police of this kind (Smith, 1987:70-71).

According to Smith the hostility can be accounted for by reference to what he calls 'the extra element' in the formation of the views of Black-Caribbean people which means their sense of solidarity within the ethnic group provides a 'collective consciousness' which forms 'some kind of political ideology' (Smith,

1983:72). Jefferson interprets this to mean that the 'collective experiences' of racial discrimination appears to have produced both a 'collective consciousness' and 'political ideology', which is above the experiences of discrimination suffered by individuals within the group.

Jefferson then notes that it could be a different 'collective consciousness', which is informing the markedly more conforming behaviour and attitudes of Asians. Furthermore, he speculates that if the 'mutual hostility' between Black-Caribbeans and the police is a 'self fulfilling prophecy' it may well be that more positive and conforming Asian attitudes are 'rewarded' with more positive police attitudes. Jefferson continues by stating 'what we are witnessing in police-Asian relations is a self-fulfilling prophecy of a more positive kind' (Jefferson, 1991:181). The author quotes an example of his Leeds research to illustrate the point that Asian juveniles are significantly more likely to be cautioned than other ethnic groups and adults to have 'No Further Action' taken after arrest. Jefferson does observe, however, that there is evidence of conflict between police and 'some' sections of Asian youths in places like Southall and Bradford (NCCL, 1980). Now one may add the Bradford riots of 1995 and the lesser-known Blackburn riots of the same year (Marshall, 1997). However, although the author quotes the work of Bains (1988) in Southall regarding youth politics, he goes no further than stating that 'the picture is fraught with complications such that generalizations in this area are very hazardous' (Jefferson, 1991:185).

To summarize Jefferson's observations regarding Asian crime, one can say that while his work illustrates the importance of crime and 'social disadvantage' it also demonstrates that this link is problematic when we consider the differences betweens Blacks and Asians. Jefferson advocates that the apparently different response of Asians to similar levels of disadvantage places the need to take cultural as well as structural factors seriously firmly on the agenda (Jefferson, 1991).

The author also notes that there is no simple 'one to one' equation between experiences and attitudes, and that in the case of Asians, high levels of disadvantage and discrimination can be associated with positive attitudes to the police. Indeed with regard to the latter one may have to investigate whether it is respect for the police or fear which influences such attitudes in addition to the cultural factors the author suggests. Once more, however, the work illustrates the need for further research into this largely uncharted criminological field.

Elsewhere in *Out of Order* the authors only mention matters relating to Asians briefly albeit raising important points. Ruth Chigwada in her chapter 'The Policing of Black Women' illustrates some of the discrimination experienced by Asians. Chigwada notes the findings of Jalna Hanmer in her research relating to the enforcement of nationality and immigration laws. Hamner noted that in certain districts:

> the first response officers make to Asian calls for assistance, whether complaints of violence in the home or racist assaults, is to investigate the status and rights of the complainant to be in the country (Hamner, 1989:104).

Indeed it would be worthwhile investigating the latter in the 1990s with regard to the establishment of specific bilingual (civilian and police) staffed Domestic Violence Units at police stations.

Chigwada also discusses the stereotypes regarding Black women as suspects. Asian women are seen as 'passive' or 'hysterical' and subject to oppressive practices within the family. Furthermore, such stereotyping, according to Chigwada, has deterred police from taking action or prosecuting in cases of domestic violence involving Black women as they are viewed as 'macho' and therefore able to look after themselves.

Ellis Cashmore in his chapter 'Black Cops Inc.' notes the New York Police Department's actions in 1973 when it lowered its minimum height requirement to accommodate Hispanic recruits, whose average height tended to be too short by NYPD standards. Cashmore notes that the Metropolitan force did the same thing to attract South Asian officers in 1989 (Cashmore and McLaughlin, 1991). One may note here that all forces in the UK have abolished an official minimum height requirement.

Out of Order provides minimal material for the criminological evaluation of Asians in the UK. However the importance of the comparative nature of such texts cannot be understated and the experiences of minorities in the USA can provide an illuminating theoretical comparison for research in the UK.

Muslims in Prison

The discussion so far has concentrated upon criminal statistics largely sourced from court and police records and qualitative studies in particular localities. We have observed that official statistics traditionally homogenized and grouped ethnic minorities in unhelpful generic categories before eventually differentiating individuals based upon ethnic origin (FitzGerald, 1997).

Hence, when seeking to evaluate Muslims, and South Asian Muslims in particular, researchers traditionally could only estimate religious denomination of offenders from country of ethnic origin. That is to say where studies have mentioned Asians, and these are mainly from Pakistan or Bangladesh, it is implied rather than explicit that these samples are also Muslim. Police and court records do not register religion and so in the absence of any standardized collation of this information, one is prompted to use ethnic origin as an indicator of probable religious affinity. However, the Prison Act 1952 prompted the registration of religious affiliation in British prisons. Based upon prison service statistics the registered Muslim population in prison has experienced rapid growth and in 2000 the figure was approximately 4500 (Wilson, 1999). There was a ninety per cent increase in the registration of Muslim prisoners between 1991 and 1997 and this lead to the appointment of a full time Muslim Advisor to the Prison Service in

1999 (Wilson, 2000). Current estimates of registered Muslims in prison are approximately 5000[10].

This represents more than 7 per cent of the prison population whereas the Muslim presence in British society as a whole is estimated to be approximately 2 to 3 per cent (Lewis, 1994). The Muslim prison population therefore represents almost three times the population density of Muslims in wider society and this has prompted significant research interest (Beckford and Gilliat, 1998; Beckford 2002; Quraishi 2002b).

The rise in Muslim prisoners has prompted an assessment of Muslim needs by the Prison Service and this has influenced political changes at Prison Service Head Quarters. Certain factors have arguably influenced the degree to which the Muslim prisoner population has become the setting for an assessment of how the state accommodates and institutionalizes Islam. The factors are: the appointment of a Muslim Advisor, the transfer of 'other faith' matters from the Chaplain General to the Prison Administration Group, the National Council for the Welfare of Muslim Prisoners overseeing Muslim Visiting Ministers (Muslims Chaplains), and the appointment of a Chaplain General in favour of a 'multi-faith' or 'inclusive' philosophy (Beckford, 2002). These political and administrative changes have also, arguably, enabled a broadening and greater reception of research in this field by funding bodies and prison establishments in the UK (Quraishi, 2002b).

Whilst is may be clear that the number of registered Muslims in prison is rising and constitutes overrepresentation, the picture is fraught with complications. The prison service presently registers faith using computer software known as the Local Inmate Data System (LIDS). LIDS is only presently used to maintain a positive record of prisoners and cannot therefore trace conversion from either 'nil' religion or another religion to Islam. Therefore, whilst the registered numbers of Muslims is rising there is no record of how many have converted to Islam in prison. However, more recently the Home Office have released data detailing the ethnic composition of the prison population matched against religion. If we examine the South Asian incarceration rate per 100,000 of the general population was 168, as compared to 1245 for black people and 185 for white people (Home Office, 1999a). The total male Asian prison population in 1998 was 3 per cent, compared to 12 per cent for Black males and 82 per cent for white males (Home Office, 1999b). It must be noted that this represents the total South Asian male prison population; therefore this includes adherents to various faiths and not exclusively Islam. However, if we disaggregate the Asian prison population in terms of faith, we can observe an interesting trend with regard to the Muslim male prison population.

In 2000, Asian male prisoners constituted 42 per cent of the total Muslim male prison population, with 34 per cent declaring Black ethnicity (Guessous, Hooper and Moorthy, 2001). Therefore, whilst the Muslim Asian population in prison does not account for the majority of Muslim prisoners, it does constitute the largest singular Muslim ethnic group, followed closely by Black prisoners

---

[10] Presentation to Centre for Research In Ethnic Relations, University of Warwick, by the Muslim Advisor to the Prison Service - Maqsood Ahmed, 13 November 2001.

(Guessous, Hooper and Moorthy, 2001). This representation is for the prison estate of England and Wales as a whole. However, if we turn to individual prisons the Asian Muslim population is often in the minority, with Black Caribbean prisoners (principally converts to Islam) accounting substantially for the Muslim total (Quraishi, 2002b). Muslim prisoners are most likely to be found in the London Prison Service area, and there are higher than average proportions of Muslim prisoners in Eastern and High Security areas (Guessous, Hooper and Moorthy, 2001).

After consultations with the Muslim Advisor to the Prison Service, it has been made clear that there are plans to make monitoring of religious change in prison population possible in the near future (Quraishi, 2002b).

There are many reasons attributed to the relatively high levels of conversion to Islam in prison and this is interpreted from two diametrically opposed perspectives. For the prison management, officers and some Chaplains it is met with a degree of suspicion and cynicism, in that prisoners are viewed as registering as Muslim simply to acquire perceived benefits such as halal diet, rights to celebrate festivals and join in weekly congregational prayers. These suspicions are less justified when we consider all prisoners may choose halal food from their menus irrespective of faith, and that other faith groups have often more frequent congregations and social gatherings. I do not wish to discuss the dynamics of these issues here because of the danger of pre-empting the research which is still in progress, however regardless of the reasons for conversion what is important is that in general British society Muslims are largely represented by South Asians. Whilst there are significant numbers of South Asian Muslims in the prison population the ethnic composition of Muslim prisoners is skewed and has not traditionally been a reflection of that in the wider society (NACRO, 2001). The Muslim Asian prison population may finally be shifting to mirror more closely their population density in British society as a whole (Guessous, Hooper and Moorthy, 2001).

This is important in terms of understanding the fact that discourse about the Muslim prison population resonates in the public's perception with reference to South Asians, since the general British Muslim population is largely represented by Pakistanis and Bangladeshis (Anwar, 1996).

Furthermore, in the minds of law enforcement agencies and the courts, perceptions of a permanent and rising Muslim prisoner population could have an influence on the normalization and justification of custodial sentences for South Asian defendants. That is to say, where in the past stereotypes of conformity produced low incarceration rates for Muslim South Asian defendants, the stereotype of a deviant and criminal Muslim South Asian defendant may have arrived (Mawby and Batta, 1980, Webster, 1997).

Criminology in Pakistan

The discipline known as criminology in the West is not easily defined. The very identity of the discipline is problematic due to the nature and manner in which the study of crime has evolved. Contributions have been offered from the disciplines of jurisprudence, sociology and law among others. Attempts to place the discipline within neatly categorized boxes is to demonstrate ignorance of the incremental, multi-disciplinary and, arguably, relative youth of criminology.

Nonetheless, there are those who assert that criminology is a discipline of unique and independent standing with its prime focus being the study, recording and explaining of crime (Nelken, 1994). Within criminology there remain rifts between methodological perspectives and conceptions of the social world (Barak, 1994). These differences in world-views provide for a diversity of approaches to the phenomenon of crime. The methodological wrangling that occupies the academic arena in the West may often find voice within the practices and policy-making of some governments, as well as in university syllabi and academic press. The West considers itself the home of the latest methodological brilliance, latest insights and intellectual innovations.

Whether one agrees with this or not, what is clear is that the teachings and contributions to criminology are essentially Western-led phenomena (Young, 1997). This may of course, simply be a Eurocentric view, replicated here and once again finding voice through the interpretation of a researcher schooled in the West and taught in the English medium. One should qualify the statement by emphasizing that criminology, as it is understood in the West, is essentially an amalgam of contributions by European and American scholars. The sum result of this is that in countries, such as those of the former Commonwealth, where scholars are encouraged to study overseas in European or American institutions, we see the perpetuation of the dominance of Western scholars and Western philosophies.

The latter is strongly evident within the position and status of criminology in Pakistan. As with the majority of developing countries, the academic effort and financial governmental impetus is inevitably disproportionately centred upon achieving economic strength and longevity of fiscal stability. The focus for governments in Pakistan has been the advancement of the country's infrastructure by promotion of the classical sciences, engineering and financial disciplines. A direct consequence of this is the under-funding, neglect and correspondingly secondary position of the humanities and social sciences in Pakistan. This position must be contrasted with that of India, where criminological university instruction began in the 1940s and 1950s with undergraduate and postgraduate degrees at the University of Lucknow. Subsequent developments included the establishment of an Institute of Criminology and Forensic Science at New Delhi in the early 1970s (Sandhu, 1983).

It is not surprising, therefore, that despite significant crime problems very few contributions have been made in this field by indigenous scholars. This statement refers to research published in the English medium. One must acknowledge that scholars in the Urdu-medium may have more closely addressed the issues. It should be stressed, however, that English is the main language of commerce and business in Pakistan and strongly encouraged as a language for the scholar. After discussions with a professor of Applied Criminological Studies at the University of Karachi, it became clear that the governments in Pakistan have not given prominence to the study of criminology. Furthermore, within the private education sphere in Pakistan, there are very few current providers of degree programmes in criminology.

At the University of Karachi, a perusal of the syllabi and reading lists for degree courses in sociology and criminology reveal a concentration upon traditional criminological texts, overwhelmingly by American scholars. The works of Wolfgang, Park and his colleagues at the Chicago School are strongly recommended key texts for the few Pakistani students of criminology. One can observe, in Pakistan, that there is a very marked absence of the study of more contemporary criminological theories. This is not to say that the Karachi scholars are intellectually blinkered, but rather that the restrictions of finance and the attitude to research by the government produces a particularly positivistic research programme. Scholars must either practice within such a programme or become defunct. The Institute of Applied Criminological Studies, at Karachi University, provides an example of such a positivistic research culture, where criminal psychology and the like are taught as part of a socio-medical discipline.

A further factor that could help to account for the traditional overlooking of criminology as a distinct discipline in Pakistan is the presence of institutions of legal education and Islamic colleges, where sharī'ah and fiqh are taught. The prominence of such madaris[11] in Pakistan, and the focus upon Islamic law taught via the Arabic medium, could help explain the relatively minor position of criminology, in so far as it is defined from a Western perspective. Muslim scholars in other Islamic countries have undertaken explorations of crime and these often evaluate sharī'ah against secular criminal codes (see for example Hussinat, 1997)[12].

For the Muslim, crime is inevitable. What is needed for the ummah is the scholarly pursuit of the written sources of Islamic law to enable contemporary interpretation, application and the imparting of knowledge of such to future generations. It is not surprising, therefore, that the area of concentration for Pakistani scholars of crime is sharī'ah. However, as long as Pakistan continues to maintain a constitutional and legal infrastructure centred upon a secular common-law philosophy (inherited from the British colonial period), the insights and usefulness of contemporary Western criminology cannot be overlooked by Pakistani scholars.

One must stress that the discussion of crime in Pakistan, does take place within the academic arena, but that this arena is more likely to be occupied by scholars of politics than scholars of criminology. Further, as we shall see, the daily experiences of, reactions to and hypothesizing about crime in Karachi amongst ordinary residents, illustrates the seemingly pervasive nature of offending in Pakistan.

Scholars who have been educated outside of Pakistan, particularly in Europe and North America, often make the few contributions to Pakistani criminology in the English language. One such work is 'Crime and Criminology' by Khan, Aoulakh and Ajmal (1995). This study demonstrates the affinity and

---

[11] Islamic seminaries/schools also known as a madrasah.

[12] See Hussinat (1997) for an exploration of crime and leisure in Jordanian society.

often perceived inseparability of criminology from law. All the contributors to the text are scholars of law and criminal justice. Crime and Criminology is a truly unique text in that it claims to provide a comparative study of crime in Pakistan and the USA.

The text is indeed a comprehensive evaluation of criminological theories and the applicability, or inappropriateness, of such to our contemporary understanding of crime in Pakistan. The strengths of the text lie in its attempt to place a 'Qur'ānic analysis of crime against Western, largely American-led hypothesizing.

In Chapter four the authors demonstrate the pitfalls and patchiness of official crime statistics in Pakistan and therefore advise researchers to look beyond the official statistics, they argue that:

> The government of Pakistan and each of the four Provincial Police Headquarters release the raw data for statistical use according to their own politico-administrative needs and bureaucratic performance interests (Khan, Aoulakh, Ajmal, 1995:78).

The text provides a rich source of data regarding the constitutional framework of criminal justice in Pakistan and offers comparisons with European and American judicial structures (Khan, Aoulakh, Ajmal, 1995)

A particular problem, detailed by the authors, is the dire situation of juvenile justice in Pakistan. The authors are critical of the current absence of specific juvenile laws in Pakistan which means, inter alia, that there are no separate facilities to hold juveniles apart from adult offenders. Further, the authors highlight that:

> Children are treated as property of parents, the society and prison authorities. They have no 'say' in their stay at the institution in Pakistan (Khan, Aoulakh, Ajmal, 1995:363).

The work must be praised for its acknowledgement and attempt to push the historical cultural triad of 'zer' (money), 'zameen' (land) and 'zun' (woman), as the causes of crime in Pakistan, towards the inclusion of criminals as victims, who are often forced to violate the law because of 'shuhrat' (valour), 'zaroorat' (need) and 'ghyrat' (frustration).

The authors wisely advocate that Pakistan must fill the gap in crime research by introducing the discipline of criminology via institutions of higher learning. They believe criminological research will improve the criminal justice system by providing humane and cost-beneficial reactions to crime (Khan, Aoulakh, Ajmal, 1995:335).

The work of Mahfooz Kanwar provides a comprehensive evaluation of murder and homicide in Pakistan (Kanwar, 1989). The study is particularly original because of the qualitative methodology adopted and corresponding concentration upon case studies of people convicted of murder and homicide in Pakistan. Kanwar is able to demonstrate that, in Pakistan, specific cultural traditions such as safeguarding of the family, land, historic notions of vengeance, biraderi (kinship) ties and the concept of honour are all related to the cause and effect of murder and homicide.

The author also offers an 'international frame of reference' though this is confined to a statistical analysis of murder and homicide in various European and American countries. Kanwar is critical of official statistics in Pakistan generally and asserts that the 'corruption in the criminal justice system of Pakistan further clouds the reliability of homicide statistics in that country' (Kanwar, 1989:178). Kanwar's descriptive qualitative evaluation of the bureaucratic loopholes and barriers to access demonstrate the importance of 'negotiating a role' as a researcher of crime in Pakistan.

It should be stressed that Kanwar's sample group was of persons formally convicted of murder and homicide. By its own submission the work highlights that there is, unsurprisingly, an overrepresentation of economically disadvantaged persons serving sentences for murder and homicide in Pakistan. Kanwar asserts that the reason for high incidence of offending by the poor is due to their reactions to various cultural and traditional pressures such as honour and biraderi. Although Kanwar advocates addressing state corruption in the various limbs of the criminal justice system, he does not make explicit the significance of politically motivated and extra-judicial killings in Pakistan[13].

To summarize, the current contributions to an understanding of Muslims and crime contain both limitations and insights, each within the specific contexts of the research undertaken. Taken cumulatively, we can begin to observe the picture of Asian crime involvement and victimization more clearly. First, one must conclude that the present contributions are indeed minimal, a fact repeatedly stated by the contributors themselves. What little work exists tends to have been excessively involved with statistical analysis, arguably at the expense of qualitative studies.

The traditional picture is one of relatively low levels of crime and high levels of conformity for Asians in Britain. The early studies of criminality, although restricted in their application for the reasons stated, all suggest lower crime rates among Asians as compared to Black and white ethnic groups. We have also observed that, for demographic reasons, commentators predict a rise in Asian crime. It must be noted that such predictions have not yet been wholly realized.

With regard to Muslims in prison, statistical evidence records rapid increases over the last ten years (Home Office, 1999a). As discussed, South Asian Muslims constitute only between 2 and 3 per cent of the total Muslim prison population (Home Office, 1999b). Present data collection does not record conversion to Islam, but research in progress tends to illustrate significant rates of conversion to Islam in prison by Black prisoners (Quraishi, 2002b).

---

[13] See Report of the Humans Rights Commission of Pakistan 1997.

Latest Developments

Although qualitative studies of Muslims and crime remain scarce, the neglect has, more recently, begun to be addressed by academics[14]. New research has been prompted by governmental and institutional interest in British Muslims following the events of September 11th 2001. One of the most comprehensive examinations of British Muslims and criminal justice was commissioned by the Open Society Institute in January 2004, culminating in a report by Dr Basia Spalek of the Institute of Applied Social Studies, University of Birmingham (Spalek, 2004). This report has provided a detailed review of the representation and studies of experience of British Muslims and the criminal justice system. Further, the paper has provided direct policy recommendations to curb racism, exclusion and promote fair treatment of Muslims by criminal justice institutions in Britain. The recommendations include developing diversity training for the police to include Islamophobia, religious discrimination and the experiences of crime for Muslims (recommendation 11); disaggregating crime data from a general Asian category (recommendation 1); and providing a booster sample of Muslims in the next British Crime Survey (recommendation 5) (Spalek, 2004).

Summary

Evaluation of the literature and studies mentioned here allows us to make the following observations. The use of terms suggesting homogeneity amongst British Asians is problematic. Pockets of data and qualitative studies exist regarding Muslims and crime in Britain. However, the historical inconsistency amongst official criminal justice agencies regarding the classification of ethnicity and religion has prohibited more coherent analysis of Muslims in the British criminal justice system. There needs to be an academic deconstruction of discourse in the media and among criminal justice agencies regarding the Muslim criminal.

Early studies of British Asians illustrate traditional under-representation in official criminal statistics. However, more recent prison data reveals a higher incarceration rate per 100,000 population for British born Pakistani males when compared to the white, Bangladeshi and Indian prison populations (Home Office, 1999). The data may indicate a number of developments in criminological terms. First, that the rise in incarceration rates for Pakistani males is a reflection of a genuine rise in offending amongst this population. Second, that the rise is simply a reflection of the youthful demographic profile of this population. Third, that the increase in incarceration rates is a reflection of Pakistani (Muslim) youth coming under the increasing scrutiny of a prejudicial public, police and criminal justice system.

---

[14] See Macey, 1999; Desai, 1998; Alexander, 2000a, 2000b, Spalek, 2002.

If we turn to comparative studies, research which compares crime issues between countries must give due consideration to the particular social contexts of the societies being studied and make these contexts explicit.

We have observed that the contributors suggest the need for further investigations of the cultural institutions that influence and regulate Muslim criminality. The present should therefore be a period of initiating such studies, evaluating such institutions and uncovering the reality beyond the mere statistical projections.

Particular historical and institutional practices have had resounding impact on the Muslim community globally and in the next chapter we turn to discussions of colonialism, criminal tribes and the 'demonization' of Islam.

Having discussed the principal criminological contributions to the field, we may now consider the historical practices that help position the Muslims in Britain and Pakistan within a colonial past and post-colonial present.

Chapter 3

Colonialism, Criminalized Tribes and Islamophobia

The purpose of the following discussion is to locate the British South Asian Muslim within the broader historical picture and to elucidate how far institutionalized identity manipulation strategies used by the British during colonial rule in India have influenced the current terrain of post-colonialism.

One must note that there are distinct issues to be clarified here. First there must be clarity about the intention of the British through their colonial plans. Second, there must be a process of uncovering how those plans were actualized. Finally, there must be an assessment of consequences within the social, political and racial terrains affected, re-constituted or invented via the colonial encounter.

It is submitted that the pursuit of these three factors represents a Herculean task, which scholars of various disciplines have addressed and neglected in varying degrees. What is certain is that, in the context of Pakistan, criminologists have rarely sought to locate the present criminological terrain within the broader historical spectrum and to assess how far the present reflects the past.

The following therefore represents an illustration of how certain colonial practices constituted the manipulation of identities and alerts the reader to consider to what extent these strategies have shaped the current criminal justice systems in the Indian subcontinent. Furthermore, the following discussion highlights how the concepts of 'deviant', 'criminal' and 'martial' have been internalized by the subjects of colonization and questions how far these concepts have entered the discourse of British criminology within the context of how Muslims are viewed as perpetrators and/or victims of crime and deviance.

Colonialism

Some scholars assert that it was to reconcile colonial domination with the ideals of freedom and equality, that colonial powers adopted a discourse of racial difference and hierarchy when referring to the colonized (Mahmud, 1999). Within such discourse 'capacity and eligibility to freedom and progress were deemed biologically determined, and colonialism was legitimated as the natural subordination of lesser races to higher ones' (Mahmud, 1999:1219). Furthermore, according to Mahmud:

Traces of racialized discursive structures of Europe's colonial encounter remain visible in post-colonial terrains, where many a public policy and legal regime are animated by racialized categories and classifications (Mahmud, 1999:1220).

The colonial governance strategy of 'divide and rule' in colonial India was encouraged by the regional, cultural, linguistic, religious and political heterogeneity of pre-colonial India. For those who doubt the definite adoption of such strategies reference should be made to the correspondence of colonial officials. For example, Lieutenant-Colonel Coke, Commandant of Moradabad is recorded as voicing the following:

> Uphold in full force the (for us fortunate) separation which exists between the different religions and races, not to endeavour to amalgamate them. *Divide et impera* should be the principle of Indian government (Dutt, 1949).

There exists a conflicting dialogue about the degree to which colonial practices were of benefit or detriment to those colonized in India. Much of the earliest discussion centred upon economic benefits versus economic detriments. This discourse appears to have been conducted with minimal attention to questions of the social or cultural consequences of colonialism. This is so despite early acknowledgement and awareness of the spiritual and cultural implications of colonialism. For example in 1583 Sir George Peckham, casting around for arguments to interest Elizabeth I in colonial ventures wrote that 'We shall be planting there the glory of the gospel and from England plant sincere religion' (Bolton, 1973: 97).

The publicists Dadabhai Naoroji (1901) and later Romesh C. Dutt (1906), traced the roots of India's poverty to:

> economic exploitation in the form of drainage of resources through undervalued exports, Home Charges, and the heavy cost of deploying the Indian Army for Imperial purposes (Raychaudhuri, 1999:225).

Defenders of the Imperial record who urged that the strengthening of India's infrastructure via investments during the colonial period had enabled a positive transformation of the Indian economy challenged such assertions (Knowles, 1924; Anstey, 1931). Estimates of national income, agricultural output and trends in India's international trade in the 1950s and 1960s provided a quantitative basis for similar studies but did not really terminate the controversy which had strong ideological overtones.

According to some scholars, the impact of colonial rule on Indian Muslims was an 'unmitigated disaster' (Ahmed, 2002: 117). Ahmed highlights the negative impact of Lord Macaulay's 'Minute on Education' in 1835 which introduced English as the medium of instruction in colonial India (Ahmed, 2002). According to Ahmed:

> When English replaced Persian, the court language of the Mughals, Muslims found
> themselves at a crippling disadvantage. A reluctance, a mental block, to speak or
> learn English grew among them (Ahmed, 2002:126).

Furthermore, Ahmed details the disintegration of Muslim Indian society during
colonial rule under which their leaders were ridiculed, rebellion was met with
draconian punishment and noble Islamic titles were applied in humiliating ways
(Ahmed, 2002).

Some obstacles in seeking clarity about the consequences of colonialism are
demonstrated by an analysis of the 'top-down' or 'Orientalist' nature of the early
contributions to our understanding of British rule in India. The historian Robert
Frykenberg notes:

> The India discovered by national historians was, in short, just the mirror image of
> the Empire described by Imperial historians...Often Eurocentric in tone, such
> historians dealt with the impacts of Indo-British personalities, perspectives and
> policies (Frykenberg, 1999).

The words of commentators such as G. Bolton in his text 'Britain's Legacy
Overseas' demonstrate that such Eurocentric perspectives were not simply
confined to the early twentieth century:

> Previous British ventures in colonization involved the subjugation of a technically
> under-developed indigenous people, and the imposition on them of what could be
> seen as the manifestly superior culture and economic organization of Britain
> (Bolton, 1973:14).

Elsewhere in the same text Bolton notes:

> It is rather that the spread of British culture into many environments enriched and
> diversified the local traditions because it drew in its turn on so many disparate.
> However involuntarily it occurred, this mingling of cultures was one of the few
> unquestionably beneficial after-effects of the British Empire (Bolton, 1973:108).

Amongst those who would question the beneficial nature of such 'mingling
of cultures' are commentators such as Edward Said, Ranjit Guha, Gayatri Spivak
and Bernard S. Cohn. The work of such scholars' marks a trend that began during
the 1930s prompted by closer attention to historic research and the adoption of a
'bottom-up' or 'Indocentric' approach. An interesting dimension to such work is its
attempt to demonstrate that whatever British aims may have been, it was Indian
realities that shaped the course of events. According to Frykenberg:

> Local conditions and circumstances, as reflected in local conflicts between social
> entities rooted in family, caste and village, language and culture, or religion or
> culture...Indigenous institutions rather than high imperial policy or national
> aspirations were examined more carefully (Frykenberg, 1999:194).

The critique of Orientalism has itself come under tough criticism. Scholars such as David Kopf, Ernst Gellner and Bernard Lewis have opposed Said's views, asserting that the whole body of anti-Orientalist 'colonial discourse analysis' is itself a form of neo-colonialist Eurocentric nihilism (Kopf, 1980).

Acknowledgement of such theoretical and methodological perspectives is crucial to our evaluation of the body of literature proposing to catalogue what is presented as being the true picture of India under colonial rule. Whilst the philosophy and subjectivity of the historian often prompts the scholar to query what is purported to be historical fact, certain factual sources are less susceptible to such criticism. Legislation and legal documents provide an example of such factual sources. A contemporary evaluation of such texts can demonstrate the intention of the colonizer to classify, subjugate and manipulate the colonized. The Criminal Tribes Act 1871 represents a clear example of the repressive and manipulative nature of certain colonial legislation.

The Criminal Tribes Act (Act XXVII of 1871)

This Act was specifically passed to 'provide for the registration, surveillance and control of certain tribes…. [designated] criminal' (Mahmud, 1999:1236). By the early twentieth century 13 million people were classified as such (Yang, 1985). The Act empowered local governments to designate 'any tribe, gang or class of persons' as a 'criminal tribe' if they were 'addicted to the systematic commission of non-bailable offences' (Mahmud, 1999:1236). A comprehensive registration of such tribes was set in motion, and the District Magistrate in India during the colonial period was responsible for supervising and maintaining a record of such groups. A notice of registration was posted in the villages where the tribe resided. Once officially notified, these groups had no recourse to the judicial system for repealing such notices.

The fact that the people now deemed criminal were illiterate and often unaware of their perceived criminal status demonstrates a particularly draconian adherence to the principle *ignorantia juris non excusat*. The movement of the 'criminal tribes' was closely monitored via a system of passes. These passes specified where the holder could travel or reside and incorporated compulsory reporting of movement at designated police stations. Local officials were empowered to resettle criminal tribes or to remove them to 'a reformatory settlement' (Mahmud, 1999:1236).

The tribes were subject to penal sanctions for breach of the pass system, which included imprisonment, fines and whipping. These policies reflected a philosophy of biological determinism, and in order to guard against the passing on of 'criminal genes' intermarriage within a criminal tribe was prohibited. Children were separated from their parents and kept in custody (Mahmud, 1999:1236).

Scholars such as Radhika Singha (1993), C.A. Bayley (1996) and G. Bruce (1968) have highlighted the most celebrated of Indian folk devils through their analyses of the Thuggee or Thugs. The Thuggee (or Thagi) were identified by the British as 'a Hindu-cult of assassin priests who preyed on travellers'. Under Lord

William Bentinck, governor-general from 1828 to 1835, systematic measures were adopted to eradicate them. The penalties for belonging to 'any gang of Thugs included, for example, branding on the forehead' (James, 1995:75). The case of Thuggee demonstrates the impact of British authority upon native society and the need to categorize the colonized Indians (Brown, 2002).

In 1897 the Criminal Tribes Act was amended to enable local governments to establish a separate reformatory settlement for minors of parents designated members of a criminal tribe. Further amendments provided for stricter punitive measures and the requirement for compulsory fingerprinting of all members of criminal tribes. Scholars have noted how the Criminal Tribes Act 1871 formed part of the aggressive and suppressive legislation passed by the British post-1857 to hamper the likelihood of a further revolt (Mahmud, 1999; Stokes, 1959; Brown, 2002).

Unsurprisingly the 1871 Act was used to control and label other small communities: 'wandering gangs, nomadic petty traders and pastoralists, gypsies and forest dwellers, in short, it was used against a wide variety of marginals who did not conform to the colonial pattern of settled agriculture and wage labour' (Mahmud, 1999:1237). Mahmud notes that, paradoxically, the criminalization of these people stemmed from social changes prompted by colonial economic policies such as state monopolies on commodities and regulation of forest harvesting (Mahmud, 1999).

There also existed the colonial objective of putting 'unproductive communities' to useful and law-abiding activity, and many of those classified under the Act were often put to work on tea and coffee estates and in textile mills. The Criminal Tribes Acts of 1871 and 1897 were supplemented by two further Acts in 1911 and 1924 before finally being repealed in 1952, five years after decolonization. Some scholars assert that the post independence decriminalization of the tribes resulted in resettlement on agricultural land and an end to their criminality (Sandhu, 1983). However, the stereotyping has permeated into the twenty first century. The latter is evident from an analysis of the discourse amongst law enforcement agencies and non-governmental organizations in Pakistan, such as the Citizen-Police Liaison Committee, where the practices of categorizing the criminal type demonstrates an obsession with biological determinism and the classification of the criminal group. In addition to the institutional discourse, there exists highly racialized dialogue amongst resident Karachiites about who the criminals are in their society[1].

The Martial Races Theory

The martial races theory centres upon the assumption that certain races are born with a 'military instinct' and that this was inherent in European races, especially the British, but was not true for all the races in India (Mahmud, 1999:1231).

---

[1] See Chapter 6.

Traditionally the soldiers of Bengal were the backbone of the Indian Army. The 'native Black troops' there were seen as 'fine men' who 'would not...disgrace even the Prussian ranks' (Heathcote, 1974)[2]. Scholars observe that the 1857 Revolt resulted in rapid reorganizing of the ethnic composition of the Indian Army (Cohen 1971; Heathcote, 1974). According to Mahmud 'deliberation to reorganize the Indian Army centred around loyalty and disloyalty displayed by different sections of the native population' (Mahmud, 1999:1231).

The British shifted their recruitment from Bengal and raised fresh battalions mainly from the Punjab and Nepal. The post-1857 reorganization of the army entailed a dramatic fall in recruitment from the traditional areas in the east and south of India and a rise in recruitment from the north and the west. Recruitment of Bengalis was prohibited. Almost overnight, formerly known as the backbone of the colonial army, the Bengalis became defined as 'feeble, even to effeminacy' for whom 'courage, independence, veracity are qualities to which his constitution and his situation are equally unfavourable' (Gordon, 1974)[3]. Those from southern India were declared to 'fall short, as a race in possessing the courage and military instincts', and Punjab was anointed 'the home of the most martial races of India'[4] (Omissi, 1994).

Such was the obsession of the British with the martial races theory that they codified it through a series of official recruiting handbooks for the Indian Army. In these manuals 'Indians appeared not as individuals but as specimens; photographs of suitable recruit types were included, the ideal measurements and physique were described in great detail' (Mahmud, 1999:1232).

The Commander in Chief took the view that 'no comparison can be made between...A regiment recruited amongst the warlike races of northern India and of one recruited amongst the effeminate races of the South'[5] (Mason, 1974).

The British saw some of their favourite martial races, particularly Rajputs and Punjabis, as the descendants of the Aryan invaders. Caste and tribe were often equated with race. In the case of the Rajputs, for example, it was held that they had maintained their Aryan racial 'purity' through strict adherence to the caste system. Colonial recruiting strategies, therefore, favoured those groups who followed restrictive marriage practices and who thus promised to be racially pure (Mason, 1974).

T.A. Heathcote details how service in the Indian Army in the late nineteenth and early twentieth centuries was, in the main, restricted to the following groups:

> Pathans from the NW Frontier districts and the independent tribal regions;
> Baluchis and Brahuis from Kalat and British Baluchistan;
> Sikhs, Jats, Dogras, and Muslims from the Punjab;

---

[2] Quoting Lord Cornwallis in a letter to the Duke of York in 1790.
[3] Quoting Thomas Macaulay (1800-59), he spent three and a half years in India as a member of the Supreme Council under the East India Company.
[4] Omissi Quoting Commander in Chief of Madras Army and Report to the Parliament on the Indian Army 1879.
[5] Quoting Lord Roberts of Kandahar, Commander in Chief of the Indian Army 1885-1893.

Garhwalis, Kumaonis, and Gurkhas from the Himalayan regions;
Rajputs, Brahmans, and Muslims from the Delhi and Hindustan regions;
Rajputs, Jats, Mers, and Muslims from Rajastan and central India;
Marathas and Deccani Muslims from Western India;
Christians, Untouchables, Tamils, and Muslims from Southern India.
(Heathcote, 1974:94).

Though the idea of a martial race in India pre-dates the British presence there, Lord Roberts of Kandahar, who served as Commander in Chief of the Indian Army from 1885 to 1893, can be cited as being responsible for the introduction of a policy of fostering so-called martial races (Cohen, 1971).

Mahmud claims the martial race theory was instrumental in the construction of a separate identity. He asserts that prior to the spread of the martial race theory the Hindu/Sikh distinction was not clearly marked. Furthermore, that Sikh identities, practices and beliefs of various sorts intermixed. According to Mahmud 'It was the colonial Army that consolidated Sikhism as a separate religion and the Sikh as a separate identity' (Mahmud, 1999:1233). Mahmud, continues:

A colonial official noted that Sikhs in the Indian Army have been studiously nationalized or encouraged to regard themselves as a totally distinct and separate nation. Their national pride has been fostered by every available means. Sikh as a martial race was not discovered, it was created (Mahmud, 1999:1233).

Importantly the British recruitment policy reflects two other nationalistic policies, which fed into a broader policy of geographical and theoretical constructions of regions, religions, identities and races during the colonial period. First we can observe the exclusion of the emerging urban middle classes from the colonial army and second, the recruitment of Gurkhas from Nepal. The latter policy did not fit into the Aryan-brotherhood notion, which purported to account for the martial traits amongst some indigenous Indians. Instead, with regard to the Gurkhas we see a modification of the martial race theory to include the philosophy that cooler climates contribute to the development of martial races (Cohen, 1971).

With regard to the exclusion of the urban middle classes, educated urban Bengalis were particularly excluded from the army and peasants from rural localities were favoured. Peasants were considered politically conservative and less likely than city-dwellers to question authority. The urban middle class was presented stereotypically as 'effeminate, sly and scheming' (Mahmud, 1999:1233).

A further colonial practice centred upon logistic considerations. With the emergence of Czarist Russia and the perceived threat to colonial India, the British felt it was necessary to strengthen their frontiers between the subcontinent and Central Asia. The Punjab was the chosen location for such strengthening projects. The Punjab was restructured to fit the martial races theory as a suitable place for soldiers through the most extensive form of socio-economic and demographic engineering attempted by the British in South Asia (Ali, 1988).

The construction of Punjab to fit the martial races theory involved huge civil and infra-structural engineering. First hydraulic 'canal colonies' were created in western Punjab, converting desert to fertile agricultural land. Second there followed a structured programme of 'in-migration' from other parts of Punjab of selected families and clans that had remained loyal to the British during the 1857 Revolt.

These groups helped to create a new landed aristocracy who expressed political allegiance to the British. These groups were dubbed 'agricultural castes' on whom the British relied for political support, military recruitment and raising of cattle and horses for the military.

Third, via the Punjab Alienation of Land Bill 1900, the passing of land from 'agricultural castes' to 'non-agricultural castes' was prohibited. Lastly, recruitment from rural areas and land grants made to ex-soldiers ensured the creation of a culture of soldiering in the canal colonies. By the time of decolonization, nearly half of the colonial Indian Army was recruited from the Punjab (Mahmud, 1999:1234).

What is important about the martial races theory in the present context is its pervasiveness and permeability into the twenty first century. The historian Stephen Cohen claims that the terms and meanings of martial races are 'in common use today among military and civilians, especially amongst those from the Punjab' (Cohen, 1971:45). Cohen also notes that 'Robert's theory of military deterioration never waned, and is widespread today in India' (Cohen, 1971:47).

Theoretically there should be no great imbalance in the composition of the Pakistani military, either in terms of numbers or ethnic distribution among units. In fact, however, the Pakistani military (especially the army) is more unbalanced than the British Indian Army was, or the contemporary Indian army is today. Writing prior to the independence of Bangladesh in 1971, Cohen notes how distrust was mounting amongst the East Pakistanis. Cohen asserts units drawn largely from the Punjab and West Wing dominated the post-Partition Pakistani Army. This fact is important to our understanding of the fears felt by the East Pakistanis who had vivid memories of tough Pathan and Punjabi police and military units imported by the British for law enforcement and suppression of nationalistic agitation prior to the partition of India (Cohen, 1971).

Furthermore, Mahmud believes that the resurrection of the colonial discourse of martial and non-martial races by General Ayub Khan enabled Pakistan to form a racialized construction of a 'state-nation' that culminated in the genocide of Bengalis by the Pakistan military in 1971 (Mahmud, 1999).

Cohen offers a further tracing of how colonial practices have continued into the present:

> Since all Indian and Pakistanis now have the legal right to serve in the military, the military has to some extent come to reflect nationalist and equalitarian doctrine. But, since recruitment to some units (especially the prestigious infantry units) is restricted to specific ethnic groups, the military has not abandoned its ties to traditional Indian and British patterns (Cohen, 1971:194).

Indentured Labour

Slavery was abolished by the British via the Act of Emancipation in 1833 and the French, Danish and Dutch colonial powers followed suit over the next thirty years. The economic dependency of plantation owners on slave labour needed a cost-effective replacement. The solution came in the form of indentured labour.

Between 1834 and 1927, 30 million Indians left India as part of the global division of labour, and just under 24 million returned (Davis, 1951). Most of this migration formed part of the 'coolie system' whereby Asian labour, primarily from China and India, went to colonies governed by Europeans to work on plantations, mines, railroads, and canals. The coolie system was a hybrid of various labour systems but may be located somewhere between slavery and free wage labour (Banaji, 1933).

Tayyab Mahmud details the history and discourse surrounding the practice of indentured labour (1997; 1999). His work illustrates how colonial powers actively deployed racial stereotypes as part of their project of governing the colonized. Mahmud cites sources, such as correspondence between a plantation owner and a British recruiting firm, to highlight the racial stereotypes operating to guide the increasing global division of labour. Indian workers were to be used to assert control and discipline over Black-Caribbean workers since the latter became labelled as 'lazy, unreliable, dishonest and incapable of honouring a contract' (Mahmud, 1997:643). The author notes that such portrayals were also reproduced in Parliamentary and Royal reports. The Indian workers were initially praised for their 'industriousness, familiarity with agriculture, strong family ties, respect of authority and respect for the sanctity of contracts' (Mahmud, 1997:644).

However these positive constructions did not last beyond the Indian's experiences of conditions in the plantations that lead to actions of resistance and self-preservation. Indians now became labelled as 'avaricious, jealous, dishonest, idolatrous and filthy' (Mahmud, 1997:644). The planter's dissatisfaction prompted them to shift to recruiting Chinese labour. The Chinese were the next ethnic group to be viewed, at least temporarily, in a positive light.

However, of what significance are such practices to the present? In demographic terms the deliberate distribution of forced labour explains the contemporary racial composition of former plantation colonies in regions such as the South Pacific, Africa and the West Indies. The birth of ethnic conflicts and political struggles in such former colonies can be traced to the divisive colonial practices and racial constructions that essentially displaced communities from their geographical and cultural homes.

Through an acknowledgment of the interaction of global economics, demand for cheap labour and contingent immigration policies and legislation, the case of the indentured labourer may be compared with that of the twentieth century migrant to the UK. Whilst the penal sanctions for breach of contract have gone, the experiences of the first Muslim settlers in Britain provide some striking parallels.

The migrants entered British society as minorities and remain as such. Racial discourse, however, has perpetually sought to homogenize their diverse identities into neat categories. This is reflected no more strongly than in the early Home Office criminal statistics for ethnic minorities (FitzGerald, 1993).

Initially welcomed as participants in the post-war re-building efforts the initial 'open-door' policies soon deteriorated into a racialized and prejudicial discourse about the status of such migrants (Cook, 1993). Integral to such prejudicial perceptions is the projection of groups such as Muslims as a 'threat to order', 'fanatic', 'terrorist', 'fundamentalist', 'wife-beater', and 'book-burner' (Runnymede, 1997). An examination of such Islamophobia will be provided in due course.

Ethnographic Showcases

The obsession of the European colonial powers with the identification, classification and 'exhibiting' of the colonized races is vividly demonstrated by the ethnographic showcases of 1870 to 1930. These international world fairs such as the Great Exhibition 1851, Colonial and Indian Exhibition 1886 and Worlds' Columbian Exposition 1893 were very large-scale events. Such events combined features of 'trade and industrial fairs, carnival, music festivals, political manifestations, museums and art galleries' (Corbey, 1995:56).

These exhibitions focused upon the industrial, agricultural, artistic, scientific and cultural progress of the colonizer and were the sites for ritualized competition amongst the social and economic elites of the period. The World Fair in Paris marked the first exhibition in which people from non-western cultures were exhibited. Four hundred natives from the French colonies of Indochina, Senegal and Tahiti were displayed in 'native villages' and owing to their success such displays remained a standard part of world fairs from 1878 onwards.

Corbey details a comprehensive list of native peoples who were subjugated, 'tamed' and commercially displayed at such exhibitions, such as several South African peoples who comprised the 'Kaffir Kraal' at The Greater Britain Exhibition of 1899 (Corbey, 1995:61).

A brochure commenting upon the 'Village from Dahomey' at the Imperial International Exhibition of 1909 stressed the violent brutality of indigenous Africa, especially Dahomey with its 'bloodthirsty potentates' and women warriors or 'Amazons' who were one of the main attractions of the village. The exhibition was presented as light against dark, order against violence and as a European nation bringing civilization to Africa. The exhibited 'Amazons' - depicted as both barbarous and alluring, true personifications of the so-called Dark Continent - performed throughout Europe. When they appeared in the Moskauer Panoptikum in Frankfurt in 1899, they were introduced as 'wild females'. A group of women from Samoa, however, were described by the press and in brochures as a 'breathtakingly beautiful, always cheery, erotically permissive and lazy people from the paradisiacal Pacific Ocean'[6].

---

[6] Plakate 1880-1914:257 (n.d.) exhibition catalogue, Historisches Museum Frankfurt.

Many Europeans viewed a Black African as some sort of monster. France consciously played on such fears in the French-German War of 1870-1871 by pitting Black 'tirailleurs indigenes', trained in Algeria, against German troops (Goldman, 1985:258). Whilst most sources highlight the exhibiting of natives of Africa the showcase selection did extend to people from India, for instance a prominent exhibitor Carl Hagenback is reported to have been exhibiting people from India since 1874 (Corbey, 1995).

The underlying philosophy of events such as the British Exhibition at Wembley in 1924 was to provide visual spectacles to promote the triumph of the civilized over the barbaric. Commentators, such as Corbey, believe that deconstructing such events illustrates the origins of contemporary notions of 'primitiveness tied up with imperialist ideology and social Darwinism' (Corbey, 1995:59).

The question to ask is how far have these notions of the 'dark, primitive savage', 'tamed or controlled' by a 'white civilized just and righteous race' permeated the present criminological terrain?

Islam in the Indian Subcontinent During Colonial Rule

The preceding discussion has provided a broad analysis of colonialism in India and focused on the specific aspects of institutionalized identity construction. South Asian Muslims were members of these colonized peoples, and this section explores in more detail how Muslims have been affected by colonialism.

Since colonization is a complex process, academic de-colonization presents a difficult deconstruction of such complexity. Whilst the objectives and policies of the colonizer may be relatively easily identified, in the words of some scholars 'it is extremely difficult to identify what values, institutions and identities are foreign and part of colonial legacy' (Pieterse and Parekh, 1995: 2). Nevertheless it is argued here that such complexity should not prevent the task from being executed.

With regard to the Muslim world there are perhaps significant instances where colonization marks a clear encroachment upon their governance. According to Francis Robinson:

> By the 1920s the British Empire embraced substantially more than half the Muslim peoples of the world. For much of the Twentieth Century Britain was the greatest influence over their development…The British Empire was the context in which many Muslims experienced the transition to modernity (Robinson, 1999:398).

Indeed there is undeniable evidence that the strategic and economic needs of Empire combined with local forces to carve the shapes of modern Muslim states, and in which many Muslims live, out of former Muslim empires, caliphates, sultanates and sheikdoms (Robinson, 1999:400).

In 1914 a colony of Muslims was created in Nigeria. The 'Hausa' Muslims of northern Nigeria, who had peopled the Fulani caliphate of Sokoto, were forcibly thrust together with peoples from central and southern regions. The religions and traditions of each geographical group were different, but here they were compelled to co-exist.

In Uganda, Kenya and Tanganyika (Tanzania) there were Muslim communities formed initially from the Swahili-speaking peoples who during the nineteenth century had been pressing inland from the coast. Through East Africa from Uganda to South Africa there were also Muslims of Indian origins. Amongst this group were the 'Nizari Ismaili' followers of the Aga Khan, whose migration the British had encouraged to assist in developing the resources of the region (Robinson, 1999).

In addition to such institutional practices the very fact of colonization in the Indian subcontinent influenced the emergence of particular Muslim sects. The collapse of the Mughal Empire, following Aurangzeb's death in 1707, had initiated a process of re-evaluation amongst all religious groups in India. For the Muslims of India, however, the stripping of Mughal sovereignty prompted particular anguish since British colonialism marked the toppling of an Islamic Empire and its replacement by a Christian people (Lewis, 1994:35).

One should note there is considerable debate as to when the British period of Indian history commences. Historians usually quote The Battle of Plessy in 1757 as the start of British rule in India, although it is often predated to 1740 with the War of the Austrian Succession, or postponed to the Battle of Paniput in 1761 or even to 1774 with the establishment of Governor General following the Regulating Act. What is more clearly observed is that, in any event, the process of political transition took eighty years to accomplish (Smith, 1998).

Following the short-term failure of the first War of Independence (Great Mutiny) in 1857, the Indian Muslims were prompted to adopt various strategies, which shifted from isolation from, to accommodation of, the new rulers (Lewis, 1994). The post-1857 period saw the emergence of particular sectarian groups. Furthermore, this period is of direct relevance to the contemporary expressions of Islam in South Asia and the transplanting of such to Britain via in-migration of South Asian Muslims. According to Philip Lewis, five traditions are of particular importance since they are the product of the colonial encounter and have been transferred to British cities such as Bradford: namely the reformist Deobandis, the quietist and revivalist Tablighi Jama'at, the conservative and populist Barelwis, the Islamist Jamm'at-I-Islami and the modernists (Lewis, 1994). These Islamic traditions are also prevalent within the British Muslim population in cities such as Birmingham (Joly, 1995)[7].

Islamophobia

According to the Oxford Dictionary the first recorded use of the term 'Islamophobia' was in an article in the journal 'Insight' on 4 Feb 1991 in reference to political affairs between Moscow and Afghanistan. The Runnymede

---

[7] See Chapter 1 for a discussion of these traditions.

Commission Report on British Muslims and Islamophobia suggests the term was first coined around the late 1980s and they define it as being similar to 'xenophobia' and 'Europhobia' in origin, and is taken to mean a 'dread or hatred of Islam and therefore, to the fear and dislike of all Muslims' (Runnymede 1997:1). The same report acknowledges that it is not an 'ideal' word but refers to behaviour which effectively excludes Muslims from the 'economic, social and public life of the nation' (Runnymede, 1997:1).

Fred Halliday questions the term 'Islamophobia' and argues that a more accurate term would be 'Anti-Muslimism' (Halliday, 1999:898). The reason for Halliday's view is that he believes that while in the past Islam as a faith was challenged, in times such as the Crusades or *Reconquista* for example, this is not the case in contemporary society. Halliday believes that the attack now is not on Islam as a faith but on 'Muslims' as a people. His rejection of the term Islamophobia is also based upon a belief that use of such a term reproduces a distortion that there is one 'Islam', which denies the diversity within Islam. Further, to view Islam in a homogeneous term enables certain members of the Muslim communities to offer their own selective interpretation of the tradition, be this on women, rights of free speech, the right to renounce the religion or anything else. According to Halliday, 'Islamophobia' indulges conformism and authority within Muslim communities' (Halliday, 1999:899).

Whether we refer to behaviour as 'Anti-Muslimism' or 'Islamophobia' seems a moot point. If we are agreed that either term refers to behaviour encapsulating hatred, and/or dislike to the extent of social and economic exclusion of Muslims, we must move to consider the extent of such behaviour and to evaluate how this influences crime and victimization amongst Muslims in Britain. The questions raised are to what extent do Muslims feel victims of such prejudicial behaviour and how far does this influence their sense of identity in Britain?

The Runnymede Report provides a detailed analysis of the complex social, historical, and political practices which constitute and aid the perpetuation of Islamophobia or anti-Muslim sentiments. The Report identifies eight distinctions pertaining to closed and open views about Islam. Since the bulk of the report revolves around these themes or distinctions, it is worth detailing them here. The eight distinctions between closed and open views of Islam are monolithic/diverse; separate/interacting; inferior/different; enemy/partner; manipulative/sincere; criticism of the West rejected/ considered; discrimination defended/ criticized and Islamophobia seen as natural/problematic (Runnymede, 1997:5). Taking each in turn, a closed view of Islam is one which considers it monolithic and unchanging, this is contrasted with an open view which acknowledges the diversity and progression of Islam. The history and data in Chapter 1 of this book has already illustrated the diversity and development of Islam refuting assertions about its monolithic character. Islam is often perceived within a closed perspective as separate and having few aims and objectives in common with other faiths or cultures. An open view of this distinction is that Islam acknowledges interdependence with other faiths and cultures both having certain shared values, being affected by them and further enriching them. Once again, given its Abrahamic origin, commonalities of theology, world-views and practices in Islam with other faiths such as Judaism and Christianity are inevitable. Islamophobic language and discourse indicts Islam as being barbaric, primitive, inferior and sexist, instead of different and equally worthy of respect. Muslims are projected as the enemy with Islam promoting violence, terrorism and a clash of civilizations. A more open view would emphasize that Muslims should be viewed as potential partners in co-operative initiatives to resolve common problems. When Muslims speak critically of Western politics, trade policies or practices a closed view would reject this as anti-West without engaging in debates where meaningful and informed critiques are considered. When discrimination is evidenced a closed response would be to attempt to justify the practice instead of attempting to diminish or challenge it. Finally, where Islamophobia is viewed as natural and normal this denies legitimate challenges to critical views of Islam (Runnymede, 1997).

The Runnymede Report details the role of the media in perpetuating stereotypical and discriminatory images and perceptions of Islam and Muslims. There is undeniable evidence of national and local press coverage which tends to project Muslims as a homogenous, antagonistic and fanatical group (Desai, 1999; Webster, 1997; Alexander, 2000). This must be contrasted with previous images of relative conformity amongst Asian, rather than Muslim, populations in the UK (Mawby and Batta, 1980).

Following the terrorist attacks on September 11th 2001, anti-Muslim sentiment and assaults upon Muslims in Europe intensified. According to the European Monitoring Centre on Racism and Xenophobia there was a noticeable rise in verbal attacks upon Muslims in all 14 member states, with a rise in physical attacks in the Netherlands, Sweden and the UK immediately following September 11th (EUMC, 2001). In the Netherlands the attacks against Muslims included acts of arson against an Islamic School in Nijmegen (17/9/01); telephone threats to a mosque in Roosendaal (17/9/01) and the words 'death to the Muslims' being written on the walls of an Islamic centre in Barneveld (17/9/01) (EUMC, 2001:annex). In Sweden, the attacks included Nazi graffiti on Muslim business premises; skirmishes between Muslim and non-Muslim pupils in schools and the mobilization of the anti-immigration campaign party, Sweden Democrats, in support of Israel in an attempt to foster anti-Muslim and anti-Arab sentiments in Sweden (EUMC, 2001:annex). In the UK an Afghan minicab driver was seriously assaulted and left paralyzed from the neck down by three men who, according to the police, referred to the attacks in New York; a 19 year old Asian women in Swindon was beaten around the head by two men with a baseball bat, the perpetrators were reported to have said 'here's a Muslim' prior to the assault. Furthermore, a mosque in Bolton was firebombed, whilst bricks were thrown at mosques in Belfast, Manchester, London, Southend and Glasgow (EUMC, 2001:annex). These are just a few of the incidents which were registered by the EUMC. Whilst the EUMC report states that the media tended to provide balanced coverage of the attacks in the USA, there were some incidents of sensationalism and 'anti-Islamic headlines' within member states (EUMC, 2001:3).

Considerable debate was prompted about the extent of 'Islamophobia' following the inner city riots in Bradford and Oldham (IHRC, 2001). The disadvantaged economic positions of the Muslim communities in these urban localities have been cited as evidence of Islamophobia at an institutional level, depriving such communities of adequate resources (IHRC, 2001). An evaluation of the socio-economic profiles of these communities provides a useful context through which to make sense of the disturbances (IHRC, 2001). Indeed, there has been evidence of poverty within the Muslim communities of Britain for a number of years as concluded by the Child Poverty Action Group in 1996 (Q-News, 1996)[8]. However, the principal incitement and impetus for the disturbances has been linked to agitation by the British National Party (IHRC 2001:12; The Independent 2001)[9].

Further, the BBC recently attempted to address the issue of Islamophobia through investigative journalism and concluded there was some limited evidence of discriminatory practices against Muslims in Britain[10]. Certainly, as far as the present study is concerned, the majority of Muslim respondents expressed a perceived general intolerance and negativity in the public projection of Islam and Muslims in the West (see Chapter 5). As discussed in Chapter 1, the few studies exploring issues of Muslims and crime in Britain suggest Muslims are excluded and marginalized from mainstream British society (Wardak, 2000; Webster, 1997). It is more difficult to deconstruct precisely how this exclusion process occurs, although it is certain that issues of discrimination, racism, xenophobia and Islamophobia are intertwined in the lived experiences of Muslims (see Chapter 5). That is to say South Asian Muslims in Britain are part of a religious as well as an ethnic minority group. When facing explicit or implicit prejudice they may not be able to differentiate between whether discrimination directed at them is due to their ethnic or religious disposition. A discussion of how South Asian Muslims have experienced Islamophobia and discrimination is presented in the analysis of the primary research in Chapter 5.

From the preceding discussions it is clear that certain attitudes, practices and legislative policies, adopted by the British during colonial rule in India, constituted identity-manipulation and racialized constructions. With reference to the construction of the 'racial criminal other', the Criminal Tribes Act of 1871 is one tangible empirical example of determinist and racist criminal and penal policy. Elements of such racialized constructions have arguably been traced into the terrain of post-colonialism in Pakistan, with reference to contemporary discourses about criminogenic people and corresponding policing strategies (CPLC, 1999).

This chapter discussed policies and practices, such as the resurrection of the martial races theory, the economic strategy of indentured labour and racial stereotyping via ethnographic showcases, by means of 'un-telling' the historical past. The discussion highlights and further compounds the significance of plotting practices of discrimination in order to shape and guide contemporary discussions about historically manipulated peoples.

---

[8] Q-News 19 April-9 May 1996 page 3.

[9] Raymond Whitaker - *The Independent on Sunday* 1 July 2001 page 9 and Indira Das-Gupta - *The Independent on Sunday* 8 July 2001 page 4.

[10] Jeremy Bowen - 'Islamophobia' - Part of BBC Islam UK series w/c 13/08/01.

The theoretical movement that prompted such an evaluation in the present study is critical race theory (CRT). We shall discuss CRT further in Chapter 6, but it is the overarching perspective that frames the present study and the reason why certain methodologies were adopted in analyzing the data gathered.

Chapter 4

Background to Fieldwork Locations

In addition to undertaking criminological interviews and observations, the research study undertook the collection of historical and socio-demographic data regarding the fieldwork locations. Such information is deemed essential in explaining contemporary social relations, population migration, settlement and the development of political dynamics for the sample selected.

This Chapter begins with a brief history of Karachi before describing the specific research location in Sharifabad. The Chapter then continues to discuss the location of this study in England and details some of the interaction and problems experienced by the first generation Muslim settlers in Haslingden.

Karachi, Pakistan: A Brief History of the Development of Karachi

Karachi's prominence in the Indian subcontinent arose following the Partition of India and the creation of Pakistan in 1947. Activity by the British, since 1843, had transformed the walled city of 14,000 to 57,000 population by 1862 following efforts to expand the commercial activity of this port city (Mannheim and Winter, 1996). However, it was to be political developments that initiated the massive expansion of Karachi, which is now one of the most populous cities of the world, with approximately 14 million population. The last census in Pakistan was undertaken in 1997/1998, and according to the Bureau of Statistics, the latest population figure for Karachi is said to be around 11 million (Bureau of Statistics, 2000). Critics believe this figure to be conservative in light of the Federal Award, which is related to population. The higher the population, the higher the Federal Award, hence some argue Karachi's population has been deliberately recorded at a lower figure. One source claims the population to be at least over 12 million, the statistics are still awaiting official final analysis (Urban Resource Centre, 2005)[1].

Partition in 1947 led to the arrival of thousands of refugees from the Central and Northern Provinces of India. The influx was so dramatic that Karachi's population rose from 420,000 in 1948 to over one million by 1951 (Fernandes and Fernandes, 1994). Over 60 per cent of Karachi's population at this time were immigrants, bringing with them a social and cultural heritage distinct from both the indigenous Karachiites and the rural peoples of Sindh. The significance of this migrant population to the contemporary political life in Karachi cannot be

---

[1] Urban Resource Centre, Karachi http://www.urckarachi.org/home.htm, 28/2/05.

overstated. Upon Partition, the Mohajirs[2], as the migrants subsequently became known, began to dominate politics, commerce and the social life of Karachi, and indeed of Pakistan as a whole (Mahmud, 1997).

A study by the Pakistan Institute of Development Economics in 1994 estimates that 1.40 million migrants settled in Karachi during 1947-58. Of these 1.14 million came from India and 0.26 million from Punjab and the North West Frontier Province in the new Pakistan. (Fernandes and Fernandes, 1994). Despite the political decision by General Ayub Khan to move the nation's capital from Karachi to Islamabad in 1960, the city of Karachi continues to sprawl, thus forming the country's largest conurbation. The city's status as a true 'Eldorado' for migrants remains firmly so, and it has become host to waves of migrants from India, Bangladesh, Afghanistan and various parts of rural Pakistan. (Kool, Verboom, and Linden, 1988). Ten per cent of Pakistan's population live in Karachi, which comprises 22 per cent of the country's urban population. Furthermore, Karachi contributes 15 per cent of the nations' GDP, 25 per cent of the Federal Reserve, 50 per cent of all bank deposits and 72 per cent of issued capital (Bureau of Statistics, 1990).

This rapid expansion has not resulted in corresponding planned development and therefore the infrastructure of the city is suffering from heavy over-subscription. In Karachi, between 2.5 and 3 million people live in kaatchi abaadis or squatter settlements, and the national squatter population is around 45 million (Human Rights Commission of Pakistan Report 1997).

Sharifabad, Karachi, Sindh, Pakistan

Sharifabad is an area of approximately 1-mile square in the Federal 'B' District of Karachi and has a population of approximately 15,000. The area is typical of a planned residential settlement in Karachi and was initially intended to providing housing for civil servants. However, with the stripping of Karachi's capital status in 1960, Sharifabad, and other areas like it in Karachi, became areas for the middle class Mohajirs to settle, propelled initially by the over-crowding of the old central parts of the city such as Saddar. The area is named after Mr Sharif, a builder who was responsible for its development and is still a local resident. The first residents moved into Sharifabad in the mid to late 1960s, when it formed an area on the northern fringes of the old city. The rapid urban sprawl in Karachi has meant Sharifabad is now more accurately understood as being within central metropolitan Karachi.

The Political Significance of the Mohajir Population

Prior to the Partition of India in 1947 the Urdu-speaking Muslim minority, subsequently known as 'Mohajirs', had formed communities in urban areas of

---

[2] Mohajir: Arabic, literally meaning migrant or refugee, originating from the Flight of the Prophet Mohammed, (p.b.u.h.), from Makkah to Medina in 622 AD; subsequently asserted as a distinct racial group by the Mohajir Quomi Mahaz (Migrant National Front) in 1984.

North Central India where they constituted twenty per cent of the population (Mahmud, 1997). Mohajirs had been closely associated with the Mughal Empire which meant they had relatively high levels of literacy and had acquired an elite status within Indian society. It was from within this ethnic group that the All Indian Muslim League was founded in 1906 (Moorhouse, 1983). Indeed, it can be said that the principal political articulation of the concept of a separate Muslim State came essentially from this group of people who adopted Chaudri Rahmat Ali's term via the Pakistan Resolution in 1940. In 1947 the Mohajirs constituted some twenty per cent of the eight million that migrated to Pakistan following Partition, but only constituted five per cent of the total population of the new Islamic Republic of Pakistan (Mahmud, 1997).

The majority of the Mohajirs settled in Karachi declared it a capital and began to dominate the politics, commerce and culture of the newly formed country (Hussain, 1996). According to Tayyab Mahmud, the case of the Mohajirs represents a unique attempt by a state to create a nation (Mahmud, 1997). The initial dominance of the Mohajirs was short-lived as their attempts to deny federalism grew increasingly weaker and ineffective. Opposition to their dominance was demonstrated, for example, by the stripping of Karachi's capital status in 1960 (Mannheim and Winter, 1996). The Mohajir dominance lasted for approximately twenty years post-Partition and then began to implode for a number of reasons. Partition had created mass upheaval, displacement and economic deprivation for the majority. Those who had managed to succeed financially were increasingly viewed to be enlarging the gulf between the affluent and impoverished. The ethnic groups marginalized by social division began to mobilize via resistance movements. At the same time the financial gap between rich and poor began to alienate the intelligentsia, professionals and urban student groups to whom the denial of civil liberties became increasingly intolerable (Mahmud, 1997).

With the overriding of civilian governments and successive military dictatorships the once elite Mohajir population has experienced marginalization, particularly with regard to government policies deemed discriminatory (Shaheed, 1996). The frustrations of the Mohajirs were politicized via the formation of the Mohajir Qaumi Mahaz (MQM, Migrant National Front) in 1984. The party subsequently splintered into two factions culminating in the formation of the Haqiqi (real or true) MQM and the renaming of the original MQM to Muttahida (people's) National Front in the 1990s.

The political dynamics of groups in Karachi frame a turbulent recent history of ethnic and politically motivated violence (Hussain, 1996; Shaheed, 1996). The conflicts can be viewed within three categories, first, the annual clashes between two major sects of Islam, Sunnis and Shi'ites; second, the periodic clashes against Ahmadi[3] groups and third, the more frequent clashes between different ethnic groups (Shaheed, 1996).

---

[3] Ahmadi - adherents to a sect founded by Mirza Gulam Ahmad (1835-1908) of Qadian, Punjab. Orthodox Muslims have claimed them to be a heretic group due to its founder's claim to be a prophet (Nigosian, 1987).

Some of the most destructive riots and disturbances took place in December of 1986 between Mohajirs and Pathans[4] (Hussain, 1996). The catalyst for the riots was the government's Sohrab Goth Operation on 12 December 1986. Sohrab Goth was an area on the outskirts of Karachi known as being the location for the storage, distribution and sale of heroin. The community serving this area comprised mainly of Pathans and some Afghan refugees, both groups occupied squats which provided tunnels for the illegal storage of drugs and weapons. The drugs mafia instigated propaganda to mobilize the Pathan community alleging that Mohajirs were to blame for the forced evictions at Sohrab Goth as part of a wider plot to evict Pathans from Karachi (Hussain, 1996). On 13 December, several hundred armed Pathan men commenced acts of murder, assault, arson and riot against Mohajir homes. This initial act claimed over forty lives, the days following witnessed retaliation from the Mohajirs and unchecked rioting spread to many parts of Karachi for four days (Hussain, 1996; Shaheed, 1996).

The urban conflicts in Karachi are reflective of an ingrained crisis between the state and civil society. There is little public trust, dependence or respect for governmental institutions due to significant evidence of corruption, poor civic amenities and economic inequity. Furthermore, as Akmal Hussain highlights, the availability of firearms following the end of the Afghan war and the 'collapse of state authority in large parts of Sind' has prompted civilians to seek community support mechanisms to redress injustice and provide protection from physical assaults (Hussain, 1996:193).

Haslingden, Rossendale, Lancashire, England: A Brief History of Haslingden

Haslingden is historically a Lancastrian mill town located 17 miles north of Manchester in the North West of England. Set in the Rossendale Valley, the town is surrounded by the West Pennine Moors and is famous for its flagstones, which are exported throughout the world and form the paving of Trafalgar Square. Haslingden is situated on the edge of the Pennine Chain, which makes it one of the highest towns in Lancashire, at approximately 1000 feet above sea level. The surrounding moorland rises in places to a height of 1300 feet above sea level. The town is thought to have derived its name from the Anglo-Saxon words 'haesel' and 'denn', meaning 'valley of the hazels'.

The first recorded mention of the town is often cited as 1242 when 'Heselingedon' was assigned by King Henry III as part of the dower of countess Margaret on the death of her husband, John de Lacy, Earl of Lincoln (Cruise and Dunnachie, 1994). During the Middle Ages, Haslingden was the scene of cattle rearing, lead mining and smelting and its history is connected with that of the Forest of Rossendale.

There is evidence that Haslingden experienced various economic activities during the 13th and 15th centuries, including deer breeding and sheep farming.

---

[4] Pathans - see glossary.

Following the deforestation of the Forest of Rossendale and the rise in wool production, the town entered a period of prosperity during the 16th century. The main industrial activity at this time was woollen manufacturing. By 1821 the population of Haslingden was estimated at 6,595. Road improvements, at the end of the 18th century and beginning of the 19th century, led to further population increases and by 1851 it had reached 9,000. The town was home to an influx of Irish migrants between the years 1845 to 1849, following the Irish potato famine. The increase in population gave rise to various social and public health problems, which led to the establishment of a Local Board in 1875 and subsequent incorporation of the town in 1891. Between the years 1935 and 1939, 810 people were re-housed by the local authority in the first phase of a scheme to rectify problems of overcrowding, poor sanitation and related health risks (Cruise and Dunnachie, 1994). By the outbreak of World War II, 77.5 per cent of the town's population were still employed in the textile industry (Rossendale Archives Collection, 1992).

The Arrival of the Muslims

There is little documentation of migration from the Indian subcontinent and settlement in Haslingden, beginning in the 1950s. The only source that mentions the migration pattern of Asians to the locality to any significant extent is a pamphlet published by Hyndburn and Rossendale Community Relations Council (Smallridge, 1981).

The absence of substantial written records has contributed to the adoption of a life history approach in an attempt to document the experiences of the first Muslim settlers to Haslingden. The following is a summary of a life history of a 68-year-old Pakistani male who has been a resident of Haslingden since 1960. According to his account, there was a population of approximately one hundred male Pakistanis (from both East and West) in 1960. The majority were from West Pakistan, this being a time prior to the creation of Bangladesh in 1971.

As for previous indigenous generations, it was the textile industry that had attracted the first wave of Muslim migrants to Lancashire and Haslingden. The textile industry was a labour intensive one and hence the semi-skilled and unskilled migrant could find employment relatively easily:

> Pakistanis came because it was quite low skill, it didn't need much training, within a matter of two weeks a man could run the machines, become an operator[5].

The attraction to the textile industry was not contained to Lancashire, with West Yorkshire experiencing the trend on a much larger scale; for example, in the 1960s 94 per cent of the Asian migrant population in Keighley were employed in the textile industry (Webster, 1994). The first wave migrants were encouraged to work in the textile industry, which paid them lower wages than the indigenous

---

[5] Life history of Pakistani resident of Haslingden since 1960, field notes and interview transcript.

workforce. The migrants accepted lower wages because it was considerably more than they could earn in their countries of origin. Employees were also encouraged to call their male relatives over to the UK in order to provide a cheap source of labour. Migrants lived in poor conditions, in houses that were poorly maintained, not desirable to others and extremely cramped. It was not uncommon for fifteen men to share a two-bedroom terraced house, with no inside toilet or bathroom. Those in Haslingden worked mainly in one of the large local textile factories. There was originally no mosque and they rarely arranged for collective worship. In response to an economic demand, some local grocers began to stock some of the basic provisions requested by these new settlers, such as spices.

In reaction to an environment of poor housing and lack of amenities deemed essential to their needs, migrants gradually developed local networks and were aided by enterprising local residents. There were some who befriended a local lady who acted as their interpreter, banker and prostitute. The period was one of dramatic change for the migrants and there is oral evidence to suggest that practices prohibited by Islam, such as extra-marital relationships, some first settlers experienced alcohol consumption and gambling.

The first settlers claimed that they did not wish or expect to settle permanently in the UK. However, from the mid 1960s to early 1970s, according to the respondent, this attitude or philosophy was modified. Migrants began to invite their spouses and family to the UK. With the beginning of such chain-migration, the responsibilities of the lone male dramatically shifted towards improving children's education, family health, better housing and places of collective worship.

Talk of a permanent Islamic centre began in 1966, although at that time there were doubts amongst the settlers as to whether such a permanent investment was necessary in view of the intention of the vast majority of the community to return to Pakistan. Fund raising began in 1967 and a deposit was paid on a building in Blackburn Road, close to where the majority of the migrants resided. By 1968 a rudimentary Islamic centre with basic facilities for ablution and congregational prayers was functioning. The initial settlers expressed particular concern at having to use Haslingden Public Baths for washing where there was no privacy and facilities were poor. The Islamic centre helped to alleviate some of their concerns about bathing in public. The Mayor of Haslingden officially opened the Islamic centre in 1968. However, at festivals such as *'Īd* when there were large congregations the growing community had to hire public halls. Migrants also found it particularly difficult to obtain halal meat and some resorted to buying live chickens from a local farmer and then illegally slaughtering them in their own cellars.

Although the first migrants to Haslingden were collectively from Pakistan, use of this nationalistic identity denies the subtleties and specifics of their cultural origins. In Haslingden, the initial settlers were overwhelmingly from two specific regions, one each in the former East and West Pakistan. The East Pakistanis (subsequently Bangladeshis) were from Sylhet (in present day North Bangladesh), and the West Pakistanis were from 'Chach', which is the modern day Attock otherwise known as the Campbellpur District of the Punjab in North Pakistan. Both groups were mainly from rural locations in these locations and had poor levels of education. The West Pakistanis spoke Pushto or Hindko, whilst the Bangladeshis spoke Sylheti.

With the arrival of the wives of the first settlers, family formation developed and many first generation children were born in the locality from the 1970s onwards. Demographic analysis in other larger towns and cities illustrates that in Britain Bangladeshis are the most recent South Asian ethnic groups to have undergone family re-union (Webster, 1994).

A useful source of information regarding the interaction between the first Muslim migrants and locals as well as the social problems the migrants experienced was located in the local press archives of Rawtenstall public library. In 1977 the Rossendale Valley Community Relations Council issued a report, which highlighted problems facing the local Pakistani and Bangladeshi population[6]. The report predicted a doubling of the Asian community in Rossendale from 900 in 1977 to a forecast of nearly 2000 by 1987. The projected population increase was based on the entitlement of male migrants to bring their wives and children into the UK. It was also reported that 'the wives involved are said to be almost all of child-bearing age and may be expected to have more children in the first years they are in this country, in a situation which has similarities to the post-war bulge' (Rossendale Free Press, 1977).

The report claimed that the Asian population of Rossendale were facing problems revolving around the health service, education, language difficulties, housing and jobs. Further, it was reported that both communities lived generally in areas of poor housing and worked mainly in the textile industry. Significantly the report also stated that the majority of the Pakistanis and Bangladeshis in Rossendale lived almost entirely in Haslingden and neighbouring Rawtenstall.

The influx of such migrants was reported in the local press to present particular strains on local amenities. There was significant attention given to the reporting of the language barriers for the migrant population[7]. The public reporting of the relationship between the migrants and the indigenous community depicts a general picture of tolerance, despite the problems that faced the migrant community. There are no reported accounts of racism or prejudice against the migrants. However absence of reported racism cannot exclude the possibility that such behaviour was indeed occurring. The very absence of media reports of racism is perhaps a reflection of the limited capacity and means by which migrants could articulate their concerns about these issues at this time.

There are reports that demonstrate a favourable attitude towards the migrant community, insofar as they represented a significant supply of manual labour. For example, there is one particularly well-reported incident regarding the legal 'battle'

---

[6] 'Valley Asians will Double in 10 years' Rossendale Free Press, 11/06/77, Rawtenstall Public Library News cuttings Archive.
[7] 'New help for Asians to topple barrier' Rossendale Free Press 14/01/78, 'Overtime rush for lessons in English' Rossendale Free Press 18/03/78, 'Help sought to fell language barrier' Rossendale Free Press 28/04/79. 'Leaflets make life easier for immigrants' Rossendale Free Press 26/01/85.

of a local white boss who opposed the deportation of his Pakistani employee. The boss is reported to have said the following about his employee:

> I do not want to see him sent from this country...we want to hold on to him. He has paid a lot of income tax and I think he is entitled to have some of the human rights we keep preaching about. He has never had a day off work, never had a holiday since he came to work for me. He is reliable and honest and I would stake my life on him. I will put up £30,000 for his bail if they let me, even if it means selling my house (Rossendale Free Press, 09/02/80).

When the textile industry experienced recession in the late 1970s and early 1980s the corresponding redundancies particularly affected the local Pakistani and Bangladeshi communities who accounted for 90 per cent of the work force in some mills[8].

The Present Socio-demographic Profile of Haslingden

Haslingden falls within the three Rossendale Census wards of Worsley, Greenfield and Helmshore. These wards, together with the rest of the Rossendale wards, form the County and Electoral division of Haslingden and the Parliamentary Constituency of Rossendale and Darwen (Home Office, 1991).

Haslingden has a population of 14,443 of which 371 (2.57%) are Pakistani, 200 (1.38%) are Bangladeshi and 20 (0.14%) are Indian (Home Office, 1991). A total of just over 4 per cent of the town's population are therefore of South Asian origin. The majority of the Pakistanis and Bangladeshis in Haslingden reside within the Greenfield and Worsley wards. In the Worsley ward the total population or residents is 4066 of which 1 person is Indian (0.02%), 172 (4.2%) are Pakistani, 196 (4.8%) are Bangladeshi and 3633 (89.3%) are white. In the Greenfield Ward the total population of residents is 5649 of which 21 (0.37%) are Indian, 209 (3.6%) are Pakistani, 25 (0.44%) are Bangladeshi and 5342 (94.56%) are white. The majority of the Muslims (Pakistani and Bangladeshi) (86.79%) reside in privately owned accommodation; the percentage for whites is below this at 71.68%. The percentage of Asian households that rent privately is 3.77%, which is slightly higher than the white figure at 2.33%. Whilst home owning is favoured to renting by the Asian groups and indicates relative prosperity a high percentage did not have facilities such as central heating (47%), compared to a white population without central heating at 15% (Home Office, 1991).

Haslingden has an unemployment rate of 7.7%, this is higher than the county average of 4.89% (Home Office, 1991). Furthermore Haslingden does not have an NHS hospital, local authority old people's home or youth and community centre. It does have three sheltered accommodation blocks and one hostel (Lancashire County Council, 1993). The main concentration of industry is now centred on Carrs Industrial Estate employing approximately 1,100 people.

---

[8] 'Immigrants hit by textile redundancies' Rossendale Free Press, 29/06/81.

More recently, Haslingden has experienced the establishment of two mosques, one in Beaconsfield Street in 1988[9], and a second mosque in Union Street in 1997[10]. When the research was undertaken there are two halal meat suppliers and three Asian grocers. Haslingden's increasing multiculturalism is reflected by the establishment of a community group called Project One-o-One, formed as a partnership between The Government Challenge Fund, Action For Haslingden and Mid-Pennine Arts. This voluntary based organization arranges events such as poetry recitals and music and fashion evenings for the local community, which includes the Muslims community.

The historical descriptions explain present settlement patterns in each location. The differences in empirical detail as between each location reflect contrasting methods and accuracy of collating social and demographic statistics in the respective countries. Where the UK has benefited from generations of detailed statistical recording of populations, housing and amenities, in Karachi statistical records are not as sophisticated, reliable or comprehensive.

Though the two locations are separated by thousands of miles they are similar in a number of respects. Both locations house displaced peoples, those in Haslingden claim ethnic origin from the Indian subcontinent (principally Northern Pakistan and Sylhet in Bangladesh), those in Karachi are the displaced refugees from Central and Northern India propelled to a newly constituted Pakistan in 1947. As discussed in Chapter 3, both populations have been influenced by British colonial and foreign policy, and both groups selected are South Asian Sunni Muslims. These community profiles must be referred to in order to fully comprehend the evaluation of the criminological data discussed in the next chapter.

---

[9] Masjid-e-Bilal.
[10] Masjid-e-Baitul Mukarram.

Chapter 5

Crime, Deviance and Victimization in Britain and Pakistan

Introduction

The research in Pakistan and the UK enabled a comprehensive collection of primary and secondary data. Whilst references to secondary sources are made throughout the text, the following themes represent an analysis of the core qualitative primary data, namely interviews with persons in Pakistan and England and field observations in both countries.

The topics discussed represent recurring themes and articulations from across the research sample. Each observation is substantiated by transcript extracts from interviews with individuals residing in or proximate to each locality. The data also includes extracts of interviews with officials in Karachi. To protect the identity of the respondents pseudonyms have been used throughout.

Perceptions of Crime

The findings presented here should be located in the context of the community profiles contained in the previous chapter. All respondents were asked what type of crime was of most concern to them. In Karachi virtually all interviewees indicated that politically motivated violence and corruption was the most important area of concern for them. For example, in the opinion of students such as Aliyah:

> People are more afraid of political crimes, because it is a web in which once you've got entangled you cannot get out.

Similarly, Bilquis spoke of how she felt that crime in Karachi was largely due to political groups that recruit students to fight literally for their cause. Also, Chanda emphasized that political corruption and crime within the ruling strata of society had a profound influence upon the rest of society. Chanda also highlighted the despair felt by citizens who contributed to government income, legitimately or illegitimately; yet saw no positive reinvestment of such monies in their social welfare.

Similar views were held amongst the residents of Sharifabad, for example, in the opinion of Abdul:

The main tension is between political groups, so politically motivated crimes concern me most in Karachi.

Babu and Cairul echoed the concerns of the majority of respondents interviewed emphasizing the direct negative effect of politically motivated violence upon their daily social existence. Babu spoke of the effect of political violence and civil unrest on his studies:

Well political crimes and strikes they affect my studies, the schools and colleges are closed, sometimes for a day or two, we can't do anything about it, even the government can't do anything.

For Karachiites the political environment dictates their daily lives in extremely significant ways. The political instability of the country has instilled an almost universal despair, as well as loathing for political in-fighting and constitutional wranglings. Of greatest concern is the manifestation of such instability by violent means. This serves to explain the priority placed on such issues by the Karachiites. It should also be noted that the sample interviewed were overwhelmingly Mohajir, educated and middle class, for whom political issues such as graduate employment and the racial quota system for government recruitment are of direct concern. Indeed, a principal objection was raised to the racial quota system, which is enforced in Sind but allegedly not in other states of Pakistan.

On the whole the formulation of such perceptions amongst Karachiites is a reflection of their life experiences of such politically motivated violence. There was an acknowledgement that political affiliation is often used as a mask behind which a host of criminal activity may be executed, with little or no relation to the political objectives of the group, which is being misrepresented by their actions. Bodrul spoke of the reasons why many are attracted to join political parties in Karachi:

Here, for example, if I am a villain, terrorist or dacoit, I will attempt to gain political affiliation and support, after which I will become the king of the neighbourhood and untouchable regardless of what I say or do.

In contrast, the British respondents gave mixed responses as to which crimes concerned them most, varying from zina (fornication and adultery), and drug and alcohol abuse to racially motivated violence. For example:

Anwar: Drugs and alcohol, if this ends there could be a reduction in global crime rates.
Faheem: Zina is also one of the biggest crimes and the majority of our lads, if they get a chance, will commit zina (July 1999, Memorial Gardens, Haslingden).

Significantly, the British respondents classified zina as a crime despite it not being so within the British criminal justice system. This indicates at least a basic awareness of sharī'ah. The relative political stability of Britain and virtual absence of politically motivated violence can be said to account for the stark contrast in concerns between British and Pakistani respondents. However, it could be argued that the experiences of certain British Muslims of racially motivated abuse equates to a form of politically motivated violence. We shall return to a discussion of these crimes in due course.

Perceptions of Policing

In Karachi all respondents expressed knowledge of police corruption, frauds and injustice. There was correspondingly overwhelming disrespect for the police. As with issues of politically motivated crime, the respondents had formed their opinions about the police following either direct or indirect encounters with corrupt police officers and paramilitary rangers in Karachi.

The citizens of Karachi interviewed believed the police to be overwhelmingly corrupt, and thought that a number of factors were responsible for this corruption. Abdul explained why he did not respect the police:

> They (the police) do not have any status...I don't respect the police because they don't provide security to the citizens of Pakistan. So why should I respect the police? They have a duty to protect the citizen but they don't fulfil this.

One fifteen year old youth in Sharifabad, Babu, expressed particular distrust of the police believing them to be involved in false arrests, bribe-taking and inflicting torture. Babu felt that rank and file police officers, and paramilitary rangers, were subjected to oppressive demands from their superior officers to supply the latter with bribes. A further motivation for corruption, expressed by Babu, was the need for district police stations to present sufficiently high arrest rates to appease their superiors and in turn the politicians and wider public. This may be prompted by a crime rate perceived to be spiralling out of control. Therefore, Babu had little confidence in the police:

> ...And if anything happens to me I would never report it to the police because my problems would be increased. Because they wouldn't solve anything, they would just trouble my family and disturb my family life and no solution.

Chacha, a 42-year-old resident of Sharifabad, held similar views but highlighted the practice of bribe-taking by the police from street pedlars to permit them to sell their produce:

> The police do not purchase meat with their own money, vegetables with their own money, or milk with their own money. The pedlars give one policeman a kilo of meat, a pint of milk here and there. This I have seen with my own eyes, it's common.

One interviewee, Danyaal, gave a detailed account of how his brother had been falsely arrested for terrorist charges, detained, bound, denied legal representation and family visits and kept in prison for one year before being unconditionally released.

Bodrul described how he was falsely arrested following allegations of terrorist involvement. He was detained in the back of a police vehicle and eventually released a few hours later after consenting to pay a bribe at the request of those holding him:

> The end result was simply they said if you feed us dinner we will let you go. There were eight officers so I gave them money for eight biryanis[1] and I was eventually allowed to go on my way.

A pamphlet written by the Citizens-Police Liaison Committee (CPLC) of Karachi claims to illustrate significant inroads in making the policing institution a service-orientated system (CPLC, 1999). The CPLC is a non-governmental organization that was founded by two businessmen, Jameel Yusuf and Nazim F. Haji, in 1989 in Karachi. Both men were given powers of an honorary magistrate and used their business influence to initiate changes in procedural and administrative practices.

The CPLC has, indeed, simplified and streamlined many procedural practices such as introducing a more effective police emergency response system. More recently it has concentrated on modernizing the Pakistani police force in line with international standards through developing information technology. After meeting both founders and discussing the CPLC with them, their responses provide mixed views upon the relative success of the enterprise. The current Chief of the CPLC, Jameel Yusuf, is extremely proud of the achievements of this organization and believes it will continue to provide a continuous check upon the corruption and inefficiencies of the Karachi police force. However, Nazim Haji, now disengaged from the activities of the CPLC, is more critical of the present and future usefulness of this organization. Haji left the CPLC because he felt its independent status as a true non-governmental organization was being eroded by concessions to increasingly influential politicians and bureaucrats.

Certainly, as far as the majority of the respondents are concerned, the perceptions of a corrupt and untrustworthy police force still remain and these are fuelled by their personal experiences.

In Britain disrespect for the police is also demonstrated by the views of the Lancastrian respondents. This reflects other research which claims that Asian people are less likely than white people to be satisfied with police services (Britton, 2000). Such disrespect or suspicion is not a new phenomenon within this area. For example, a community elder discussed how police officers were perceived to have been harassing the early Muslim settlers in the locality during the 1960s. Mr Khan, a community elder and resident of Haslingden since 1960, spoke of harassment experienced by the first Muslim migrants to the locality:

---

[1] Urdu - fragrant rice dish.

Then there were problems and people started referring to me when there was trouble with the police…the police would go and knock on Asian homes without warrant, they will enter the house, at night even, at one o'clock, two o'clock, early in the morning.

Some of the residents of Haslingden were particularly vocal about incidents where they perceived the police to have been acting in a prejudicial manner. For example, Ashraf expressed how he felt the local police officers to be 'detached', 'arrogant' and 'uninvolved with the community as a whole'.

What Ashraf appeared to be demanding was policing with a greater personal community involvement and his views were echoed by the views of some of the Karachiites. For example, Danyaal in Karachi, was concerned about the lack of local police officers in the neighbourhood:

In every area and province there should be a local police force, so that they know the residents, for example, in Sharifabad, there's a new police station, if there is a local officer and he is doing wrong or sees others doing wrong everyone will know about it. But a person from afar doesn't know the locals, who is who, what is what.

In another incident in Haslingden, one respondent (Choudri) claimed that the police had been acting in a racially prejudicial manner when he became the victim of a violent racist assault. Similarly, a group of Bangladeshi youths in the town held firm views that some police officers were racist. However they also expressed the view that relations between local Asians and the police had improved following a successful recent meeting with the police and local community leaders and elders[2].

The fundamental differences in the mistrust and disrespect of the police expressed in both fieldwork locations centre upon the perceived motivation for the alleged prejudice and corruption. In Karachi, whilst it was acknowledged that corruption was widespread, most respondents acknowledged that it was economic factors that propelled the individual police officer towards corruption. The Karachi respondents listed poor pay, education and resources for the police as factors that accounted for the taking of bribes. This view co-exists with an understanding of broader institutionally racist practices, political in nature, which account for the overall corruption of the entire criminal justice system of which the police are a part. Whereas racism and prejudice are cited as factors that account for the broader political instability in Pakistan, the individual police officer is still viewed as reacting to such structural constraints in a manner viewed as survivalist.

In Britain little reference was made to broader institutional racism in other parts of the criminal justice system or government. The focus for concern was at community level and with the local police. The motivating factor for such prejudice amongst officers was not linked to economic survival or need but was considered to be a demonstration of racism, xenophobia and Islamophobia.

---

[2] Group Interview, 16/7/99, Union Street Mosque, Haslingden.

Haslingden: The Festivals of 'Īd[3] and their Policing

A point of conflict between the police and Muslims in the North West of England centres upon the biannual 'Īd celebrations. For a number of years the celebration of 'Īd for many Muslim youth has involved frequenting Wilmslow Road in the Rusholme district of Manchester. Muslim restaurants, eateries, grocers and general stores dominate this location, colloquially dubbed 'the curry mile'. In addition to Rusholme, Blackpool and Alton Towers have also figured prominently as destinations during 'Īd celebrations.

At all the locations mentioned there have occurred public order incidents some of which have resulted in the arrest and conviction of Muslim youths. The celebrations could be said to provide an illustration of Cohen's 'deviancy amplification spiral' (Cohen, 1972). A particular dimension of the celebrations centres upon car culture and the commission of both minor and major driving offences.

The following accounts describe the involvement of some of the respondents in 'Īd celebrations at the locations mentioned, and suggest the reasons why some Muslim youth are attracted to celebrating 'Īd in such a manner.

Mr Khan, a community elder, expressed his concern about the manner in which 'Īd is celebrated by some youths in Manchester, as well as recognizing that the police consider policing the festivals to be a biannual problem:

> Manchester is quite a commotion really, they make, very unpleasant, the local residents hate the day when it's going to happen and there are some of them [Muslim youth] racing to Blackpool. Somehow the word would go round to set off and get to Blackpool on motorway, which caused lot of concern and worry to the police.

Ashraf felt that 'Īd was an opportunity for Muslims to get together, and the fact that shop premises and businesses in Rusholme are mainly Muslim-owned makes it a natural destination for Muslim youths. Ashraf acknowledged that public order offences had been committed by some Muslims on these occasions, and believed this was a reflection of the idea that people wanted to 'make a spectacle of themselves' and 'show off to each other'. Ashraf discussed a well-publicized incident that took place in 1996 at Rusholme where a Muslim youth was falsely arrested and suffered serious personal injuries due to excessive force used by Greater Manchester police officers during the arrest. Despite this case, Ashraf felt that some youths frequented Rusholme on 'Īd with the firm intent to commit public order offences:

> I think they go to impress the other lads saying we are here, we are present, should there be any disorder we can say we've been there, we had conflict with police, I mean consciously go to cause some disturbance.

---

[3] See Glossary.

Further interviews revealed similar acknowledgement of 'Īd-day problems, for example an interview with Bangladeshi youths yielded similar responses:

> I: What about 'Īd? How many of you are aware of what happens on 'Īd in Rusholme and in Blackpool and Alton Towers? What's the usual scenario on 'Īd?
> R: The Islamic culture goes out of the window and instead they divert to a British culture, which is to have a good time, spinning around, drinking (Group Interview, Haslingden, Union Street Mosque, 16/7/99).

In addition to the views expressed by the respondents, detailed field notes written during 'Īd celebrations at Rusholme in early 1998, provide further evidence of the activities at this location:

> There was a heavy police presence, there were four TAG[4] units parked on Victoria Avenue (off Wilmslow Road), and numerous police motorcyclists and officers on foot. Barriers were in place on the side roads but traffic was being allowed to travel along Wilmslow Road. Police cones marked out no-parking zones all along the main road and in the adjoining side streets. There was a vast volume of cars clogging the street and pedestrians clogging the pavements. We arrived at the restaurant and it was extremely busy. I was eventually seated with my friends (personal friends mainly from Oldham) and I sat next to the window and observed what was going on outside. There was a continuous flow of people, predominantly Asian males, but a significant percentage of Asian females walking past the window. I recognized a group of lads from my hometown, they walked past the window three times in a matter of minutes. There was a continuous passage of cars, music was blaring out from many of them. There were numerous police officers on foot mingling with the crowds. Cars were getting tickets for being illegally parked. I saw a white limousine drive slowly past, Asian males rolled the window down and waved and shouted to the crowds. A white Ford Escort cabriolet drove past, with two Asian females, they had the roof down despite the cold weather. Numerous vehicles had the Bangladeshi or Pakistani flag draped over the bonnet or on poles attached to various parts of the car. Other cars also had 'Eid Mubarak' sprayed in fake snow on the side. Many drove recklessly or quickly with horns blaring (Field notes, 1998, Wilmslow Road, Manchester, late evening).

The 'Īd phenomenon provides a stark contrast to the traditional conformist Asian stereotype attached to the first generation. It can be understood, in sociological terms, as an expression or venting of generational anxieties, a releasing of the Durkheimian 'pressure valve' or a violent demonstration of cultural self-assertion. The question to ask however is which culture is being asserted? It could be argued that the practices of the youths emulate football hooliganism more than a controlled assertion of civil liberties.

The dynamics of policing 'Īd, too complicated to explore thoroughly here, illustrates the sensitivities of policing the Muslim community in general. Initial confrontational tactics resulted in agitating Muslim youths and a corresponding snowballing of public order problems. The latest approach, demonstrated by

---

[4] Abbreviation - Tactical Aid Group.

persuasive community messaging, appears to favour softer pleadings to youths disseminated via mosques shortly before 'Īd. In Rusholme tactics in recent years have included closing Wilmslow Road entirely to traffic and a compulsory riot-equipped police presence.

Behaviour such as that experienced during 'Īd in Manchester, may be understood as a demonstration of 'the second life of the people' (Bakhtin, 1984). This refers to a dimension of social existence where commonly held beliefs and norms are capable of being inverted. Therefore, where ideological mainstream political discourse arguably attempts to project conformity, harmony and consensus, the reality for many is located in a 'second life' where dissent, destruction and conflict find voice. This 'second life' is inaccessible and out of the reach of the 'official world' of scientific rationality of modernity and its politics, parties and politicians (Presdee, 2000).

As politics and social policies shape social life, homogenizing communities, denying diversity and pluralism, a corresponding coercion towards the 'second life' occurs when people are denied what Holquist calls a 'usable past' (Presdee, 2000). Eventually there are no barriers between the 'second life' and true life. The 'second life' becomes the space where the fears and anxieties of true life are expressed, prompted by the experiences and the pain, poverty and inequality of official life (Presdee, 2000). Expressions of the 'second life' within the official life would result in those expressions becoming criminalized and demonized. In essence, therefore, the 'second life' enables 'freedom, equality and abundance' in a true life of 'oppression, inequality and poverty' (Bakhtin, 1984:9).

Is celebrating 'Īd in a rebellious manner by Muslim youth therefore a reflection of the 'second life' for minorities? Is this more plausible if we consider that British Pakistanis and Bangladeshis experience high levels of socio-economic deprivation (Runnymede, 1997)? Is the conflict between police and those celebrating an expression of powerlessness and the loosening of cultural imperatives, as Presdee (2000) would argue? The celebration of 'Īd in the manner described can certainly be understood as a carnival, where disrespect, defiance and the celebration of the irrational reign.

In terms of location, it is fitting that the prime public disorder conflicts occur in a cityscape essentially understood as the 'street'. Presdee notes that the street has 'long been a site of social performance and protest and the place *par excellence*, where carnival has become crime' (Presdee, 2000:138). He continues:

> in some sense there is a continuing struggle by young people to take possession of the street as their own space whilst much policing is aimed at reclaiming what is perceived as public space. It is therefore no surprise to see young people defending the street, which often becomes the place where battle takes place (Presdee, 2000:139).

Certainly, as far as Rusholme is concerned, the above comment is particularly pertinent. Muslim ownership of property here is predominant and it can be argued Muslim youths feel they have a sort of territorial cultural right to frequent the premises and urban space proximate to this area.

'No-go' Zones

Many respondents in Sharifabad expressed their view that there existed certain no-go zones in their neighbourhood and city as a whole. Such areas were to be avoided due to risks of becoming a victim of crime (Sibley, 1995).

Abdul expressed that for him there did exist certain no-go zones, namely Al-Akram Square (near Sharifabad) and Gharibabad, a kaatchi abaadi[5] neighbouring Sharifabad. The principal reason for avoiding these areas was the belief that he might get caught and falsely arrested during a police raid on political activists who reside in these locations. Abdul also expressed an overwhelming perception of such locations as 'dangerous' even though he had not actually visited these locations:

> There's a kaatchi abaadi and it's a very dangerous place because you are not sure of your security so if you just go there you don't know where you might get caught.

Babu and Ali held similar views about frequenting such localities. Ali spoke of certain places 'never being safe' whilst Babu's fears were perpetuated by the reality of violent exchanges in these localities between law-enforcers and others. Danyaal explained that, for him, vast warrens of narrow congested alleys and routes characterized the kaatchi abaadis. In his opinion, people could easily get lost in them and they enabled criminals to execute their activities within a hidden environment. Most respondents, when speaking about kaatchi abaadis, spoke with reference to feelings of perceived 'threat', 'danger', 'strangeness' and 'safety' within these settlements.

Importantly, the few respondents who physically frequented areas commonly cited as 'no-go' zones spoke of no feelings of animosity or fear when visiting such locations. For example, Daanish spoke of his perceptions of localities others considered unsafe, which he has had to frequent:

> There aren't such places for me because I reside in such neighbourhoods, where I have observed so much that the fear has been ground out of me. I go wherever now, and now there's nothing going on anyhow.

Similarly, Hassan spoke of frequenting such localities in order to visit relatives:

> No, not really, I go everywhere, no problem, I mean I have relatives there so I frequent these places, I don't fear them.

Extensive fieldwork conducted in Karachi has facilitated the gathering of a detailed understanding of the complex meanings of 'no-go' areas for the residents.

There was a general consensus about which areas clearly constituted a 'no-go' zone. These were most often characterized in terms of geographical identity,

---

[5] Urdu - squatter settlements, shanty towns see Glossary.

for example Liaqatabad or Gharibabad. It must be noted that the majority of the respondents were Mohajir and many of the 'no-go zones', such as Landhi, were considered 'ethnically different' zones. Therefore, to a large extent, the zones demarked ethnically defined residence patterns. Risks to Mohajirs were considered higher in non-Mohajir dominated areas. The source of such perceptions often stemmed from first-hand experience of racially motivated violence against the Mohajirs in these areas. However the majority of the respondents indicated little direct experience of frequenting the perceived 'no-go' zone.

A general perception of such 'no-go' zones centred upon the belief and observation that these were the sites of on-going conflicts between groups such as rival political parties, police and activists, landowners and squatters and that simply being in these locations would automatically place the individual within the line of crossfire. This is a practical philosophy of simply avoiding areas reputed to have regular civil unrest.

Following the military coup of October 1999, the civil unrest in Karachi considerably lessened whilst rival political parties entered a 'honeymoon' phase with the incoming dictatorship. The police were also understood to be 'under military control' and hence corrupt practices, raids and illegal stop and searches were considered by the residents to be less frequent than in previous months.

The fact that certain 'no-go' zones had now become more accessible to the respondents is reflective of the reduction in the civil unrest and conflict in the city as a whole. However, many respondents still perceived these locations as problematic even in the absence of genuine unrest, and hence their status as 'no-go zones' has remained psychologically engrained (Sibley, 1995). For example, Esaah described the long-lasting nature of labelling a certain geographical area as criminogenic:

> Yes, Lines Area (Jacobline), but even though it's not a big threat now, it's remained in our heads that we should avoid that area.

The fact that certain areas can shift in and out of the 'no-go' classification illustrates the transitory and temporary nature of such perceptions for some areas. The kaatchi abaadis however, never seemed to be considered areas where Mohajirs felt they could visit without serious risks of becoming victims of crime.

Regarding 'no-go zones' in British research Webster (1993; 1997), for example, has demonstrated the importance of deconstructing the urban environment in terms of racially defined zones. As in Karachi, British Muslim youth in Haslingden spoke of areas they considered 'no-go zones'. The prime reason for avoiding such areas was to reduce the risk of racially motivated conflict. In Haslingden the extra dimension of time was considered to be important in assessing risk. Night time was associated with drinking and respondents mainly classified locations near to public houses in the town centre as areas to avoid. For example:

I: Are there any areas you wouldn't go in Haslingden?
R: Not really, probably Lower Deardengate at night near pubs, when all the white guys are outside the pubs.
Group Interview, 16/7/99, Bangladeshi Youths, Union Street Mosque.

Whereas in Karachi the areas avoided were also considered areas of the destitute and poor, in Haslingden the 'no-go' areas were considered mainly to be near pubs and the main threat to Muslim youth was from white males drinking at such locations. Indeed, many of the respondents cited having to walk past the pubs during the evening as a main point of anxiety.

Broad institutional practices within social policy and media construction have an influential part to play in the formation and perpetuation of urban localities personified as criminal and deviant. Whether the initial perception is sparked by genuine criminal activity is therefore less relevant than the projection and 'holding-out' of a particular locality as a 'no-go' zone.

In Karachi, where ethnic and class segregation is particularly marked, it is easy to see how the perception of a 'no-go' zone is conceived and perpetuated as an integral aspect of power relations between the 'haves' and 'have nots'; for the latter the construction of their social and physical environment is largely out of their hands. There are locations in Karachi, such as kaatchi abaadis, which are essentially residential in nature, impoverished and poorly resourced. Nearly two million people reside in such localities in the city (Human Rights Commission of Pakistan, 1997). It can be understood that the need to frequent them by non-residents is indeed minimal. That is to say, for most residents of Sharifabad there is no need or reason to travel into a kaatchi abaadi. Not only do these locations represent a class barrier but also a racial barrier, as often these places are the home to the newest migrants seeking refuge in Pakistan's largest conurbation.

Therefore, although the origin of a particular locality's reputation as a 'dangerous' place may well be founded on a 'once-in-the-past' reality of urban conflict and victimization within it, there is a further process of perpetuation of this image by agencies such as the media. This is capable of sealing the fate of whether a particular urban location becomes a 'no-go' zone for non-residents or outsiders.

Whilst the individual may be strongly influenced by institutional projections of a locality's reputation, he or she is still free to make a subjective assessment of the 'risk-factor' of becoming a victim whilst frequenting a zone thus labelled. Such an assessment is weighed against a *need to frequent* as opposed to a *desire* or *wish* to frequent a particular locality. The 'no-go' zone for one person, therefore, is wholly capable of being the refuge of another and what determines this pertains to race, education and stratification (Quraishi, 2005b).

Victimization in Karachi

In Karachi the majority of the respondents declared that they had been victims of crime. The offences against them varied from minor to major incidents. These experiences may be considered within two categories, victims of the police and paramilitary, and victims of crime by unknown assailants.

Victims of the Police and Paramilitary

The police and paramilitary rangers in Karachi have developed a significant history of, and reputation for, corruption. Reports have frequently uncovered police involvement in both petty and serious organized crime including illegal trade in narcotics, firearms, prostitution and stolen vehicles (Pakistan Human Rights Commission Report 1997).

The majority of the respondents in Karachi had experienced police corruption (see the previous section on perceptions of policing). The following cases illustrate the levels of victimization experienced by some respondents. For example Danyaal in Sharifabad in January 1999 gave a detailed account of how his brother had been falsely detained and charged as an MQM activist. The respondent's brother had been bound, blindfolded, shackled, denied legal representation and family visits for the duration of one year before being unconditionally released without a trial.

Chacha disclosed that the police had stopped him frequently but he had never paid a bribe although his passengers had. Elahi discussed the armed robbery of three of his friends. Although they were masked, the assailants wore police uniforms and brandished police issue firearms, and these factors prompted the victims to assume that they were police officers.

Cairul gave a detailed account of how he had been stopped frequently by the police and paramilitary forces allegedly checking for known criminals, firearms and ammunitions. Cairul routinely paid bribes to be allowed to go on his way. Faiyaaz gave the following account:

> Many friends and family I know have all been stopped by the police and they take even Rs5[6], if you have it, Rs5, 10, 25 whatever. My cousin was stopped once and they checked his wallet. There was a kaleidoscope calendar in it, a photograph calendar. The officer said, you keep photographs of naked women and then he planted some marijuana on my cousin. My cousin had to give Rs25 to escape. They do this a lot, money's always on their lips. It's not the individual police officer's fault, the SSP demands certain sums that they have to collect for him, by whatever means.

The accounts depict a police force that is corrupt and oppressive, yet most of the behaviour appears to be financially motivated. The victims themselves often explained the behaviour by citing the extremely low earnings the police make in Pakistan, which forces them to find alternative illegal incomes.

---

[6] Rs - abbreviation for Pakistani Rupee.

Victimization from Unknown Assailants

In addition to incidents where it was clear that law enforcement officers (police and paramilitary) were involved, a substantial number of respondents in Karachi discussed incidents where the identities and affiliations of the criminals was not known. For example, Bodrul explained how his friend was robbed at gunpoint:

> A friend of mine advertised his laptop for sale in a newspaper, some guys came and checked it out. They left and returned the next day, they held a revolver to my friend's head and stole the computer, there were three of them.

Cairul gave a detailed account of the racially motivated violence he and his family were subjected to:

> Well when I was in Model Colony (Karachi), there were many groups. We are Mohajirs, the other groups were different, Punjabi, Pathan, plus Sindhi. These groups wanted to get rid of the Mohajirs from that neighbourhood so there were attacks upon us. Shooting and all sorts of threatening behaviour. Because of this we were forced to relocate to Sharifabad. Because, of course, if you get 20 lads stood outside your home with firearms and ammunition then there's no security of life or honour. Your family is inside, the guys could get inside the house at anytime. So you can't live there, we had to leave and come to Sharifabad.

Faiyaaz described the attempted murder of his uncle:

> Well, I think my cousin has told you about the car theft. They stole my cousin's car at gunpoint. A separate incident was that my uncle was shot at whilst driving. The MQM had called for a strike the next working day so my uncle was returning from work by car the day before the planned strike. Buses weren't running because they had begun to set them alight. So he was at Aisha Manzil when he noticed two guys following him on a motorbike. Some kids were playing cricket in the street so my uncle had to slow down for them. The guys behind him moved in front and pointed a gun at the windscreen; he stuck the car in reverse and tried to get away when they opened fire at his head. The windscreen shattered but luckily he was not hit by a bullet.

The three incidents detailed here demonstrate the often very violent nature of offences being committed in Karachi. Due to the proliferation of firearms in Sindh, following the end of the Afghan war, coupled with the fact that the law enforcement officers are armed, it is unsurprising that many incidents involve firearms (Shamsi, 1998).

The last account centres upon alleged racially motivated violence, although it could also be understood in terms of economic relations. All the incidents clearly depict attempts to acquire property by illegal means. In Karachi, land, amenities and resources are overstretched and infrastructural weaknesses and imbalances are often reflected in conflicts, which can find expression as ethnically categorized outbursts.

These accounts describe incidents of violent exchanges where individuals can be seen as victims of offences against the person. However the respondents in Karachi spoke of a far more fundamental process of victimization, which was political and institutional in nature. The following accounts document the principal anxieties felt by respondents in terms of how they consider themselves to be victims. Victimization is understood within a broad political context, especially with regard to reaction to the racial quota system operating for recruitment to government posts. Bilquis explained it thus:

> In a way politicians are involved because if car theft or anything is happening... I agree that if I have the qualification and I am not getting the job and I will have to support my family, how will I do that? I will have to move to such things. If we had the job facility and this and that then possibly the students will not move to that other side, the criminal side, because I think we have the talent but the government is not using our talent, they are just destroying us.

Similarly, Dhillon emphasized societal strains and nepotism as causal factors for certain crimes:

> Youths themselves are very good in nature, they are very good basically, but they have no other way, they don't have any jobs or any facilities. If, for example, there are two persons, one person is very much qualified and the other is under qualified but he has the sources and the influences he will get the job, but what will the other do? Of course he will get frustrated and he will snatch different things from the other people.

Ehsaan, a female postgraduate student, explained that she felt that political parties, such as the MQM in particular, were brainwashing youths who were easily influenced in view of their dire financial positions. Ehsaan expressed that she was aware of the problems political affiliation could cause having experienced her own brother's involvement in MQM activism. She spoke of the pain and suffering of families who had lost sons through violent clashes between activists, their political rivals and law enforcement officers. Importantly, Ehsaan emphasized that universities were the prime recruiting ground for political parties.

Several respondents identified the issue of the racial quota for government posts as the linchpin of urban conflicts. Chacha, for example, believed the racial quota system to be the main contributory factor to civil unrest in Karachi:

> ...for eighteen years there's been a ban on employment. Those who graduated when eighteen are now approaching their thirties and are without government jobs. There's a ban, it's a racial quota. So the root of the problem in Karachi is that the youth are barred from employment in government jobs because of race, even after graduating.

The majority of the respondents echoed the concerns of Chacha regarding the racial quota system; Danyaal for example expressed particular frustration highlighting the anomaly. In his opinion the most educated are denied jobs, which were instead being offered to the lesser educated:

> …due to overpopulation there are many burdens. Then there's the job quota system. Only two per cent are allowed to apply for jobs in the government from Karachi. In the whole of Pakistan people of Karachi tend to be the most educated and the central area, Azizabad, the majority are educated. A high percentage of them vote. The vote in the village is tied to the landowner, but here this is not the case.

Farida, a civil servant working in education, gave a detailed submission of the mounting problems facing youths and students in Karachi, and she highlighted the struggles students face to get into university. Farida believes there should be at least four government universities in a city the size of Karachi against a reality of just one. Issues of lack of funding and the development of college facilities further exacerbate the problems:

> The students, when facing rejection, become worthless in their own eyes and are tempted to go into criminal activities. There are limited seats at Karachi University, there should be at least four state universities in Karachi. One university has been operating for twenty-five years, which isn't enough. The graduates are subject to a quota system, only two per cent of government jobs are open to Karachiites and more for people from Interior Sindh who do not have the same level of education.

Victimization in Haslingden

When the Haslingden respondents were asked about victimization, they automatically associated such enquiries with racially motivated incidents. This demonstrates that, in the minds of the respondents at least, racially motivated crime and the risk of becoming a victim figured most prominently in the construction of victim risk assessment.

A significant number of those interviewed had been victims of racially motivated abuse, some of which was extremely violent. For example, one elderly respondent detailed how he lost four teeth in an unprovoked racist attack in 1991 by four white youths who had allegedly called him a 'Muslim bastard'. Another respondent gave a detailed account of how he and his friends were involved in a violent unprovoked racist attack, which involved serious bodily harm and hospital treatment.

In addition to such violent incidents the Muslim respondents explained how attending prayers at the local mosque brings them into potentially hostile encounters with people drinking in and outside local public houses. The following account by Faheem describes one such experience:

> I was walking past the Commercial Inn one evening and I had traditional shalwar kameez[7] on, I don't usually wear them. There were many people stood outside the

---

[7] Traditional attire and national dress of Pakistan which consists of a knee-length shirt and

pub, as I passed by one guy spat his beer over me. I hadn't done or said anything to aggravate them. I crossed the road and saw a bottle on the floor. I was thinking of picking it up but there were six or seven of them or possibly more. I suppressed my anger but I was thinking of taking that bottle and smashing it on his head and then running, he spat on me for no reason. I stood opposite the pub thinking about this but I thought someone might recognize me so I didn't do it.

The Runnymede Trust report on Islamophobia[8] submits that there is widespread anecdotal evidence in Muslim communities that an individual Muslim is 'more likely to be a victim of racist violence if he or she is wearing Islamic dress or symbols'. The same report also argues that 'Muslims are particularly likely to be attacked when going to and from their local mosque' (Runnymede Trust, 1997: 41).

Respondents also spoke of a 'racist climate at the moment' (Choudri) and 'I get verbal abuse everyday whilst walking the streets, Black bastard, Paki bastard etc.' (Bashir).

An interesting observation centres upon the analysis of the elders' reaction to racism and that of the younger generation. The younger generation seemingly is far less likely to 'sit back and take' the abuse than the elders. This is confirmed by research such as that of Webster (1993, 1997).

The broad parallels between the British and Pakistani submissions are that both groups consider themselves to be marginalized minorities. Mohajirs are considered minorities in Sindh and Pakistan as a whole, and Muslims are considered as religious and racial minorities in the United Kingdom. Both groups speak of violent racially motivated incidents. Whilst for the Karachiites such racism manifests in the state-driven suppression and politically motivated violence, for the Lancastrian Muslims the oppression is from a homogenously conceived prejudiced white majority, which is also perceived to be reflected in the local police-force.

---

loose fitting trousers - see Glossary.
[8] Note discussion in Chapter 3.

Religion in Sharifabad and Haslingden

All the respondents, in both locations, were Muslim and in particular Sunni Muslims. The interviews assessed the influence of Islam on their daily lives as well as an evaluation of how Islamic jurisprudence directly or indirectly influenced their world-view, practice, behaviour and philosophy.

In both locations all respondents expressed that Islam figured prominently in their lives. In particular, the respondents claimed that they identified strongly with religion and in turn it gave them their identity. These findings confirm recent research that British Muslims are more likely to actively practice their religion than other religious groups (Modood, 1997). However recent research by the Policy Studies Institute suggests a downturn in religious observance amongst younger Muslims (Modood and Berthoud, 1997). Nevertheless, the importance of a Muslim identity may not depend solely or exclusively on religious practice but may rather be a reflection of ethnic categorisation of groups pursuant to political objectives. For example, under the former Yugoslavian communist regime Bosnian Muslims were 'officially designated' to distinguish them from (Orthodox) Serbs and (Catholic) Croats (Ruthven, 1997:3).

The very notion of identity is far from being unproblematic and a comprehensive analysis of the concept is not the remit of this study. However, for purposes of this discussion, the concept as defined within post-psychological definitions, as an essentially 'psycho-social' phenomenon is helpful here. Thus, the definition by Erik Erikson of identity where the sense of 'me' or 'myself' is formed in relation to others and their responses is how it may be understood on an individual level. Here the process of identity-formation is incremental but with particular stages of the life cycle, such as adolescence, as critical points of development (Erikson, 1980).

Regarding the notion of identity and religion, however, Hans Mol's work 'Identity and the Sacred' offers a helpful discussion and notes 'religious practices give special underpinning to particular conceptions of order and views of reality within a culture making the security of the individual less precarious' (Mol 1976:9). Therefore, a religion 'has the potential to justify and legitimate norms and values, as well as social institutions and the interpretation of reality that lies behind religious customs' (Gilliat-Ray, 1998:348).

In Karachi youths spoke of how a 'Muslim identity' stood above any other notion of nationhood or national identity. For example Abdul (14) spoke about his faith as follows:

> I: Would you say that you are religious?
> R: Not fully, I'm not a pure Muslim, I'm a so-called Muslim.
> I: How important is it to you?
> R: Well we are known by our religion, so religion provides a very meaningful identity for us...first I would say I am a Muslim and then a Pakistani and then Mohajir and all that stuff.
> I: Have you done things prohibited in Islam?
> R: No, no I don't drink, I don't smoke. I don't take anything.

Similarly Babu, Chacha, Danyaal, and Elahi all placed a strong emphasis on religion playing a fundamental role in constructing their identity, for example Danyaal:

> I: Would you consider yourself religious?
> R: Yes absolutely, this is very important. If I had no religion I would be nothing, because our religion forms our whole life. This religion, Islam, decides my rights and wrongs.

A point to note is that in Pakistan the mainstream, infrastructural, institutional and interpersonal environment is loosely Islamic with emphasis upon compulsory Islamic education in state school curricula and common practices of tutoring children privately in Qur'ānic recitation and learning. Therefore, when assessing whether a person perceives himself or herself to be a 'good' Muslim the definition of this in Karachi is arguably different to how that term is understood in Britain.

The Karachiite may well have a fuller understanding of what, according to Islam, is required of a practising Muslim than in the case of British Muslims. To illustrate this point many youths in Karachi would consider themselves 'poor' or 'lesser' Muslims because they did not pray five times daily. In terms of how they lived their lives many confessed that this was as far as their religious rule breaking went. Whilst indeed praying five times daily is fundamental to the Muslim faith, in Britain what constitutes a 'good' Muslim could mean a person who has not committed any serious religious offence such as zina or drinking alcohol, but not necessarily someone who prays five times daily. To summarize, the expectations of what constitutes a 'good' Muslim are relative and in Karachi the standards are probably higher than in Britain.

British respondents also placed a high degree of emphasis on being identified as Muslim. For example Ashraf spoke of Islam in the following manner:

> I: How important is Islam to you and why?
> R: Essential, it comes above all else. One thing about Islam is that we believe in the unseen. We often emphasise that we regard life as a journey, real life is in the afterlife, everything is secondary to religion. The way we walk, dress, study, eat, everything. Islam means a way of life rather than a religion for twenty-four hours a day, literally we make every effort.

The Bangladeshi youths interviewed in Haslingden also expressed that their religion was a way of life that was of prime importance and any concepts of nationality came second to religious identity.

Therefore piety, in terms of acknowledging the fundamentals of Islam, is highly regarded amongst the sample respondents. More probing questions enabled a deeper assessment of how far such ideals are understood, internalized and practiced. Each respondent was asked about his or her knowledge of sharī'ah (Islamic law) and fiqh (Islamic jurisprudence). The overwhelming response was that respondents had only a superficial knowledge of such matters. In Karachi, for example, respondents were asked about whether they could define the three classifications of Islamic criminal laws. The vast majority of respondents were unable to correctly define the classifications but a greater proportion was able to identify hudūd offences. This appears to be a direct result of political educational programmes in Pakistan that have emphasized the study of hudūd offences, following the Hudūd Ordinance in 1979.

Also the existence of conflicting legal constitutions in Pakistan may account for the confusion and ignorance of such matters amongst the respondents. Several respondents expressed an awareness of the duality of Pakistan's criminal law; that is, that it comprises secular as well as Islamic law (sharī'ah). The majority believed that Islamic law, however, was not being properly practiced or enforced at an official level. For example, Danyaal highlighted that, in his opinion, not only was sharī'ah being marginalized at a constitutional level, but also in terms of religious education, in that scholars and tutors did not place significant emphasis upon sharī'ah. Danyaal spoke of these issues as follows:

> I: Are you familiar with Islamic law and jurisprudence?
> R: No, actually in Pakistan we don't follow the true Islamic laws. There are a lot of laws being followed here. Islamic and British. I think most people don't know the full evidential practice in any depth. Sharī'ah is not really being taught here. Islamic education here is mainly only about learning how to read the Qur'ān. This is wrong because as Muslims we should teach the meanings and practice of Islam. This is why our children are ignorant of faith. Faith, our religion stops you from wrong and bad things. If they read the meanings of the Qur'ān they can be saved from committing crimes.

Elahi also expressed similar views:

> I: Are you aware of Sharī'ah?
> R: No I don't know that much.
> I: Do you think that most know much about it?
> R: No most people don't. The reason being that most of us are illiterate or uneducated. Then also, this subject is not taught. In the mosque you are taught how to pray, law is not taught.

Similarly, in the UK knowledge of sharī'ah was limited and superficial. However the vagueness about sharī'ah was contained to the dynamics and classification of offences rather than an ignorance of what and what is not generally permitted in Islam. All respondents seemed to acknowledge the fundamental concepts of what a Muslim must not do.

Part of the reason for such limitation is the acknowledgement that legal issues are of such complexity that they should be left to learned scholars of sharī'ah and fiqh within the ummah. In counter-argument to such a response it must be noted that the questions asked were purely elementary in nature. Religious scholars, such as Imam Hamza Yusuf, emphasize that such ignorance of basic Islamic laws is demonstrative of the general demise of true scholars of sharī'ah and fiqh within the global ummah[9]. Many respondents emphasized that the scholarly pursuit of such issues was being undertaken in Islamic colleges. The point to note, however, is that by virtue of declaring oneself Muslim one is required to submit to the commands of Allah (SWT) and if those commands are, as Muslims believe, contained in the Qur'ān and hadīth, then there must be a corresponding ideological practice of ascertaining such laws and attempt to live by them for all Muslims.

In practice the transfer of knowledge, and hence adoption of such laws and rules, is a complex process. The Muslims find themselves within a nexus of conflicting theological and social frameworks. Whilst the religious law is often clear about certain prohibitions, the contemporary Muslim must process what does and does not apply to his or her lifestyle, resulting in varied interpretations of Islam as it is lived today. The fact that Muslim scholars assert that the law is in fact clear cannot alleviate the confusion when the elementary philosophy and skills required to comprehend sharī'ah and fiqh are lacking. In this sense, it is not the law that is problematic, but the co-existence of this law with secular non-Islamic value systems and legal constitutions. This is the challenge for both Muslim scholars and the Muslim community in general.

How Respondents Viewed the Global Image of Muslims in Sharifabad and Haslingden

In both locations respondents were asked what they considered the global image of Muslims to be and in particular what the image was like in Europe. That is, how did the respondents feel Islam and Muslims were represented in social and political discourse on a global scale? In Karachi, the majority of respondents observed that they felt the global image of Muslims, particularly in western countries, was negative. Respondents felt that Muslims had been subjected to western-inspired Islamophobia, where Islam has been cast as a faith with worshippers stereotypically depicted as oppressors, fanatics, fundamentalists and terrorists. The following discussion with Cairul helps to illustrate this point:

> I: How do you perceive the image of Muslims in Europe?
> R: I think, from my own observations through TV, because I have never been there or met an Englishman. I think they have had their heads filled with the view that Muslims are terrorists. That they are constantly fighting, so I don't think they have a good image of Muslims. From just what I have observed in the media, it could be otherwise, they say each finger on the hand is a different size. But my friend is studying in the US and he tells me that the common perception of Muslims is that they are always fighting Jihad. That expression seems to be in circulation, then he has to explain the meaning of Jihad. But I think that the people and media over there have corrupted reality and put it in their heads that all Muslims do is fight and commit acts of terrorism.

---

[9] Speech to Conference: Setting The Foundations of a Humane Society, Aston Villa Community Centre, Co-ordination Committee, 29/8/1999.

Daanish held a similar belief about the negative labelling of Muslims by the West:

> I think that in the eyes of others there is no respect for Muslims, they just want to end Muslims and Islam … my cousins live overseas, they tell me, for example, if a Muslim accomplishes an achievement they are treated with envy and jealousy as a result of it. They keep their distance from any Muslim that achieves success.

Esaah highlighted concerns about propaganda from the Islamic fundamentalists as well as from the West:

> I think that the image was originally good but it's forever being tainted…firstly there's the Islamic propaganda and misconceptions based on views of fundamentalists, others then paint all Muslims with the same brush. I read papers and on the Internet, there's a lot of propaganda.

Faiyaaz was critical of the Western media's depiction of Islam:

> They have made films depicting Muslims as fundamentalists who simultaneously pray to Allah (SWT) whilst murdering.

Similarly, Hassan felt Hindus had a better global image than Muslims:

> These days it's bad…newspapers, they have bad-named Muslims so much that they've effectively separated us from the rest of humanity. If you look at Hindus they have an image that is respected. Like, for example, Clinton [President of USA at the time] is going to India first, and it's not even been confirmed whether he's coming here and he's supposed to be our friend, but he's going to India.

The extracts mentioned here illustrate a general feeling of despair and anger amongst respondents about how their faith is being depicted by non-Muslims. Their sentiments are reflected in the responses of British Muslims who speak of alienation, ostracism and prejudice due, directly or indirectly, to their religious identity (Runnymede, 1997). There are two forms of prejudice identified by the research. One form is at the 'street-level' and may refer to verbal abuse and assaults. These form the bulk of the main forms of racism perceived by the respondents in Haslingden. However, there were also concerns expressed about a far more fundamentally socially damaging aspect of Islamophobia, which was the perceived institutionalised and political marginalizing of Muslims within a global setting. Concerns about the latter form of Islamophobia tended to come from respondents in Karachi. This is reflective, perhaps, of the State-initiated anti-Western propaganda pursued in the national press and political discourse in Pakistan (Human Rights Commission of Pakistan, 1997)[10].

As argued earlier, offending and victimization should be viewed as interactive processes. The South Asian youth not only face racial prejudice but a

---

[10] Lapse of Freedom of Information Ordinance.

perceived ignorance of his or her faith by the majority and, as discussed, this faith is intertwined in formulating self-identity. Given such social facts, Muslim youth involvement in a struggle to reassert identity through deviance and crime becomes more plausible. Thus, crime here may be viewed as an act of empowerment against a broader social picture of youth powerlessness.

Offending Behaviour in Sharifabad

A central goal of the research was to assess the involvement of Muslims, and in particular Muslim youths, in crime and deviance. As noted in Chapter 4, there are inherent methodological problems with enquiries which request personal accounts of offending. As expected, the overwhelming response in both locations was of limited self-confession of involvement in offending. This may be interpreted in two ways, either that the respondents interviewed had not in fact committed any serious crime or deviance or if they had, they were not prepared to discuss it. However, the majority of respondents were prepared to discuss the offending and deviance of friends and people whom they knew. In some cases, this may have been a covert way of discussing their own involvement.

Where respondents did confess to crimes or deviance, these tended to be minor in nature. The inclusion of deviance in addition to crime was intended, as discussed in Chapter 3, to enable an assessment of how influential Islamic law was upon Muslims. The comparative dimension to the work enabled an analysis of how influential cultural and religious rules and laws are within Islamic and non-Islamic State contexts.

The notion of observing rules has a particular dimension in Karachi. In Karachi, and in Pakistan as a whole, there is little clear understanding of what constitutes a legal wrong. The concept of a rule of law in Pakistan that is State-inspired is not self-evident. Instead citizens, communities and provinces have created a working reality of legal observance, these laws neither being officially codified nor universally accepted. What must be emphasised is that Pakistan, like many countries, has a written constitution, highly documented legal procedures and extensive legislation that includes a comprehensive Penal Code (1860), deriving from the time of British rule. Theoretically, therefore, the rule of law and the apparatus for transferring authority to state officials, the judiciary and law enforcement officers all exist. In reality, however, a properly functioning criminal justice system remains largely an ideological goal. Such criticism could be levied at various criminal justice systems including that of Britain. However, the level of corruption, inequality and injustice experienced in Karachi particularly make a mockery of any commonly understood meaning of the rule of law (Human Rights Commission of Pakistan, 1997). Certainly such observations were reflected in an interview with one respondent who was a former High Court Judge in Pakistan[11].

---

[11] Unpublished field notes, Karachi, 1999.

Given the corruption within the Pakistani legal system, how then do citizens understand, interpret and defend their civil liberties? What becomes acceptable and unacceptable behaviour in the eyes of the citizen and the state? Which legal system informs the citizens of their parameters of behaviour, Islamic, secular or both? The interviews enabled a closer understanding of these issues, and it is only through understanding these broader institutional practices that criminal offending can be placed in context.

In Karachi there emerged a pattern of acknowledgement of rule breaking. That is to say, certain behaviour was deemed acceptable even though it was technically criminal. This is a reflection of the low status attached to the State apparatus responsible for law enforcement, coupled with a survivalist rule-breaking philosophy. This philosophy of 'normalizing' crime applied largely to what could be considered minor offences, such as traffic offences. Respondents rarely acknowledged that what was often deemed 'minor offending' could have significant consequences. For example, that serious bodily harm or even fatalities for the victim could result from failing to keep a vehicle in a safe working state. The justification for rule- breaking for one type of behaviour and not others at first appears contradictory. However, it is more a reflection of citizens defining their rules of governance within a highly complex process of evaluating what is and what is not socially accepted behaviour. Within such an evaluation certain behaviour appears to be universally understood as transgressing norms, and in Karachi the rules thus defined tended to be those sanctioned by religion.

Therefore, jumping a red light, not declaring income for taxation, failing to report an accident, or having no licence were considered part of everyday matters of minor concern, but drinking alcohol, fornication and blasphemy were considered serious social and moral ills. This was so even for those who confessed to committing such acts, the fact that they had done so did not detract from how morally wrong they felt those actions to be. For example, Ali and Cairul expressed guilt for drinking alcohol. Cairul gave the following account:

> I have consumed alcohol, I have drunk alcohol definitely, but I have left it now, this is considered a very bad thing in our faith. I drank alcohol in Pakistan, I knew some guys who used to drink and I became friendly with them and began to drink out of desire and intrigue. But when I saw how wrong it was in our faith and in reality it does lead to many problems, I left drinking alcohol.

For the following discussion criminal and deviant acts may be understood as either those committed as part of a political struggle or those committed as criminal offences per se, or in some cases as behaviour that transcends both categories.

Since most respondents in Karachi indicated that politically motivated crime was of most concern to them, a significant number observed how friends or family members had committed acts which could be deemed criminal through their involvement with political parties. For example, one respondent, Chanda, noted how a friend's brother had been involved in terrorist activities for a political party and eventually escaped overseas seeking asylum.

Cairul spoke of how his cousin had been arrested and imprisoned for breach of a public order law:

> My cousin was involved in the Muttahida (MQM) in 1990 and he was attending a meeting which the police raided. At that time meeting were subject to s144[12] which limited such political meetings to four members, there were between one and two hundred at that meeting. When the police raided it they all tried to run away but my cousin was caught. He spent time in prison whilst waiting for his trial date.

Daanish disclosed that he knew certain terrorists in the neighbourhood:

I: Have any of your friends committed crime?
R: I know of many people who are terrorists, two or three people I know.
I: How do you know this?
R: They've not done anything to me but to other people, I know from them directly and from other people they hang out with.
I: Are they all in this neighbourhood?'
R: Yes, they are all from here, Sharifabad, Al-Azam, Liaqatabad, they go elsewhere to commit crime, thefts, terrorism and then they return to their homes in this locality.
I: Do they do it in the name of politics?
R: Yes in the name of politics but they are terrorists.

Faiyaaz's account illustrates the level of fatal violence many of his peers experienced:

> It's been a long time but I knew people by face and when there was an outbreak of dacoity and murders these same guys, whom I grew up with were involved. They were younger than us. But most of that group has not remained alive, killed in encounters, in one way or another they were killed, eighty per cent of these guys are dead now.

Any discussion about offending implicitly prompted respondents to evaluate all types of rule breaking, whether state-defined crimes or infractions of religious law. In Karachi, at least on a theoretical level, there are close parallels between what the State defines as criminal and what sharī'ah declares criminal. Therefore, when the question was put to respondents - 'have you ever committed crime?', it yielded disclosure of activity prohibited within Islam, such as consumption of intoxicants, alongside confessions of offences against the criminal law such as committing fraud or minor traffic offences.

Interestingly, although sharī'ah places significant emphasis upon refraining from all criminal activity, even that which is defined by a secular state, respondents expressed greater respect for sharī'ah than for secular laws. This was so despite confessions that little was known or comprehended about the dynamics of sharī'ah in Karachi.

In Karachi, the awareness and self-confessions of infractions of sharī'ah were given priority over State law in the minds of some respondents. State law is

---

[12] Pakistan Penal Code s144 grants general public order powers to the police.

thus viewed by some as corrupt, and as having been generated by oppressive colonial powers in particular. Not only is State law considered corrupt, it is seen as a product of humans, whereas sharīʻah, in the eyes of Muslims, is irrefutable due to its divine origin. This distinction enables critical discourse to develop regarding secular laws as opposed to religious law. The fact that this divine law compels Muslims to abide by State law, as long as it does not oppress them in worship, is somehow lost in the construction of which rules may or may not be broken.

Central to this discussion is the evaluation, by Karachiites, of the legal nature of the Constitution of Pakistan. No respondent believed Pakistan to be a true Islamic State. Seeking clarification of this opinion prompted requests to evaluate the practices of State-orientated denial of minority rights in Karachi, political frauds of overwhelming magnitude, such as those alleged against the former Prime Minister Nawaz Sharif, and most importantly the preference of a secular constitution over one based on sharīʻah (Mehdi, 1994). The argument put is that the state, irrespective of religious bearings, must be just, tolerant and protective of minority rights, qualities deemed redundant in the present Pakistani criminal justice system. There is correspondingly little respect for prohibitive laws in the face of such perceived injustice. Religious law provides an 'untouched purity' for the citizens, hence its appeal, yet it lacks the official state legal framework in which to operate, instead becoming subject to multiple interpretations and expression via religious leaders.

For example, Gafoor spoke of his experiences of drinking and relationships outside of marriage:

> I: Have you ever done anything not permitted in Islam, drinking, drugs, relationships outside marriage?
> R: You can say, during teenage, I was with my friends, I did taste such things, alcohol once, I tried it but I did feel that it wasn't for me, it's been ten years since then. Also the other things you mention, women.
> I: Women?
> R: Yes, not deeply, but I got involved in things I shouldn't.

Javaid spoke of persons he knew who had committed crimes:

> I: Have any of your friends committed crimes, or do you know of people locally who have done so?
> R: Yes I know.
> I: What type of crimes?
> R: Dacoity.
> I: Do you know these people, have they spoken to you about it or do you simply know them by face?
> R: I know them by face.

Offending Behaviour in Haslingden

As in Karachi, few respondents stated that they had committed any serious crimes. Some respondents did acknowledge having committed less serious offences such as criminal damage:

> I: Have you ever committed a crime?
> R: A crime could be taking a floppy disk from school.
> I: It could be.
> R: To our perception I have yeah.
> I: What type of offence?
> R: Minor ones.
> I: What would you say are minor?
> R: Breaking windows.
> I: Breaking of windows which are vacant or occupied?
> R: Occupied.
> I: What was the purpose of this?
> R: Just for the hell of it.
> I: Were you caught for it?
> R: No.
> I: (Turning to another respondent) so were you involved in the same thing or different things?
> R: Separate things, when I was in school, property damage in school (Group Interview, Bangladeshi Youths).

Self-confessions were not generally forthcoming, although it can perhaps be assumed that some respondents did have such an involvement in crime. Many more cited the crimes and deviance of friends or people they knew. For example Ashraf informed me of the following:

> I: Have you any Asian friends or family whom you know to have committed crime?
> R: Oh yeah, many many, especially friends, family no to be honest, but friends in Haslingden, drugs even now as we speak I can name twenty to thirty lads who are involved in drugs who are my friends.
> I: What type of drugs?
> R: Soft drugs, not going above marijuana, not heroin, cocaine or anything, it's very difficult for the lads in Haslingden to get hold of stuff like that. Break-ins happen, many break-ins.
> I: Are these Asians?
> R: Yes Asian lads.
> I: From what backgrounds?
> R: Bangladeshis, Pakistanis and you're talking from the age of 12, 13 to 24, once they get married they tend to go back down.
> I: Have you been told this or witnessed it yourself?
> R: Yes, you know being lads they brag about it perhaps, from the way they walk and talk, but because of my character I still got involved with them. I mean they occasionally go with us on these religious trips for three days every month, they're brilliant lads at the end of the day but still involved in crime. Lads who I know have bragged about the way they have broken into houses and cars. I know lads who have mugged old ladies and mention it.

Therefore, regardless of the fact that few self-confessions of crime and deviance were made there is an underlying belief amongst the respondents that local Muslims are indeed involved in committing crime. This ranges from drugs and alcohol abuse to criminal damage, assaults, fraud and theft. There is particular concern amongst respondents about a perceived local drug and alcohol problem in which Muslim youths are involved. In addition, respondents were concerned about non-criminal religious offences, such as Muslims having sexual relationships outside marriage. Respondents felt that such issues were a result of living in a social environment that promotes alcohol and drug abuse and sexually promiscuous lifestyles.

The fieldwork gathered accounts of crime and deviance among first–generation South Asians. These submissions help dispel the myth of a completely law-abiding, conformist parent group, and illustrate the application of a form of 'historical amnesia' regarding the lifestyles of the first settlers. For example, an elder discussed how significant numbers of the first settlers drank alcohol and indulged in relationships outside of marriage. Importantly, the submissions of some respondents suggest that the elder/conformist and youth/deviant dichotomy is not rigidly adhered to within the community. Some respondents believed that some elders were clearly known to have broken the law, mainly through benefit fraud, whereas some youths were considered to be involved in minor offences such as petty theft. For example:

> I: Do you think the elders are more law-abiding than the youth?
> Ghazan: the elders are committing different crimes. Elders may be doing fraud, youths may be breaking cars.
> I: What about crime amongst the first settlers?
> Ghazan: well if someone calls himself Haji (pilgrim) then all will know him as such, even though, as happened here, he defrauded everyone in charity collecting to fill his own stomach. Others are dealing in drugs, there was an incident where an elder was arrested recently in Blackburn. The elders have and are doing crime but for you to understand how, what and when is not an easy thing.
> Faheem: If you give me a social security job, I can get from the first row in the mosque people who are criminals. If you tell me outside and catch five to ten youths, it will be hard for me because youth are doing small types of crime, breaking a window and telephone kiosk things like that, but the main criminals will be on the front row of the mosque praying (Group Interview, Memorial Gardens, Haslingden).

Whilst the respondents' views in the last extract may appear generalised, it reflects their view that not all elders within the local community are wholly law-abiding and conformist. It is worth noting that these submissions are not only from youths but also from some elders themselves. Other respondents seemed to agree with this view, for example during the same interviews:

> Bashir: Yes those on the front row in the mosque are the criminals, but the methods are different. You might think that they are Haji (pilgrim), but we know otherwise and there are people who have committed crime in Pakistan before settling here. We

are also not helping matters if we do not police things ourselves. Like when that guy was collecting charity for twenty years we all suspected but nobody would say that he was a thief. Until that attitude changes crimes can't be reduced amongst us.

Choudri: Well that was one guy, but what about the social security fraud that's going on a massive scale?

Bashir: Some are doing it for need, but for many it's greed, the elders are keen on buying land back home, it gives them respect back in the homeland.

Choudri: Also they live in two countries, they need to spend in two countries.

Bashir: But many have their families here, their responsibilities should be here.

Faheem: I think some professionals are involved in the frauds, GPs allowing disability grants.

Bashir: But the whites do it also.

Ghazan: Our people don't actually claim their full entitlements due to stigma and ignorance (Group Interview, Memorial Gardens, Haslingden).

These conversations illustrate the complexities of how Muslims view others within their community. What is demonstrated is that there is no clear-cut picture of an easily identifiable criminal 'other', but rather that the 'other' is part of the whole. Members of the community, whether youths or elders, cannot evade the labelling of deviant or criminal being attached to them by their peers and by the wider community beyond. Whilst elders are perceived to be more involved in benefits fraud, youths are seen as going through a transient phase where crimes are considered to be minor. All does not share the latter view; with some respondents genuinely believing that the youth are now particularly rebellious, deviant and involved in minor to major criminal acts. This view is reflected in some media discourse, concentrating on a view of the once victimized minority now becoming the perpetrators of racially motivated crime (Ramesh, 1998). Similarly the rise in the proportion of prison inmates that are Muslim provides the grist to the mills of promoters of a sudden moral panic about Muslim criminals (Webster, 1997).

The 'Racialized Criminal Other' in Sharifabad and Haslingden

In Karachi the submissions made by the respondents indicate a significant racialized social construction of who the 'criminals' are. There is wide variation as to what the causes of crime are perceived to be, ranging from socio-economic to psychological factors. Many respondents expressed notions of a 'criminal other' and this could refer to the 'drug-addict', the 'free-loader', the 'squatter' or the rival 'political other'. Whilst the categories are not race-specific, when used alongside labels such as the 'Afghani' or the 'Punjabi', a more race-orientated discourse becomes apparent. The labels are used interchangeably by the respondents, so the 'squatter' does not remain simply a squatter but becomes an 'Afghani squatter' or a 'Punjabi political rival'.

Often, the socially constructed identities are posited in geographical terrains such as the 'kaatchi abaadi'[13], the 'Interior Provinces' or simply the 'village'.

---

[13] Urdu: literally translates as *raw populace*, i.e. squatter establishments or shanty towns (see

These areas and peoples are considered criminogenic. The deconstruction of such identity-formation leads to an understanding of how some people and places become scapegoats and 'folk devils'. It sheds light upon the notion of the criminal as an 'outsider' both racially and geographically.

The following accounts represent a sophisticated comprehension of the layers of criminal activity and injustice in Karachi. Crime may be understood within a number of contexts. Most respondents expressed an understanding of the broader political dynamics operating in Pakistan. Crime is viewed as directly related to a corrupt and dysfunctional legal system; dysfunctional here is understood as dysfunctional in protecting fundamental civil liberties for the citizen. The principal crimes and injustices are perceived to be those undertaken by political leaders. Those in power are considered to be denying basic human rights to the majority who are deliberately kept illiterate, ignorant and hence powerless. The corruption has become aligned, by some, along ethnic lines. The construction of 'Mohajir' identity demonstrates the struggle by a once elite minority to regain fundamental civil liberties, which have been gradually eroded.

Within a social atmosphere of political struggle the agents of political insurgency become subsumed within the generic categories of 'deviant' and 'criminal'. The political struggle operates as an umbrella and a uniform disguise for the deviance and criminality of many who have no genuine political affiliation or agenda, thus undermining any true political struggle. The community-based enquiry revealed practical daily animosities and concerns for the residents within the local terrain. Here we can trace how political observations fracture along racial lines. The police force was seen as corrupt, and considered to be a product of a corrupt criminal and civil legal system. Since the recruitment and ethnic composition of the police force is overwhelmingly from the Punjab and rural locations, the corruption becomes associated with specific ethnic groups and locations.

Respondents spoke of social problems emanating essentially from a corrupt political system. Political instability was considered by respondents to be the most influential contributory factor regarding crime in Pakistan. Respondents advocated calls for constitutional change to address the political problems. A second, but related level of comprehension was that of the day-to-day social reality of crime, stemming in part from the political instability. Within discussions about crime in the community, respondents levelled the blame at a corrupt civil and criminal justice system whilst simultaneously pointing the finger at scapegoats within a clearly racialized discourse.

The following extracts demonstrate the manner in which some respondents constructed racialized conceptions of problematic peoples. For example, Abdul expressed the following views about various groups he perceived to be 'problematic' in the neighbourhood:

> Initially it was quite a peaceful area but with the passage of time it has turned and has been involved in some political matters. And also people have come from the

Glossary).

different areas which are involved in some crime and who have some link with the political parties.

Yes tramps, they are drug addicts, this has been going on for the past six or seven years, on the corner of Al-Azam Square, they just sit there smoke and inject. You must have noticed people sitting at Hussain Square, with the cloth around them?

In response to questions about a nearby shanty town Abdul expressed his belief that the prime suspects for car lifting resided in these localities. Further, Abdul believed individuals in such localities were driven by greed as much as need. In response to questions about the ethnicity of residents in the shantytown Abdul clearly distanced himself (as a Mohajir) from those living there, despite an acknowledgement that some of them belonged to the same ethnic group as himself. Here we see the influence of class differences upon the social terrain and the status of Mohajir is clearly something elevated in the perception of the respondent, this is indicated by his use of the term 'pure' when referring to Mohajir as a racial classification whilst the term Afghani may be interpreted as impure in this context:

I: Where have these people come from, who lives in the kaatchi abaadis?
R: Well they call themselves Mohajir, but I really don't know whether they are purely Mohajir or Afghani and all.

The physical environment in which the Mohajir respondents reside was also granted an elevated status, for example Babu believed his locality, Sharifabad, to be a middle-class area that was relatively free of criminals, though not necessarily crime. The distinction between criminal concordance and locations where crimes take place is an important distinction and one that was raised by the respondents. Crime was equated with poverty and the neighbouring areas of Gharibabad and Liaqatabad were cited as economically impoverished localities making them easy targets for the drugs mafia and other criminals.

Chacha also emphasized the relatively law-abiding nature of residents of Sharifabad. Crime and deviance were considered the negative outcome of poor education whilst conformity was considered the positive product of education.

Certain respondents were strongly opposed to the existence of kaatchi abaadis whilst acknowledging that the principal cause of conflict was poverty-driven. For example in response to a question about the existence of a neighbouring kaatchi abaadi Chacha said: 'I am not happy about them because they are illegal and the beauty of the city is being destroyed'.

Danyaal also echoed Chacha's views about kaatchi abaadis. It can be argued that the process of politicising the struggle for urban space in Karachi detracts citizens from any substantial voiced critique of government policies, instead offering them easily targeted peoples to blame for increases in social problems. Chacha expressed the following views:

I: What are the causes of crime here?
R: There's limited funds for resources from the government, but the population keeps on growing, there's increasing in-migration with a limited govt. budget which puts strains on the resources, water, electric.

I: How do you feel about the kaatchi abaadis?

R: I'm not happy about them, because they are illegal and the beauty of the city is being destroyed.

I: I've seen drug addicts in the area, how common are they?

R: Yes a little outside Sharifabad, in Gharibabad, they sleep on the streets, they beg for food from the hotels.

I: What drugs are they using?

R: Heroin.

I: Where do they get it from?

R: Nearby their dealer is around.

I: Is there police involvement?

R: Yes, they have a hand in it...I've seen the police watching them take drugs.

Danyaal spoke of the term Mohajir and what he considered to be the problem behind crime in the locality:

We didn't like to be called Mohajir, we were named this by others. We used to refer to ourselves as Hindustani, but since Altaf Hussain gave prominence to this expression it became more accepted, but in educated circles it is still disapproved of. There was an acknowledgement that to be called Hindustani in Pakistan was also not acceptable. So you should just be Pakistani. But due to the relationship with India, and due to the ethnic differences and migration history, they were incapable of saying that they belonged to a particular region. The Punjabis, Sindhis etc. belonged to a region, they didn't shift during Partition. But all those that came from pre-Partition India neither did they become Sindhi, nor did they remain Hindustani. So those who say clearly that they are Mohajir, they emphasize that it was because nobody was accepting them as any other ethnic group. n Karachi all the people of Pakistan reside here, Pathan, Punjabi, Baluchi etc. In the villages where they come from, there are feuds, they capitalise on the political instability here to fuel and perpetuate such rural personal vendettas. So the political turmoil is used as a mask behind which people commit crimes.

In response to a question about kaatchi abaadis:

No. Kaatchi abaadis or unauthorised shops shouldn't be here, I'm not happy with them because the whole system goes bad, we lose track of the population, the planning fails, water, transport, electricity and sanitation problems are aggravated.
Karachi gives 70-75 per cent tax revenue throughout Pakistan. Central government views Karachiites as people of another country. Representatives from all over Pakistan will and have competed for elections in Karachi, but it's never been the case where a Karachiite for example has been elected in Lahore, or Peshawar, but people from there win votes here because here all races and cultures are represented.
In every area and province there should be a local police force so that they know the residents. But a person from afar doesn't know the locals, who is who, what is what. What happens now is that officers from village areas or outside Karachi commit theft accept bribes and take money out of Karachi. This is a very sore point amongst Karachiites.

Some respondents spoke of a 'more sociable' past where families socialised regularly in contrast to a 'less sociable' present atmosphere. The shift was accounted for, in the perception of the more established residents, by the influx of 'less sociable newcomers'. For example Elahi mentioned the following:

> People used to socialise more in Sharifabad. Now many of those that are arriving are not as sociable. There are old circles of families which keep in touch, but the newcomers don't mix.

Some respondents spoke of Karachi in positive terms emphasizing the relatively high levels of education amongst its dwellers as against a criticism of the feudal system of the villages, for example Farida said the following:

> Karachi, I like it, I view the law and order problem as temporary, Karachi is a metropolitan city and it is a unique city within Pakistan for a number of reasons. Firstly the literacy rate is relatively high, secondly the living style is such that it is open, people do not mistreat their domestic help and the rest of Pakistan is subject to feudalism where landowners mistreat the villagers. For example they don't permit the education of village children. In Baluchistan there are tribes there and similar abuses.

With regard to the criminal as an 'outsider' Bodrul's comments summarize what was a frequently repeated dialogue amongst the 'Mohajir' respondents:

> Here for example, if I am a villain, terrorist or dacoit, I will attempt to gain political affiliation and support, after which I will become the king of the neighbourhood and untouchable regardless of what I say or do... but in Karachi it's not really the Karachiites who are doing the crime, they come from Interior Sindh, Multan, Lahore, Dado, 80 per cent of them are from outside Karachi, 20 per cent are from Karachi and the reason why they are committing crime is due to unemployment and poverty, illiteracy and they get involved in crime.
> I: What crimes are most prevalent in Sharifabad in your perception?
> R: I feel there are no major crimes here, there are a few minor crimes...like for example if you have an argument with your neighbour you go to the station and we compromise, end of matter. But surrounding Sharifabad, are Gharibabad and Liaqatabad, Al-Karam and Karimabad, these are known as terrorist areas. Right in the middle of these areas is a small piece of land, Sharifabad, where the people are educated a bit more and where you find literacy then crime is less, where education is less, crime will be higher.
> I: What do you think the image of Muslims is like in Europe?
> R: I've never been abroad but I don't think the image is positive. I have friends who live in the Middle East, the Arabs have labelled the Pakistanis complete bastards, my own cousin has observed this. But the reason for this is that over there they have done many wrong things. Also the Afghans are coming into Pakistan getting Pakistani passports and then going overseas. Who will get the blame for their wrongdoings? The Pakistani government. Also there are people from Punjab, education and literacy is considerably low over there. I mean there are good and bad people in all cultures and races but people from Punjab who go overseas and get involved in dubious practices give Pakistan a bad name.

Interestingly, whilst the main blame for crime is placed on people from outside of Karachi, there is some acknowledgement that Karchiites themselves commit crime. These crimes, however, are justified due to external factors such as poverty and unemployment. Implicit in Bodrul's submission is the notion that crime committed by 'others' outside Karachi is somehow motivated beyond these forces of strain, therefore stripping from the offender the mitigating factors afforded to his fellow Mohajir Karachiites.

There was particular concern expressed by the respondents about the manner in which they felt their national identity was being projected on a global level. 'Afghans' and 'Punjabis' figured frequently in the submissions of the Mohajirs who felt these groups had 'tarnished' their image on a global scale by their involvement in organized crime such as the heroin trade. Cairul's conversation emphasizes the latter point:

> Well over there in Model Colony there were Punjabis, Pathans and Sindhis and Mohajirs, the others formed an alliance and were after the Mohajirs so that the area would be rid of Mohajirs and so they could take over the area for themselves. Here in Sharifabad everyone is a Mohajir, it's a Mohajir community and there's no trouble like we experienced in Model Colony. So when we came here we felt much more secure, there was no ill-mannered behaviour towards us.
>
> I am proud to be Pakistani but I don't think the image is a good one abroad, basically because Pakistan is represented by all Pakistanis, but the green passport also increasingly represents Afghans. So, for example, in Saudi on every Friday an Afghan can be found hanging from a noose due to involvement in heroin. He is an Afghan but he has a Pakistani passport so it's Pakistan's image that is damaged. Also go to Canada, USA or England, regarding England I have even heard that in certain hotels they have signs that say 'DOGS AND PAKISTANIS NOT ALLOWED'.
>
> I think the Punjab district has soiled Pakistan's image. I've heard and spoken to people who have been overseas and they all say that the Punjabis have done so many corrupt things that all Pakistanis are dishonoured. My father in Saudi does not wear the traditional shalwar kameez out of the shame of being recognized as a Pakistani.
>
> Whilst we are proud to be Pakistani because our image has been tarnished by Afghans and Punjabis we don't like it to be known that we are from Pakistan when we go abroad.

The questions raised during the course of the research include: what factors are operating to produce racially constructed definitions of the 'Karachi criminal', and how far are such 'modern' racial stereotypes a legacy of the colonial period? We have already noted the manner in which certain racial constructions formed part of the colonial exercise in managing the colonies (Chapter 3). The formulation of criminal tribes, for example, provides a perfect example of state-originated ethnic classification and labelling (Mahmud, 1999). Certain tribes and nomadic peoples were effectively 'demonized' by governmental policies to enable swift means of controlling what was deemed an 'unproductive' group of people. In contemporary Karachi the perceptions of tribal regions and people, such as those from Baluchistan, are overwhelmingly negative. Such negativity is reflected in recent policing strategies, which have been targeting cross-border smuggling, as well as the classification of criminogenic areas using Geographic Imaging Software in Karachi (CPLC 1999b). Whilst the Citizen-Police Liaison Committee in Karachi consciously acknowledges the legal negativities associated with legislation inherited from colonial times, this does not appear to have deterred it from subconsciously pursuing policies that are essentially designed to record, classify and generate profiles of criminal places and criminal people. The pursuit of such a statistical programme will eventually provide ammunition for the persistence of racialized discourse about who the 'problematic' peoples are in Karachi. Given the relative newness and inaccuracy of criminal data collation and analysis in Pakistan, any policies based upon such statistical projections are arguably based on extremely insecure foundations.

    In the British context the respondents themselves may be viewed as the subjects of a racialized discourse that may be considered beyond their control. The Muslim in Lancashire can be viewed as forming part of the 'racialized criminal other' within a broader institutionalized discourse about race and crime. Here the respondents found themselves to be the subjects of prejudicial labelling, just as was the case for the 'Afghan' and the 'squatter' in Karachi. In Britain the respondents viewed themselves as members of the 'Muslim' group. Whilst contemporary criminological discourse on Asians and crime has been extremely limited, there is an increasingly mounting contribution to the study of Muslims and crime[14]. The British respondents were increasingly aware of such discourse and felt that the 'Muslim' as a 'deviant', be it as a 'terrorist', 'fanatic', or 'oppressor of women', was an image they were constantly attempting to dispel.

    As we have observed, the topics discussed represent the principal articulations of the South Asian Muslim samples in Britain and Pakistan. Perceptions of problematic crime in Karachi are rooted in politically motivated crime. In Britain, Muslims tend to view racial violence, drugs and other offences within Islam, such as zina, problematic.

    With regard to policing, both communities articulate distrust of, alienation from, and discrimination towards them from the police. A significant level of police and paramilitary corruption and brutality were articulated from the lived-experiences of the Karachiites. Both communities expressed a need for a more inclusive and representative police force and articulated this with reference to 'community policing'. Such community policing centred upon individual officers physically living or spending time visiting and getting to personally know individual households and members of the community.

    The experiences of South Asian Muslim youth during the biannual 'Īd celebrations offers an insight into group deviancy. Developing ideas were presented; that the deviancy is evidence of the cultural carnival of crime whereby repressed and marginalized groups in society find temporary expression and empowerment (Presdee, 2000). The phenomenon also highlights formal interaction between the police and perceived 'brokers of control' or order (such as mosque elders) within Muslim communities.

---

[14] See Chapter 2.

The two field locations offer contrast in terms of urban geography and ecology. The location in Pakistan is one of the most populous conurbations in the Indian subcontinent (Bureau of Statistics, 1990), and indeed in the world. Political, social, urban and ecological factors combine to produce certain 'no-go zones' for the residents. These 'no-go zones' are construed as problematic localities, and both the area and the residents acquire 'racialized' identities as 'criminogenic'. In the UK, despite differences in ecology, political and urban environments, Muslims also demark certain areas in their locality as 'no-go' zones. In both Karachi and Britain it is the fear of becoming the victim of crime that prevents individuals from frequenting such 'no-go zones'. In Britain, 'no-go zones' for Muslims are areas where there are perceptions of increased risks of becoming the victim of verbal or physical racial abuse.

This study highlights the fact that South Asian Muslims perceive significant experiences of victimization. Karachiites feel themselves to be victims of state oppression, political marginalization, police and paramilitary brutality and from criminals involved in politically motivated and organized crime. British Muslims feel they are victims of prejudice, both explicit and implicit which leads to feelings of exclusion and marginalization.

For both populations there is a comprehension of a global ill will towards Muslims, culminating in 'Islamophobia'. As we shall discuss in the next chapter, the research affords an insight into how historical and institutional practices have impacted on Muslim self-identity and the construction of them as deviant. In this respect, the study records a shared sense of victimization within the ummah.

The study also explores issues of religion, in particular the comprehension of Islamic criminal law (Al-uqūbāt) by South Asian Muslims within a comparative setting. As discussed, the vast majority of respondents confessed to knowing very little about Al-uqūbāt. Knowledge of more orthodox aspects of Islamic criminal law (hūdd offences) was more apparent amongst the sample, and this was principally due to political efforts in Pakistan to enforce hūdd offences at the expense of other types of Islamic criminal legislative policy (Mehdi, 1994). However, the majority of respondents were aware of permitted (jaīz) and forbidden (harām) behaviour as these values are disseminated via the institutions of the family and local mosques.

Muslims in both countries, in their assessment of crime and deviance, favoured Islamic definitions of prohibited behaviour over secular definitions. For example, in the articulations of the British respondents, fornication and the consumption of intoxicants was considered criminal rather than deviant or permissible (as it is by secular law).

An important theme to emerge from the study is the articulations of the 'racialized criminal other', interlinked to constructions of criminogenic places. Origins of the construction and use of 'racialized criminal others' can be traced to colonial rule in India (Mahmud, 1999). The study begins to trace where colonial legacies have left their imprints upon the contemporary post-colonial terrain. Racialized and stereotypical discourses that framed legislation, such as the Criminal Tribes Act of 1871, find articulation in the contemporary crime control policies of the Karachi police, as well as in the articulations of local residents

(CPLC, 1999). Therefore, in Karachi we witness the emergence of crime being personified via the construction of the 'Afghan heroin addict', the 'Pathan squatter', the 'Punjabi-corrupt police officer' and the 'Mohajir terrorist'. In Britain, the Muslims find themselves the subject of racialized discourse of a once law-abiding conforming group becoming constructed as the latest folk-devil (Webster, 1997).

These issues and themes constitute a core of the present study. The articulations and qualitative experiences ultimately shape a discussion that offers theoretical propositions detailed in the following chapter.

Chapter 6

Theoretical Perspectives

The following chapter plots the development and emergence of a substantial theoretical evaluation of Muslims and crime. This research has led to the assertion of a theoretical perspective unknown in contemporary British criminology. The unique qualities of the study are demonstrated by its comparative dimension, its in-depth qualitative methodology, and its adoption of a critical race theory perspective.

Traditional Criminological Theories

The discipline of criminology, as is the case for all disciplines, is subject to constant redefinition and changing constitutional composition. To ignore its multi-disciplinary heritage is to undermine criminology itself. Nevertheless, it is noteworthy that European and American academic endeavours dominate founding criminological discourse (Maguire, Morgan and Reiner, 2002). The Eurocentric nature of traditional criminology is therefore a direct consequence of this legacy (Bowling and Phillips, 2003). Theory, by virtue of its very nature, is speculative and often unsupported by data or facts, but when examining traditional criminological theories and Muslims certain theoretical speculations provide more coherent explanations for crime and victimization than others.

In terms of the chronology of theoretical developments on crime, a distinction can be made between the more deterministic positivist approaches beginning with Cesare Lombroso in 1876 to counter-positivistic interpretative paradigms during the 1960s and 1970s with thinkers such as Howard Becker and Stanley Cohen (Lombroso, 1876; Becker, 1963; Cohen, 1972). It is not the remit of this text to offer a systematic critique of the early positivistic literature suffice to say that the racism and Eurocentricism voiced during the Enlightenment found purchase amongst some of the founding studies of crime and biological positivism (Eze, 1997).

The qualitative emphasis placed in counter-positivistic theories is particularly suited to deconstructing the 'truth' about culture, and in turn issues of crime and victimization (Sztompka, 1990). When considering Muslims, as noted throughout this text, there are very few directly relevant criminological contributions. The two main studies introduced in the second chapter of this text examine traditional sociological theories of social control (Wardak, 2000) and racial victimization (Webster, 1994). With regard to Muslim youth involvement in crime, these studies tend to suggest both a loosening in traditional control mechanisms meted by institutions such as the family and religion against societal strains contributing to social exclusion, discrimination and marginalization. Such marginalization is confirmed by empirical data regarding the British Muslim population (Runnymede, 1997; IHRC, 2001; OSI, 2004).

Criminological discourse about the role of the media in manipulating cultural images and initiating moral panics is comprehensive (Maguire, Morgan, Reiner, 2002; Cohen, 1972; Hall et al., 1978). More recent research has broadened the focus on how media images have contributed to stereotypes and moral panics pertaining to Muslims (Runnymede, 1997). Criminological theories about 'media deviancy amplification', 'labelling' and 'self-fulfilling' prophecies provide meaningful explanations for the emergence of the Muslim as the latest folk-devil (Cohen, 1972; Becker, 1963; Webster, 1997).

Critical Race Theory

Critical race theory (CRT) is not truly a theory in the classical understanding of this word. It is probably better defined as a perspective. The roots of the perspective lie essentially with the Black civil rights movement of the 1960s in the United States. Figures such as Martin Luther King, Malcolm X, Rosa Parks and W.E.B. DuBois are frequently cited as iconic inspiration for CRT scholars (Crenshaw et al., 1995).

However, there was a perception amongst some leading Black American scholars that the initial impetus and rush of the Black civil rights movement was stalling in the latter part of the 1960s and early 1970s. The influential writings of the late legal scholar Robert Cover, and jurist, A. Leon Higginbotham Jr., highlighted the marginalisation of the role of 'race' in the American legal academy (Crenshaw et al., 1995). Cover and Higginbotham Jr. claimed that there was a silence with regard to the sufferings and life experiences of indigenous people 'Latin, Asian and African Americans' and that such silence was maintained in American legal education.

This sense of silence and injustice with regard to indigenous and displaced peoples was developed further by the most noted figures of the CRT perspective, namely Derrick Bell Jr. and Alan Freeman, writing in the mid 1970s (Delgado and Stefanic, 2000). Therefore, central to the roots of the perspective, and indeed arguably its current dominant focus, has been the contribution of progressive intellectuals of 'colour' working within the realm of contemporary legal studies.

To focus upon the law as opposed to politics was a conscious decision by CRT scholars, for whereas politics was considered 'open-ended, subjective, discretionary and ideological', law was supposed to be 'determinate, objective, bounded and neutral' (Crenshaw et al. 1995:xviii). There is the assumption of law operating as apolitical, rational and technical; operating according to CRT scholars, as a 'regulatory principle defining what is legitimate and illegitimate to pursue in legal scholarship' (Crenshaw et al., 1995:xviii).

According to Cornell West, CRT scholarship is unified by its focus on two common themes. First to understand how a:

> Regime of white supremacy and its subordinates of people of colour have been created and maintained in America, and in particular, to examine the relationship between the social structure and professed ideals such as the 'rule of law' and 'equal protection' (West, 1995:xiii).

Second:

> A desire not to merely understand the vexed bond between law and racial power but to change it (West, 1995:xiii).

Whilst these two aims may indeed be unifying factors within the perspective, the discourse it has generated is by no means governed by a canonical set of doctrines or methodologies to which all CRT theorists subscribe. Further, since many CRT scholars have located the root of inequality and injustice in colonial times, CRT is therefore applicable to wherever such colonialism may be traced and hence is not confined purely to the American context (see Mahmud, 1997; 1999).

Regarding methodology, many contemporary CRT scholars have adopted novel and unique methods of breaking the perceived silence of suffering minorities. Techniques such as story telling offer valuable insights into myths and pre-suppositions about 'race, ethnicity and culture'. These works reject the prevailing orthodoxy that scholarship should be or could be 'neutral' or 'objective'. The emphasis is often upon a process of 'un-telling' history in order to publicize and place the current socio-economic position of marginalized communities in context (Montoya, 2000). For example, we hear the voice of Christine Zuni Cruz 'un-telling' the life experiences of Native American Indians and the issues facing tribal law programmes (Zuni Cruz, 2000). Similarly Bonita Lawrence is able to discuss 'Metisation and the regulation of native identity' as an aboriginal woman of 'Mi'kmaq, Acadian, and English heritages' (Lawrence, 1999).

Of particular relevance to the present study is the work of CRT scholars, such as Tayyab Mahmud, who have evaluated issues of colonialism and modern constructions of 'race' and 'ethnicity' (Mahmud, 1997; 1999).

Within such studies lies the strength of the CRT approach. By analyzing the past, which includes the colonial past, scholars have embarked upon a discovery of how practices during colonial periods have permeated the terrain of post-colonialism. So whilst the geographical and socio-political contexts may differ, understanding the past and the institutionalized displacement of peoples and cultures helps to clarify the contemporary social terrain of the metropolis. This aspect of CRT enables it to be applied wherever such 'displacement', 'marginalization' and 'silencing' is occurring.

CRT scholarship has prompted significant criticism from legal academics in the USA. Commentators such as Randall Kennedy and Farber Sherry have articulated a lengthy critique of CRT challenging the 'voice' and 'exclusion' theses in addition to accusations of CRT representing 'vulgar racial essentialism' (Delgado and Stefancic, 200:87-95). Kennedy questioned the notion that minority scholars spoke with a unique voice pertaining to issues of race or possessed specific expertise to do so. Kennedy asserts that by providing a voice for some minority ethnic scholars it undermines the genuine contributions from white scholars on the subject. Furthermore, Kennedy challenged the assertion, articulated by Criticalists such as Richard Delgado, that mainstream scholars ignored the work of academics belonging to an ethnic minority group (Delgado, 1995; Delgado and Stefancic, 2001).

Further criticism was raised by Daniel Farber and Suzanna Sherry of the usefulness of 'story-telling' as a methodology by CRT scholars. The same critics point to the relative success of Jewish and East Asian minority groups in the USA in relation to academic and occupational achievement. Farber and Sherry assert that CRT's critique of merit leads to the conclusion that Jews and Asians either cheated, took unfair advantage or were 'unimaginative drones' (Delgado and Stefancic, 2001:90). Farber and Sherry go further in accusing CRT scholars of being implicitly anti-Semitic and anti-Asian due to the attack by Criticalists on then notion of a meritocratic and egalitarian society.

In reply to the criticisms leveled at them, CRT scholars asserted that Kennedy failed to grasp the important issue of 'context' and 'narrative', whilst his claims for quantifiable proof of discrimination in legal scholarship echoed the 'loaded standards the conservative Supreme Court had been developing in the law of racial remedies, such as proof of intent and straight line causation[1] (Delgado and Stefancic, 2001:89).

With reference to the comments by Farber and Sherry, Richard Delgado claims they confuse the issues, for how cam a critique of an unfair conventional merits standards equate with anti-Semitic or anti-Asian sentiments? According to Delgado, Farber and Sherry are themselves responsible for viewing the discriminatory experiences of all minority groups in homogenous terms (Delgado and Stefancic, 2001). The critique asserted by Farber and Sherry illustrates a 'colour-blind' approach to the complexities of institutional and contextual racism.

The brief insight to debates within the American legal academy about race, ethnicity and the law demonstrate that CRT scholarship is challenging existing standards and provoking constructive debate about discrimination which is the raison d'être of the perspective.

---

[1] It is worth noting that in the UK the Macpherson Inquiry (1999) and Race Relations (Amendment) Act 2000 remove the emphasis on having to prove 'intent' for the prosecution of racial discrimination, unwitting racism will suffice.

CRT Applied to the Present Study

At first, CRT may appear to be an unsuitable theoretical framework to adopt given its American origins and given the absence of an American field location in the present study. However, as emphasized previously, CRT is very much a perspective or approach rather than a theory in the classical sense.

The focus and approach of certain CRT scholars emphasizes the diversity of methodological tradition in the unified struggle to facilitate qualitative evaluation of individuals belonging to ethnic, religious or cultural minorities and their experiences and relationship with crime and deviance as offenders and victims (Mahmud, 1997; Montoya 2000). CRT therefore provides a rich pool from which to select novel and unique research strategies and analysis developed by scholars belonging to disciplines of law, socio-legal studies, sociology, criminology, jurisprudence, anthropology and political studies (Crenshaw et al., 1995).

For the present study the following dimensions of CRT research have particular significance. These are: the commitment by CRT scholars to make the invisible-visible, the untold-told and the 'un-telling' of history so as to enable a tracing of the historical past into the terrain of contemporary post-colonial society (Montoya, 2000). Thus, it was important to place the articulations of individual Muslims within a broader historical context to emphasize that here we have displaced populations with common histories due to the British colonization of India. An important dimension to the sample Muslim populations chosen was the concept and experience of migration. Migration and the displacement of people prompted a concentration upon discourses in the USA where such matters have been given considerable academic attention (Lavie and Swedenburg, 1996). This is not to undermine the studies of migration and identity in the UK, however British scholars acknowledge the influence of the Chicago School upon the sociology of migration and subsequent offshoots originating in the USA (Sibley, 1995). Migration has been primarily viewed as a problem with political and popular discourse. In-migration is viewed as a threat to civic amenities based upon the fiction of race as an absolute divider (Bhattacharyya, Gabriel and Small, 2002).

The first 'act of displacement' highlighted in this study is the Partition of India in 1947. The migrants to Karachi in modern-day Pakistan form a vivid example of a population displaced, eventually leading to the construction of the Mohajir identity (Mahmud, 1997). For the British Muslims it was the legacy of colonialism and the UK immigration policies of post-World War II that maintained a nexus between the former colonies and the colonizer, leading to 'guest-worker' status for many of the elder generation of Muslims in the sample.

History is inseparable from the contemporary period, and for the Mohajirs of Karachi the constitutional and hence political environment are legacies of a colonial past that still impact on their daily lives. For example, the fundamental Civil and Criminal Codes of Pakistan have remained virtually intact since the late nineteenth century when they were introduced by the British legislature to assist in the governance of India (Mehdi, 1994).

For the British Muslim, though the colonial legal framework is less influential on their daily lives, the colonial past is nonetheless very relevant to their sense of 'belonging' and 'identity', notwithstanding their familial ties with the Indian subcontinent. If issues of offending and victimization are significantly related to issues of 'identity' and 'belonging' this raises the importance of evaluating the broader historical context for criminologists (Presdee, 2000). It is this point in particular that leads me to conclude that CRT is one theoretical vehicle through which contemporary British criminology can commence enquiry, discourse and theorizing about offending and victimization amongst the Muslim population. Furthermore, this point is not simply relevant to the UK alone, but arguably wherever Muslim communities have been displaced and influenced by the enterprise of colonization, France being a particularly relevant example[2].

Muslims and Crime: Individual, Community and Global contexts

Individual Context

It is important to emphasize that the individual, community and global contexts are not mutually exclusive dimensions but rather the individual positions himself or herself within a sense of the society or world in which he or she lives according to a variety of contexts and factors. For example, if we question whether the individual considers himself or herself to be a victim of crime, the evaluation of this is understood at a number of inter-related levels.

For those in this study the evaluation of crime and deviance, offending and victimization, prompted discussions of self-reported individual experiences. The majority did not report personal involvement in crime. The study also facilitates an insight into how, in some cases, the very definition of a 'crime' is open to subjective individual interpretation. Two examples from the research in Karachi are the normalization of traffic offences, (offenders) and the normalization of police corruption (victimization)[3].

Here lies a disjuncture between State-defined legal wrongs and socially constructed acceptable norms. All individuals had their own assessment and interpretation of the seriousness, extent and impact of crime upon their own lives. On the whole however, crimes were perceived to be committed by 'others'. In many cases the 'criminal other' was also a 'racial or ethnic other', an 'outsider' perceived to be disrupting social life in contrast with an imagined point in the past when such crime and deviance did not take place.

In Pakistan we hear of the criminal or deviant other as being an 'Afghan', 'Pathan', 'squatter' or 'village-dweller'. Here the 'criminal other' is perceived to originate from elsewhere 'geographically', elsewhere 'ethnically' and elsewhere 'culturally'.

The individual comprehends and evaluates the complex factors contributing to crime and deviance occurring in their immediate and broader social environments. Crimes are assessed against causation and poverty, destitution and

---

[2] See Sartre (2001) for discussions about the impact of French colonialism on Algeria.
[3] See Chapter 5.

marginalization are frequently cited as contributory factors. In the case of the Karachi populace, the impact of political instability, politically motivated violence and political corruption produce a social reality and discourse where the State, its various organs and those working within the criminal justice system are attributed with the label of perpetrators of crime and injustice. For the individual there emerges a sense of helplessness against deep-rooted political disenfranchisement, prejudice and corruption. The same can be applied, albeit to a lesser extent, to the articulations, perceptions and experiences of the British Muslims, who feel excluded, victimized and marginalized from mainstream British society (see Wardak, 2000; Runnymede 1997; Modood and Berthoud, 1997). Although the study specifically investigated the experiences of South Asian Muslims as perpetrators of crime, what emerges is an overwhelming discourse of victimhood.

The elder/youth dynamic   Whilst the South Asian Muslim sample spoke with a united voice regarding experiences of victimhood, there was some evidence of generational differences. The articulations of elders, or long residing members of a particular community, often spoke of the youths as being problematic and more criminal or deviant than in the past. Media reporting of criminal statistics and a rising Muslim prison population further fuel perceptions of a South Asian Muslim youth crime problem. However, the study also reveals historical amnesia about the past and the involvement in crime and deviance by first-generation South Asian Muslim settlers to Lancashire. The majority of this group now comprises elders of the Muslim community in Haslingden.

Life histories and interviews reveal a past involvement by certain first settlers in drinking alcohol, adultery, gambling and illegal immigration matters. Nevertheless, even for those who acknowledge that such deviant and criminal behaviour did occur amongst first settlers, their perception of present day deviance and crime by Muslim youths is that it is occurring at a far greater scale and by far more individuals.

The picture emerges of fragmented social relationships between certain sections of the community. Some elders spoke of different persons committing different crimes. Some elders were alleged to have been committing social benefits fraud, whilst youths were viewed to be involved in drug and alcohol abuse and drug trafficking, adultery and violence. Often the label of 'hypocrite' was attached to those individuals (youth or elder) who were deemed to be committing offences but also attending the mosque for prayers. To be dubbed 'hypocrite' is a serious accusation for a Muslim for it implies being a sinner and behaving contrary to God's commandments.

Religion   Religious observance is considered by some commentators to be evidence of an individual's degree of conformity to agencies of social control. Islam prescribes permissible and non-permissible human behaviour formally maintained via comprehensive legal codex[4]. Social and political constructions

---

[4] See Chapter 1.

have ensured that the more orthodox elements of Islamic criminal law (al-'uqūbāt) have been disseminated and imprinted upon the Muslim moral conscience arguably at the expense of equally important elements of criminal law (ta'zīr). Therefore, the Muslim remains largely ill-informed about the dynamics of sharī'ah, although he or she is more likely to be aware of the importance of abstaining from drink, fornication and blasphemy.

Religion is evidently a prominent sociological phenomenon in the lives of Muslims; in that it not only provides cultural norms and values but also effectively defines certain basic universal permitted (jāīz) and prohibited (harām) behaviour. Religious identity has also become the vehicle through which political claims and community allegiance are articulated (Bhattacharyya, Gabriel and Small, 2002). Whilst the construction and interpretation of whether certain behaviour is deviant or criminal is dependent upon contextual, historical and political variables, the comparative study reveals that particular behaviour by Muslims is universally considered to be deviant.

Fornication and adultery (zina) are two examples of behaviour understood to be deviant in both Karachi and Lancashire. The assessment of whether certain behaviour is 'legally or morally wrong' is distinguished from why individual Muslims may breach that 'legal or moral wrong'. That is to say, although individual Muslims may commit fornication, it was universally understood to be 'legally and morally wrong' for Muslims.

A reason for such universal comprehension of permitted and non-permitted human behaviour stems from the singularity of the Qur'ān. The Qur'ān in Karachi is the same as in Lancashire or anywhere else in the world for that matter; therefore where behaviour such as fornication, murder and blasphemy are concerned there is a universally understood perception of it being 'legally or morally wrong'. As discussed in Chapter 1, where the legal codex of the Qur'ān is silent on an issue it has been supplemented by the hadīth and interpretations of the classical schools of fiqh. What is revealed by this comparative study, however, is that the teaching, instruction and interpretation of sharī'ah, and specifically al-'uqūbāt, is virtually non-existent amongst the Muslims of Karachi and Lancashire. There is evidence of such matters being discussed at madaris and universities but not for the vast majority of individuals residing in the chosen localities in Britain and Pakistan.

Community Dimension

Whilst acknowledging that the concept of community is problematic and contested[5], the field locations can be understood to be part of a distinct community in each respective country. They are communities and neighbourhoods in the sense that they are the immediate social and physical environments the individual finds himself or herself residing in on a daily basis. The community or neighbourhood is arguably the next social unit and environment after the family where the individual experiences daily social interaction.

---

[5] See Crow (2000).

In the present study the community is seen as a physical but also imagined space within which the individual has a social stake. The discussions regarding crime and victimization often pivot upon the interests of the 'community' or 'moholah'[6]. Discussions centre upon perceptions of who is residing in the community 'legitimately', and who are 'illegal' or 'unwelcome' residents.

In Karachi, perceptions of criminals and deviants centre upon in-migrants, squatters, street pedlars, and drug addicts. However, these 'problematic' groups are understood to be inextricably linked to broader political instability and therefore the 'political activist' and 'corrupt politician or official' figures prominently within discourses about the 'criminal other' in Pakistan. In Britain, we observe Muslims perceived as in-migrants to an indigenous white 'community'. They are the subjects of racialized discourse about their status as citizens and involvement in crime and deviance.

Concepts of 'community' and crime are highlighted by reactions to policing. Policing represents one of the few direct and daily contacts between residents of a 'community' and a major state institution. In both countries the police represent alienation, discrimination and disenfranchisement for those policed. For Karachiites, the ethnic composition, political affiliation and perceived corruption contribute to an overwhelming disrespect, distrust and apprehension regarding the police (and paramilitary) by residents. Such evaluations are not simply the product of secondary discourse but formulated from directly lived experiences of police and paramilitary corruption, coercion and brutality.

In Britain, attitudes towards policing amongst Muslims are also riddled with suspicion, accusations of racism, prejudice and Islamophobia. In both countries there are calls for ethnic self-representation and inclusiveness in criminal justice agencies. In Karachi, distrust and disrespect of the police has lead to vigilantism and self-help alternatives in dispute-resolution[7]. In the UK, a perception of the police as 'outsiders' exacerbates and perpetuates alienation between Muslim residents and the local police. Police and community liaison groups in both countries have therefore had limited impact upon the confidence and trust granted towards the police by residents. Significantly, the latest Home Office 'Citizenship Survey' reports that some respondents perceived certain organizations, such as the police, are likely to treat ethnic minorities worse than others (Home Office, 2004). The same survey found that after white respondents, the Pakistani sample were most likely to say that there was more racial prejudice in Britain now than five years ago (Home Office, 2004:55).

With regard to racism and victimization, the present monograph adds to a steadily growing wealth of studies in the UK[8]. Researchers have evaluated the influence of the far-right on incidents of racially motivated violence. According to Husbands, far right groups can create a climate which facilitates racial violence by providing perpetrators with the confidence to engage in physical rather than verbal

---

[6] Moholah - Urdu - neighbourhood - see Glossary.

[7] Field notes: local incident of resident reprimanding thief, Karachi, April 2000.

[8] See IRR, 1979, 1987, 2001; CRE, 1979; CARF, 1981; Virdee, 1995; Bowling and Phillips, 2002.

assaults (Husbands, 1983). With regard to recent incidents of public disorder involving Muslim youths in the north of England, the inflammatory influence of the British National Party has been acknowledged (IHRC, 2001). Furthermore, the BNP has publicly articulated anti-Muslim rhetoric and prejudice hoping to isolate South Asian Muslims from other British Asian communities (Sayyid, 2002).

Similarly, Sibbet's study of racist offenders provides an interesting evaluation of the way in which racist ideology is sustained via community interaction (Sibbit, 1997). Sibbit concluded that the views of racist perpetrators were shared by the white community where they resided and this effectively legitimated their action. White racists perceive ethnic minorities to receive preferential treatment to public resources and this fuels their prejudice. This theory was offered in an earlier study by Hesse et al. in 1992. According to Hesse et al., racism is facilitated by a non-challenging and sympathetic white non-criminal population (Hesse et al., 1992). It is essentially the inaction of a broadly conformist white community which enables racist violence to grow unchallenged. The fact racist violence in the UK occurs in rural, suburban and prosperous areas challenges the notion that it is simply competition for resources which accounts for such animosity (Bowling and Phillips, 2002). Furthermore, studies of racist violence highlight that it is concentrated in areas of multiple deprivation (Virdee, 1995; Webster, 2001). A recent study explores the concept of 'shame' amongst white racists who perceive south Asians as more successful, but illegitimately so, which serves to compound prejudicial views leading to frustration and in some cases violence (Ray, Smith and Wastell, 2004).

The comparative nature of the present study enables a useful application of the theories outlined above. The experiences of those in Karachi demonstrate how prejudicial behaviour can be perpetuated without challenge from largely conformist groups. We have discussed in Chapter 5, how racially prejudicial discourses arose in relation to the criminal 'other'. In the same way that a white British community may sympathize with racist offenders, in Karachi sectarian and political divisions further complicate and compound significant indifference to the mistreatment of marginalized people in Pakistan.

The exploration of 'no-go zones' provided an insight into the complex relationship between individuals, ethnic groups and the urban environment. This data contributes to the steadily expanding academic discourse on racial victimization and social geography (Smith, 1989; Hesse et al., 1992; Webster, 1994; Sibley, 1995; Back, 1996). In Karachi, the data illustrates high levels of segregation based upon ethnic, class and political differences. The urban conflicts are indicative of a crisis between the state and civil society fueled by successive collapses of civilian governments and distrust of public institutions (Hussain, 1996). With continuous levels of in-migration and strains upon amenities and resources, conflicts arise along racialized discourses about 'outsiders', 'legitimate residents' and 'criminal others'. The contested physical space becomes personified and associated with the ethnicity and class of the people assumed to live there. The *kaatchi abaadis* were highlighted as particular points of conflict, perceived by Mohajirs to harbour criminals, illegitimately consume amenities and represent the unchecked encroachment of physical space.

In the UK, the experiences of Muslims indicate a genuine reality of negotiated urban spaces. Muslim elders and youths employ avoidance strategies based upon local knowledge to reduce the risk of incidents of racial harassment (Webster, 1994). Muslims viewed the areas around public houses as problematic in terms of urban spaces they must cross in order to walk between their homes and the local mosque. Certain areas in an urban locality become associated with an ethnic group whilst others are contested. In studies of areas with significant Muslim populations in London and Keighley, both Asian and white youths claimed stakes in territory, and local knowledge informed youths which area 'belonged' to which ethnic group (Webster, 1994; Alexander, 2000; Keith, 2004). Such studies illustrate the benefits to criminology from social geography in addition to the specific evaluation of differentiating urban space within the context of cultural, rather than physical, mapping (Campbell, 1993; Massey, 1998).

Global Context

The two field bases were separated by more than four thousand miles, yet as we have observed they share common experiences. These common experiences are those of displacement, migration, socio-economic hardships and religion. All the respondents have in some direct or indirect way been influenced by the colonization of India by the British[9].

In addition to the impact of colonial legislation on the present constitutional, criminal and civil legal codes of modern-day Pakistan, the study enables a limited insight into the construction of global 'criminal or deviant' identities to take place.

All Muslim respondents expressed a self-perception of Islam and Muslims as being projected on a global scale via the media synonymously with 'terrorism', 'fundamentalism' and 'barbarism'. Thus for the ummah, or global Muslim consciousness, the image of Muslims and Islam is a soiled and deviant one. Far from locating responsibility for the construction of stereotypes purely on non-Muslims, the study identified elements of self-critique and acceptance that the ummah is facing global challenges and apathy from within.

However, there is significant historical evidence to assert that the construction of the Muslim as 'criminal' or 'deviant', is in part the cumulative outcome of policies, practices and prejudices (direct and indirect) that constitute Islamophobia (Runnymede, 1997; Ahmed, 2000). Within parts of the British criminal justice system there are significant obstacles facing Muslims.

In summary, critical enquiry and primary fieldwork has enabled the emergence of unique theoretical evaluation within the specific contexts of the research locations. The study plots a process through which the researcher's biographical and lived experiences shaped a methodology that is inspired by critical race theory perspective. Central to this process is the emphasis on the social reality of crime and deviance for respondents, the process of 'un-telling' history

---

[9] See Chapter 3.

and making explicit the colonial past insofar as it impacts on the post-colonial social terrain.

Crime and deviance for South Asian Muslims has been evaluated at three levels, individual, community and global. These levels are not mutually exclusive but interrelated. At an individual level, the study has enabled the accumulation of lived experiences of both perpetrators and victims of crime and deviance. Individual evaluation indicates self-assessment of state-defined legal norms and socially constructed acceptable norms. Within such constructions, the criminal almost always figures as the 'other', and this may be the ethnic or religious 'other' considered an 'outsider'. Within such racialized constructions there emerges evidence of understanding by respondents of complex factors that influence crime in both Pakistan and Britain. Crime is assessed against multiple causes, strains and explanations by Muslim respondents and not viewed as a singular phenomenon.

Discussions of crime and deviance within the immediate community prompt calls for ethnic self-representation in criminal justice agencies, in both Karachi and Haslingden. The accounts of respondents depict a sense of disenfranchisement and exclusion from the police and institutions of criminal justice. Evaluation of the global self-identity of Muslims marks the emergence of an image of the Muslim as deviant. This image is one deemed by respondents to be constructed by the 'other', and the 'other' is largely seen as the West and non-Muslim. What emerges prominently from the accounts of South Asian Muslims is a sense of being victims. The final Chapter of this text includes an evaluation of this sense of being a victim via an exploration of experiences of Islamophobia in both Britain and Pakistan and also evaluates the research objectives outlined in the introduction before suggesting directions for future research in the field.

Conclusion

This study was framed by specific research objectives outlined in the preface. An evaluation of how far each objective has been realized is apparent throughout the text. However, this chapter recapitulates the salient aspects of the research as well as offering policy recommendations and directions for future research in the field.

There were four main research objectives:

1. To evaluate issues of offending and victimization amongst South Asian Muslims.
2. To develop a comprehensive understanding of Islamic criminal law (al'uqūbāt) and its influence on crime and social control.
3. To explore the nature of racism and Islamophobia and its impact on South Asian Muslims
4. To inform constructive policy strategies in relation to offending and victimization experienced by South Asian Muslims.

Offending and Victimization amongst South Asian Muslims

As highlighted by a comprehensive literature review[1], there exists a gap in contemporary British criminological academic contributions to the understanding of the qualitative experiences of South Asian Muslims and crime. The few specific studies discussed, whilst offering valuable contributions, concentrate either on aspects of social control (Wardak, 2000), intra-racial crime (Webster, 1994) or quantitative data (Mawby and Batta, 1980). No British criminological study of South Asians (Muslim or otherwise), at the time of writing this monograph, has offered a comparative dimension.

The research that does exist tends to suggest that the traditional picture of South Asians as a conformist ethnic group, subject to low levels of criminal offending as compared to other ethnic groups is now in question. The shift in contemporary discourse is towards the construction of a new 'folk devil' in the form of a Muslim criminal (Webster, 1997). This study has argued that the process of constructing criminalized identities can be traced to policies, legislation and practices established during British colonial rule in India (Mahmud, 1999)[2].

---

[1] See Chapter 2.
[2] See Chapter 3.

Whilst criminal statistics for South Asian Muslims can be interpreted as representing relative conformity (FitzGerald, 1997), prison statistics indicate a rapid increase in the registered Muslim prison population (Wilson, 1999).

As discussed in Chapter 2, whilst the public societal face of Islam in the UK is predominantly South Asian, this has not traditionally been reflected in the prison population in the UK (NACRO, 2001). More recent analysis of prison statistics has revealed an interesting trend regarding the South Asian Muslim population. In 2000, Asian male prisoners constituted 42 per cent of the total Muslim male prison population, with 34 per cent declaring Black ethnicity (Guessous, Hooper and Moorthy, 2001). Therefore, whilst the Muslim Asian population in prison does not account for the majority of Muslim prisoners, it does constitute the largest singular Muslim ethnic group, followed closely by Black prisoners (Guessous, Hooper and Moorthy, 2001). This representation is for the prison estate of England and Wales as a whole. However, if we turn to individual prisons the Asian Muslim population is often in the minority, with Black Caribbean prisoners (often converts to Islam) accounting substantially for the Muslim total (Quraishi, 2002b). Muslim prisoners are most likely to be found in the London Prison Service area, and there are higher than average proportions of Muslim prisoners in Eastern and High Security areas (Guessous, Hooper and Moorthy, 2001).

The recent rise in Muslim, and particularly Asian, prisoners may be due to a number of factors. First, the rise may reflect the youthful demographic profile of the Pakistani and Bangladeshi populations in Britain, with more people falling within the peak offending age groups (FitzGerald, 1997). Second, the rise reflects a sea change in criminal justice practices towards Asian and particularly Muslim defendants. The fact the rising numbers pre-date September 11th 2001 is significant but should not distract from the reality of Muslims becoming the subject of increased discriminatory policing, sentencing and negative media reporting (Spalek, 2004).

The institutional setting of prison offers what may be perceived as an unlikely platform for the definition and defence of Muslim human rights (Quraishi, 2002 b). In the wider British society campaigners for Muslim human rights have met with significant resistance (IHRC, 2001). However, prison has arguably provided a legitimizing voice for Muslim civil liberties.

As well as considering Muslims as offenders, by means of an investigation into the lived experiences of individuals in Britain and Pakistan, the study also offers an insight into a commonly shared sense of victimization amongst South Asian Muslims. The research has demonstrated that the ummah, as comprised by the individual, community and global Muslim population, perceives itself to be a victim of religious and racial oppression, ignorance and the construction of Muslims as deviant within Islamophobia. The study confirms the findings of existing research exploring Muslim self-perceptions as oppressed minorities and contributes to literature exploring contemporary Muslim self-identity[3] (Gilliat-Ray, 1998). The dominant discourse is one of exclusion, marginalization and global

---

[3] Also See Modood, 1996; Wardak, 2000; IHRC, 2001.

identity manipulation that gives rise to the construction of the Muslim deviant as a 'fanatic', 'fundamentalist' and 'terrorist' (Runnymede, 1997)[4].

The study also reveals, via a comparative perspective, a complex understanding by South Asian Muslims of the dynamics of crime and its impact upon daily life. The primary research process encouraged the self-reported commission of crime and deviance amongst South Asian Muslims in Pakistan and Britain. The revelation of significant deviance amongst first wave South Asian migrants to the UK demonstrates a process of 'historical amnesia' pertaining to the present elder South Asian Muslim generation.

This is important, for it frames any contemporary discourse about Muslim youth involvement in crime and highlights the fact that social reactions to crime and deviance often follow cyclic, recurrent and hence far from unique trends. In essence, the uncovering of this historical amnesia draws attention to the fact that there was a moral panic regarding the influx of first wave South Asian migrants from the former Commonwealth, which prompted a racialized discourse in Britain (Runnymede, 1997). By the twenty first century those very same migrants are now the subject of a conformist, law abiding, morally robust stereotype in tacit partnership with law enforcement agencies, against a youth population deemed to be wayward, problematic and deviant (Webster, 1997).

What links both older and younger generations of South Asians in Britain are their shared experiences as displaced, marginalized and disenfranchised people. The Runnymede Commission's report of 1997 described Islamophobia as comprising exclusion, discrimination, violence and prejudice. Exclusion includes that from the spheres of politics, government, employment, management and positions of responsibility. Muslims encounter discrimination in employment practices and in the provision of education and health services, whilst being subject to prejudice in the media and in everyday discourse. Violence levelled towards Muslims may be physical or verbal abuse, coupled with damage to property (Runnymede, 1997:11). Therefore, Muslims have been collectively the subjects of racialized constructions and the origin of such may arguably be traced to colonial rule in India by the British (Mahmud, 1999)[5].

The comparative dimension to the work reveals and emphasizes the pervasive impact of such stereotyping of groups of people deemed criminal by birth[6]. The colonization of India impacted not only on the civil and criminal justice system of present-day Pakistan, but also the social construction of persons deemed deviant, colonial practices having been traced into the post-colonial terrain (Mahmud, 1999).

---

[4] See Chapter 5.

[5] See Chapter 3.

[6] See Chapter 3, in particular the discussion of The Criminal Tribes Act (Act XXVII of 1871).

Islamic Criminal Law

As discussed in Chapter 1, Islamic jurisprudence is represented by diverse sources
of learned scholarship and interpretation from within established schools of
thought. Whilst the evaluation of fiqh in great depth was beyond the remit of the
study, the reader nonetheless has been introduced to the salient aspects of
al'uqūbāt.

Since the prime sources of law for the vast majority of the ummah are the
same (namely the Qur'ān and hadīth) there is indeed a common understanding by
Muslims of what is criminal and deviant, harām or halal. However, the study
sought to explore beyond these elementary religious norms to evaluate how much
South Asian Muslims comprehended the dynamics and application of al-'uqūbāt in
their daily lives.

By conducting interviews in an Islamic Republic (Pakistan), the work offers
a unique insight into the comprehension of al-'uqūbāt from within a country where
attempts have been made to apply sharī'ah at State level (Mehdi, 1994). Due to
socio-political dynamics and historical constitutional legacies, al-'uqūbāt in
Pakistan remains little understood by the Muslims of Karachi. The vast majority of
respondents were unable to list or differentiate between the three principal
classifications of criminal offences according to al-'uqūbāt. More respondents were
aware of hadd offences, owing to the introduction of the Hūdūd Ordinances of
1979 during the administration of General Zia ul-Haq. It is in the classification of
ta'zīr crime, where there are no specified penalties in the Qur'ān or Hadīth, where
judicial interpretation could apply to contemporary jurisprudential matters
concerning the ummah.

Similarly, in the UK, most respondents were unaware, or had little
knowledge of al-'uqūbāt, or sharī'ah for that matter. Therefore, it is not an
awareness of the dynamics of Islamic criminal law that influences the day-to-day
life of the South Asian Muslim in the UK. Moreover, it is an individual
interpretation of acceptable and unacceptable behaviour, inspired partly by Islamic
and partly by secular culture, that is of relevance, rather than specific clearly
defined legal prohibitions. Nevertheless, most Muslim respondents had a firm
awareness of the prohibition of murder, the consumption of intoxicants, blasphemy
and fornication as decreed in the Qur'ān.

Racism and Islamophobia and its Impact on South Asian Muslims

A discussion about prohibited behaviour emerged almost exclusively within a
discourse about criminogenic people and places. In Karachi political instability,
strained infrastructures, competition for resources and colonial legacies contributed
to a racialized discourse about criminogenic people and zones[7]. For example, the

---

[7] See Chapter 5.

Afghan migrant to Pakistan has been constructed as a 'dangerous and disordered other'.

In the UK, the South Asian Muslims are the subject of a racialized discourse from a wider British society they deem to be both racist and Islamophobic (Runnymede, 1997). What is clear from this research is the overwhelming sense of being victimized shared by South Asian Muslims in Britain and Pakistan. Islamophobia, or anti-Muslimism[8], is a perceived reality for the people interviewed.

Their articulations point to a perception of global political and social practices that have contributed to a picture of the Muslim as deviant, whether this be a 'terrorist', 'fundamentalist', 'fanatic' or 'oppressor of women'. The study, therefore, permits a unique insight into the self-consciousness of the ummah. It is important for our understanding of recent public disorder incidents in the northern towns of Oldham[9] and Bradford involving South Asian Muslims, for, according to some scholars, when legitimate spaces for expression are blocked (due to oppression) deviance may provide the only acceptable arena within which to act (Presdee, 2000).

To Inform Constructive Policy Strategies in Relation to Offending and Victimization Experienced by South Asian Muslims

This research was grounded in a sense of seeking to improve the social condition of the people who contributed to it. One respondent in Pakistan implored me to entitle the section on Karachi as a 'living hell'[10], whilst the majority would enquire, 'what good will come of this study of yours?'.

In significant or minor ways it is hoped the work will be of worth, first by contributing to a neglected field in contemporary British criminology, and second by suggesting areas where current practices are problematic. There are three main areas of policy-related implications, discussed below.

Ignorance and Racism

In the UK there are widespread misconceptions about Islam as a faith and Muslims as people (Runnymede, 1997). However, there is also ignorance of the law by ordinary citizens (irrespective of ethnicity or religion) (Home Office, 2001).

Cases taken from the fieldwork in Britain include an account from a South Asian elder in Haslingden that offers a persuasive illustration of where positive policy strategies can ease the friction, misunderstanding and conflict that may occur between local police and Muslim communities[11]. This respondent believed the police had been behaving in a prejudicial manner when taking a verbal

---

[8] See Halliday 1999:898.
[9] See IHRC, 2001.
[10] Field notes 5th January 1999, Sharifabad Karachi, Pakistan.
[11] See Chapter 5 for a discussion of this case.

statement from him following an assault on him. His complaint against the police seemed to centre upon the view that instead of arresting the offenders the police were wasting time taking a detailed statement from him. After explaining to him that this was standard behaviour to enable prosecutions to take place, the behaviour of the police became clearer and less threatening to the respondent.

Therefore, the Muslim community, and indeed the broader community in general, could benefit significantly by familiarising themselves with their fundamental civil rights and basic police procedures. Local police-community liaison groups could be a convenient means of disseminating such information, in addition to voluntary legal advice clinics geared not for litigation but for the promotion of broad civil rights and the provision of practical information.

The problem of institutional racism remains an unsightly aspect of contemporary British society. However, some argue that it is from the community level upwards that institutional prejudice spreads, so any policies that can help alleviate racist misconceptions and practices at a local level must be recommended. Certainly such an ideal was put forward by the Runnymede Commission as detailed in their report on Islamophobia (Runnymede, 1997)[12].

Community Policing

In both Karachi and Lancashire, the research revealed demands by respondents for a community policing approach to law enforcement[13]. In Karachi the emphasis was on the ethnic composition of local police and paramilitary, with requests by Mohajirs to have a police force with higher levels of Mohajir ethnic representation. Mohajirs expressed feelings of marginalisation and exclusion from a police force deemed ethnically and culturally different. Paramilitary rangers were viewed as outsiders and unwelcome over-stayers initially charged with border patrol but drafted into the conurbation to police public disorder following riots in Karachi during the administration of General Zia ul-Haq.

Residents in Sharifabad articulated demands for officers recruited locally and of Mohajir ethnicity. It was deemed necessary, by some respondents, for local officers to develop a nexus of familiarity between them and residents in order to establish a sense of trust where presently there was none.

The work of the Citizen's Police Liaison Committee (CPLC) demonstrates an ambitious organizational attempt to build civic trust in the police. This non-governmental organization has now arguably passed beyond the initial objectives of its founders. The CPLC has proved successful in executing duties initially performed by the police and has been granted quasi-legislative powers to police crime in Karachi (CPLC, 1999). However, the police and the paramilitary forces in Karachi are still considered to be driven by, and subject to, significant levels of corruption (Human Rights Commission of Pakistan, 1997). As previously discussed, a corrupt police force is viewed by residents as being located within the broader context of a corrupt political system.

---

[12] See Chapter 8 of this report 'Building Bridges: Inter-community projects and dialogue'.
[13] See Chapter 5.

In Britain, respondents also articulated their preference for community policing. Furthermore, residents welcomed greater Muslim representation in the local police force. More emphasis, however, was placed on policing attitudes and practices than on ethnic composition per se. Residents in Haslingden welcomed the prospect of officers developing stronger links with the local community. Such strong links would be fostered by a return to increased levels of officers on foot-patrol. Calls for such strategies serve to highlight the limited success of existing police-community liaison practices within British Muslim communities.

Statistics and Modern Techniques of Crime Control in Pakistan

One of the latest strategies employed by the CPLC in Karachi is the use of geographical information systems (GIS) mapping of Karachi's districts against crime rates. Although such criminal concordance is reflective of Chicago School techniques first attempted by Shaw and McKay in 1942, (Shaw and McKay, 1942) it also mirrors more contemporary practices used by British constabularies in crime audits conducted pursuant to the Crime and Disorder Act 1998.

Whilst criminologists acknowledge the unreliability of certain criminal statistics, they are nonetheless useful starting points from which to commence criminological enquiry (Savitz, 1982). Britain has experienced a significant history and development of sophisticated collation and analysis techniques for criminal statistics (Jupp, 1989). The same, however, cannot be said for statistical data regarding crime in Pakistan, and the implementation of any crime prevention strategies based on inaccurate statistics remains highly problematic (Khan, Auolakh and Ajmal, 1995). Therefore, before bodies such as the CPLC suggest the deployment of policing resources in Karachi based on statistical projections, they should critically evaluate the mechanisms by which such statistics are generated. Given the significant levels of inaccuracy in criminal statistics in Pakistan, as highlighted by Pakistani criminologists and the accounts by statisticians in the present study[14], criminal justice practitioners and researchers are encouraged to generate qualitative sources to aid evaluation of criminological issues in Pakistan.

The study also suggests that it is not the deployment of policing resources that is essential to curbing crime in Karachi, but rather an eradication of corruption within the institution of the police itself that is required. Qualitative accounts from this study reveal a bankruptcy in any sense of civic trust in the law enforcement and criminal justice agencies of Pakistan[15].

Methodological considerations

The study has presented significant methodological considerations prompted by the investigations[16]. It is hoped that any future project could benefit from the dynamic

---

[14] Interview with statistician at Bureau of Statistics, Karachi, 1999, field notes.

[15] Chapter 5.

[16] See Quraishi, 2003.

experiences encountered in the field. In particular the study highlights practical considerations, such as those related to health and conducting research overseas. The research process enabled an evaluation of existing criminological research methodologies and identified an important gap in guidance on health risks associated with being in the field.

Furthermore, the ethical considerations of researching with family members provided a unique exploration of the sensitivities and benefits of conducting criminological research in such a setting. The theoretical evaluations in the preceding chapter illustrate a genuine redundancy within traditional criminological theory regarding faith-based groups in the UK. Issues of spirituality and religious identity have not been sufficiently explored by criminologists. This neglect is particularly onerous given the priority many Muslims give to religious identity above ethnic identities. This monograph has discussed the marginalization of Muslim communities in relation to the construction of deviant identities. Could the neglect in criminology be attributable to the inadequacies of traditional methodological perspectives regarding the study of faith-groups? If this is the case, there needs to be a concerted effort by scholars to include methods more conducive to inclusion. One such method could involve the granting of a 'voice' to marginalized groups and adopting the dynamic research tools of legal 'story-telling' and qualitative narrative found amongst American CRT scholarship.

Theoretical Perspectives: Critical Race Theory (CRT)

As detailed in chapter six, this study found theoretical root and sustenance within the American critical race theory perspective. This diverse, multi-disciplinary perspective was deemed appropriate to an exploration of displaced peoples unified by experiences of colonisation. Existing contributions by American legal scholars on how the colonial experience impacts on the contemporary social terrain of post-colonialism proved vital to understanding the Muslim communities evaluated by the present study in Britain and Pakistan (Mahmud, 1997).

CRT is still in its developmental stages, and at the time of writing virtually no British research has attempted to incorporate the diversity and richness the approach offers for criminological scholarship.

CRT rejects certain orthodox doctrines of how academic research should progress. American scholars who identify themselves as 'people of colour' have initiated an increasing body of literature employing research methodologies that present insights into the lived experiences of ethnic minority people and aspects of the law (Crenshaw et al., 1995).

In writing about Muslims in my hometown, I felt I was in part also writing about my own lived experiences. In conducting research in Karachi, I felt I was providing an insight to another biographical aspect of my life. Rather than nullifying such subjective accounts, CRT embraces subjectivity as a means towards understanding the lived experiences of 'people of colour', and as a step towards the 'un-telling' of history (West, 1995).

CRT therefore, is one theoretical perspective through which contemporary British criminology can commence enquiry, discourse and theorizing about offending and victimization among the Muslim population.

Future Research

Fieldwork for this study was undertaken prior to the events of September 11th 2001 in the USA. Some British Muslim organizations reported increases in Islamophobic behaviour following the events of this date (IHRC, 2001). Other sources indicate a cumulative sense of increased religious and racial discrimination, following 9/11, among Muslims in British prisons (Quraishi, 2002 b). At the time of writing, Britain has experienced its most fatal terrorist attack on 7th July 2005. The alleged perpetrators of the 7/7 attacks have been identified as British Muslims, three of whom were Asian Muslims. As, with the post 9/11 backlash, Muslims in the UK have experienced increased levels of physical and verbal abuse including attacks on mosques, Asian-owned premises and individuals.

The present study highlights the global sense of victimization perceived by Muslims in the UK and Pakistan. Arguably, there is now a pressing need to evaluate the impact of 9/11 and 7/7 on Muslim communities on a global scale and how it has, if at all, influenced their experiences of victimization and offending.

The exploration of Muslims in prisons provides a most pressing prompt for further research within a number of related directions. First, there is a gap in existing criminological knowledge about the processes through which Islamic law is being interpreted and applied in the British prison estate via the work of the Muslim Advisor to HM Prison Service. Whilst Muslims in society remain free to consult myriad sources about theological issues, the closed institutional environment of the prison has become the unlikely venue for the articulation and application of shari'ah (Quraishi, 2005a). Second, the significance of Muslim converts to Islam in prison must be explored more fully. Conversion is often construed in a negative and sceptical way yet it remains to be seen whether genuine converts to Islam perceive qualitative benefits to their lifestyles once released from prison. Whilst Black Caribbean converts find themselves part of a Muslim 'brotherhood' in prison, what obstacles and challenges await them when they attempt to resettle within Muslim communities which are ethnically and culturally South Asian? Third, prison represents the end point of the criminal justice process, but the impact of Muslim prison populations upon the rest of the criminal justice system remains an under-researched field (Quraishi, 2005a).

This study highlights legislation such as the Criminal Tribes Act 1871, enacted during British colonial rule in India and the pervasiveness of practices that contributed to the construction of criminalized people[17]. The Criminal Tribes Act of 1871 did not operate in isolation to social and working practices, attitudes and policies during British rule in India. It is hoped that further studies could uncover

---

[17] See Chapter 3.

greater evidence of past colonial practices being traced forward into the post-colonial terrain. A particular focus, one that was beyond the remit of the present study, would be an evaluation of penal practices in India and Pakistan and the extent to which present practices are legacies of the Indian Penal Code of 1860.

The exploratory nature of the work in Karachi also generated numerous related potential projects, including the illegal trade in women, illegal drugs, child labour, corruption in criminal litigation and a study of organized crime in Pakistan.

This study represents an academic prompt for further research pertaining to Muslims and crime. It is hoped that future contributions by researchers will seek to further elucidate this largely neglected area of criminology.

Glossary

'Alay Salām/ AS (Arabic)	Peace be upon him
Allāh (Arabic)	God
'Ālim (Arabic)	a learned person in Islām, a scholar
'Arafāt (Arabic)	day of, part of hajj, on the lain of 'Arafāt pilgrims perform the ritual of meditation and worship in remembrance of the Original Covenant
'Askarī (Arabic)	soldier, probable origin of Anglo-Indian work 'lascars' - men from the Indian subcontinent recruited into the Merchant Navy
'Asr (Arabic)	afternoon - particularly afternoon prayers
Biraderi (Urdu)	kinship ties/networks
Deobandi (Urdu)	adherents to Islamic school founded in the village of Deoband, one hundred miles north of Delhi, Uttar Pradesh, India in 1867 by Muhammad Ya'qūb Nanatawi (d.1888) and Muhammad Qāsīm Nanatawi (d.1887)
Diya (Arabic)	compensation
Fajr (Arabic)	dawn - particularly dawn prayers
Fard (Arabic)	obligatory
Fiqh (Arabic)	literally 'understanding' the science of law or jurisprudence
Furqān (Arabic)	one of the names given to the Qur'ān, literally meaning 'The Criterion' (between truth and falsehood)
Ghyrat (Urdu)	frustration
Hadd (Arabic)	prevention, restraint or prohibition
Hadīth (Arabic)	documentation of the practices of the Prophet Muhammad (SAW)

Hajj (Arabic)	pilgrimage to Makkah, Saudi Arabia, one of the five 'pillars' of Islām
Halāl (Arabic)	lawful (opposite of harām)
Hanafī (Arabic)	School of Islamic jurisprudence founded by Abū Hanīfah (699-767 CE) in Kūfa in Iraq
Hanbalī (Arabic)	School of Islamic jurisprudence founded by Ahmad ibn Hanbal (780-855 CE)
Harām (Arabic)	forbidden
Hijrah/AH (Arabic)	The Year of the Flight of the Prophet Muhammad (SAW) from Makkah to Medina in 622 CE and from when the Islāmic calendar commences: 16 July 622 CE (1 AH)
Hijrī (Arabic)	migrant
Hizb ut-Tahrir (Arabic)	fundamentalist youth group in Britain
Hudūd (Arabic)	plural of Hadd, prevention, restraint or prohibition
'Iblīs (Arabic)	Lucifer/Satan
'Īd al-Adhā (Arabic)	Festival of Sacrifice
'Īd al-Fitr (Arabic)	this celebration marks the end of the Holy month of fasting in the Islamic calendar (Ramadān) and the first day of the Islamic month Shawwāl
Ijmā' (Arabic)	consensus of opinion, particularly regarding authenticating of hadīth
Ijtihād (Arabic)	scholarly effort, independent interpretation of the sharī'ah based on the exercise of human reason
'Ishā' (Arabic)	night, particularly night prayers
Ithna 'ashariyyah (Arabic)	Twelvers - Shī'ite sect
Izzat (Urdu)	honour
Ja'farī (Arabic)	Shī'ite School of Islāmic jurisprudence named after Ja'far al-Sādiq, who was a transmitter of hadīth
Jā'iz (Arabic)	permitted

Jamm'at-I-Islami (Arabic)	Islamic movement and political party founded in 1941 by Abul A'la Maududi (d1979) with the objective of transforming Muslim countries into Islamic ideological states
Jibrīl (Arabic)	Angel Gabriel. His duty was to reveal the words of Allah (SWT)
Jihād (Arabic)	struggle for faith
Kaatchi Abaadi(s) (Urdu)	literally meaning raw population(s), shanty town(s), squatter settlement(s) acquired through adverse possession
Kāfir (Arabic)	an unbeliever, literally the 'one who covers'. Islāmically, it refers to the one who covers his/her innate primordial nature and as a result refuses to submit himself/herself to the commands of Allah (SWT)
Kameez (Urdu)	knee-length traditional shirt
Khalīfa (Arabic)	Muslim ruler, the first four after the death of Prophet Muhammad (SAW) were: Abū Bakr (R.A), 'Umar (RA), 'Uthmān (RA) and 'Alī (RA)
Kuffār or Kāfirūn (Arabic)	plural of *kāfir*, unbelievers
Madāris (Arabic)	plural of *madrasah*
Madrasah (Arabic)	Islāmic school/seminary
Makrūh (Arabic)	discouraged behaviour, blameworthy
Mālikī (Arabic)	founded by Mālik bin Anas al-Asbahi (713-795 CE) in Medina, Saudi Arabia
Mandūb (Arabic)	recommended or praiseworthy behaviour
Mohājir (Arabic/Urdu)	literally meaning migrant or refugee. Originating from the Flight of the Prophet Muhammad (SAW) from Makkah to Medina in 622 CE Subsequently asserted as a distinct racial group by the Mohajir Quomi Mahaz (MQM - Migrant National Front) in 1984 in Karachi, Pakistan
Mohola (Urdu)	neighbourhood
Mubāh (Arabic)	permitted behaviour
Murshid (Arabic)	guide

Mustahabb (Arabic)	recommended behaviour
Nisbah (Arabic)	minimum above which zakāt becomes compulsory
Pathan (Urdu/Persian)	Pushto-speaking ethnic group from the North West Frontier Province of Pakistan
Pir (Urdu/Persian)	elder/intercessor, considered to be able to lead devotees on the mystical path - also see shaykh and murshid
Purdah (Urdu)	a curtain or veil. The term applied to the system of seclusion of Muslim women in South Asia
Qādī (Arabic)	judge or legal specialist
Qazi (Arabic)	false accusation of adultery. Subject to criminal legislation in Pakistan in the form of Hudood Order VIII of 1979
Qisās (Arabic)	law of equality or equitable retaliation. Derived from qassā - meaning he cut or he followed his track in pursuit
Qur'ān (Arabic)	literally meaning The Often Recited. It is The Holy Book of Islam, believed by Muslims to be the codification of the divine utterances of the Prophet Muhammad (SAW) between 610 CE and 632 CE
Radi Allahu 'Anha/hi /RA (Arabic)	May Allah (SWT) be pleased with him/her
Rūh-al-Amīn (Arabic)	The Spirit of Truth - Angel Jibrīl (Gabriel)
Rūh-al-Qudūs (Arabic)	The Holy Spirit - Angel Jibrīl (Gabriel)
Sadaqa (Arabic)	welfare due on 'Id al-Fītr
Salāh (Arabic)	prayer
Salallahu 'Alayhi wa Sallam /SAW (Arabic)	May the Peace and Blessings of Allah (SWT) be upon him - Islamic etiquette when mentioning the Prophet Muhammad (SAW)
Sawm (Arabic)	fasting, one of the pillars of Islam
Shāfi'ī (Arabic)	School of Islāmic jurisprudence founded by Muhammad Idrīs al-Shāfi'ī (767-820 CE) in Medina, Saudi Arabia
Shahāda (Arabic)	oral testimony, declaration of faith and the first 'pillar' of Islām. When a person converts to Islām

he/she recites 'I testify that there is no God but Allāh and I testify that Muhammad is the Messenger of Allāh'

Shalwar (Urdu) — loose fitting traditional trousers

Sharī'ah (Arabic) — Islāmic law

Shaykh (Arabic) — elder, intercessor, spiritual guide

Shī'a/Shī'ite (Arabic) — literally 'the followers (of a person) or a party. Particularly the followers of 'Alī (AS), who, as first cousin of the Prophet Muhammad (SAW), and husband of his daughter, Fātimah, regard him and his heirs as the rightful successors of the Prophet Muhammad (SAW)

Shuhrat (Urdu) — valour

Subhana wa ta 'ala /SWT (Arabic) — one of the many ways of glorifying Allah - Glory be to Allah on high, far removed is he from any imperfection

Sunnah (Arabic) — literally 'trodden path', model behaviour from the practices of the Prophet Muhammad (SAW)

Sunnī(s) (Arabic) — follower(s) of the practices of the Prophet Muhammad (SAW)

Sūra(s) (Arabic) — chapter of the Qur'ān

Tablīgh (Arabic) — to preach

Tablīghi Jama'at (Arabic) — Islamic movement established by Maū'lanā Muhammad 'Ilyas, advocating door-to-door revivalist activity

Tarāwīh (Arabic) — supererogatory congregational prayers offered during the holy month of Ramadān

Tawhīd (Arabic) — the belief in the uniqueness of Allāh (SWT) in His attributes and actions

Ta'zīr (Arabic) — literally 'deterrence', crimes for which there are no specified penalties in the Qur'ān or sunnah. The power of discretionary and variable punishment, essential corrective as opposed to the hadd punishments, which are retributive

'Ulamā' (Arabic) — plural of *'alīm*, people with knowledge, scholars

Ummah (Arabic)	the global community of Muslims
'Uqūbāt (Arabic)	Islamic criminal law
Wājib (Arabic)	required
Yawm al-Ākhir (Arabic)	Day of Judgement
Zakāt (Arabic)	almsgiving or compulsory charity, 2.5 per cent of an individual's net savings
Zameen (Urdu)	land
Zaroorat (Urdu)	need, necessity
Zāwiyah(s) (Arabic)	small mosque(s) or prayer room(s)
Zer (Urdu)	money
Zina (Arabic)	fornication, including adultery, the offence of illicit sexual relations. Subject of criminal legislation in Pakistan in the form of the Hudood Ordinance VII of 1979
Zhuhr (Arabic)	midday, particularly midday prayers
Zun (Urdu)	woman

Sources: Ahmed (2002); Coulson (1964); Doi (1984); Mehdi (1994); Metcalf (1995); Ruthven (2000); Schacht (1964); Tayob (1999); Zafar (1999).

Bibliography

Abbot, N. (1967) *Studies In Arabic Literary Papyri II: Qur'ānic Commentary and Tradition*. Oriental Institute Publications lxxxvi. Chicago: University of Chicago.

Abercrombie, N., Hill, S., Turner, B.S. (eds.) (1994) *Dictionary of Sociology*. 3rd ed. Penguin.

Adams, C. (1997) *Across Seven Seas and Thirteen Rivers: life stories of pioneer Sylhetti settlers in Britain*. London. THAP.

Ahmed, A.S. (2002) *Discovering Islam: making sense of Muslim history and society*. London. Routledge.

Albrow, M. (1997) 'Travelling Beyond Local Cultures' in Eade, J. (ed.) (1997) *Living The Global City*. London. Routledge, pp.37-35.

Alexander, C. (2000a) *The Asian Gang: Ethnicity, Identity, Masculinity*. Oxford, Berg.

Alexander, C. (2000b) '(Dis)Entangling the 'Asian Gang': Ethnicity, Identity, Masculinity' in Hesse, B. (ed) (2000) *Un/settled Multiculturalisms*. London, Zed Books.

Ali, I. (1988) *Punjab Under Imperialism 1885-1947* at 1237, in Mahmud, T. (1999) 'Colonialism and Modern Construction', University of Miami Law Review, Vol 23, Jul 1999, pp.1219-1296.

Anstey, V. (1931) *The Economic Development of India* 3rd ed. London. Longman.

Anwar, M. (1996) *British Pakistanis: demographic, social and economic position*. Birmingham City Council Race Relations Unit.

Arberry, A.J. (1964) *The Koran: Interpreted*. Oxford. Oxford University Press.

Azmi, M.M. (LC listing: al-A'zamī, M.M.) (1968) *Studies In Early Hadīth Literature*. *Beirut*: al-Maktab al-Islami

Back, L. (1996) *New Ethnicities and Urban Culture*. New York, UCL & St Martins Press.

Bains, H.S. (1988) 'Southall Youth: an old-fashioned story', in Cohen, P., and Bains, H.S. (eds.) (1988) *Multi-Racist Britain*, London: Macmillan.

Bakhtin, M. (1984) *Rabelais and His World*. Bloomington, Indiana University Press.

Banaji, D.R. (1933) *Slavery In British India*. 2nd Ed. Taraporevala, Sons and Co: Bombay.

Barak, G. (ed.) (1994) *Varieties of criminology readings from a dynamic discipline*. London. Praeger.

Barker, C. (1997) 'Television and the Reflexive Project of The Self: Soaps, Teenage Talk and Hybrid Identities'. *British Journal of Sociology*, Vol 48, No. 4. Routledge. London.

Bayley, C. A. (1996) 'Empire and Information: Intelligence Gathering And Social Communication In India 1780-1870, at 1236, in Mahmud, T. (1999) 'Colonialism and Modern Construction', *University of Miami Law Review*, Vol 23, Jul 1999, pp.1219-1296.

Beckford, J., Gilliat, S. (1998) *Religion In Prison - Equal Rites in a Multi-Faith Society*. Cambridge. Cambridge University Press.

Beckford, J. (2002) 'Research On Minority Faiths In Prison' paper to Conference: Muslim Prisoners In Europe. Swedish Islamic Council, IQRA Trust, Stockholm, 14 January 2002.

Becker, H. (1963) *The Outsiders*. New York. Free Press.

Becker, H. (1964) 'Problems In The Publication of Field Studies' in Vidich, A.J., Bensman, J., Stein, M.R. (eds.) (1964) *Reflections On Community Studies*. New York: Wiley.

Bell, C., Newby, H. (1971) *Community Studies*. London: George Allen and Unwin.

Bell, C. (1977) 'Reflections on the Banbury Re-study' in Bell, C. Newby, H. (eds.) (1977) *Doing Sociological Research*. London: George Allen and Unwin, pp. 47-67.

Bhattacharyya, G., Gabriel, J., Small, S. (2002) *Race and Power: Global Racism in the Twenty-First Century*. London. Routledge.

Bierne, P. (1983) 'Generalisation and its' Discontents' in Nelken, D. (ed.) (1997) *Issues in Comparative Criminology*. Aldershot. Ashgate/Dartmouth.

Bolton, G. (1973) *Britain's Legacy Overseas*. London. Oxford University Press.

Bourjois, P. (1989) 'Crack in Spanish Harlem: culture and economy in the inner city'. *Anthropology Today*, 5(4): 6-11.

Bowling, B., Graham, J. (1994) 'Self-reported offending among young people in England and Wales' in Junger-Tas, J., Terlouw, G-J., Klein, M.W. (eds.) (1994) *Delinquent Behaviour Among Young People in the Western World: First Results of the International Self-Report Delinquency Study*. Kugler. Amsterdam.

Brah, A. (1978) 'South Asian Teenagers In Southall'. *New Community*. Vol 1, 3, 197-206.

Brewer, J. (1990) *Inside the RUC: Routine Policing In A Divided Society*. Oxford. Oxford University Press.

Britton, N.J. (2000) 'Race and Policing: A Study of Police Custody'. *British Journal of Criminology*, Sep 2000; 40:639-658.

Brown, M. (2002) 'Crime, Governance and the Company Raj. The Discovery of Thuggee'. *The British Journal of Criminology 2002*, 42:77-95. OUP.

Bruce, G. (1968) *The Stranglers: The Cult of Thuggee and Its Overthrow In British India* London. Longman.

Bulmer, M. (1982) (ed.) *Social Research Ethics*. London: Macmillan.

Bureau of Statistics (1990) *Sindh Reference Book*. Government of Pakistan.

Bureau of Statistics (2000) Planning and Development Department, Karachi, Government of Pakistan.

Carey, J. T. (1972) 'Problems of access and risk in observing drug scenes' in Douglas, J.D. (ed) *Research On Deviance*. New York. Random House.

Campaign Against Racism and Fascism (1981) *Southall: The Birth of a Black Community*. London Institute of Race Relations and Southall Rights.

Campbell, B. (1993) *Goliath: Britain's Dangerous Places*. London. Methuen.

Cashmore, E., McLaughlin, E. (eds.) (1991) *Out Of Order? Policing Black People*. London. Routledge.

Chigwada, R. (1991) 'The Policing of Black Women' in Cashmore, E., McLaughlin, E. (eds.) (1991) *Out Of Order? Policing Black People*. London. Routledge.

Citizens Police Liaison Committee (1999) *Area Crime Statistics FB Area*. Karachi.CPLC.

Citizens Police Liaison Committee (1999b) *CPLC And It's Role In Combating and Assisting Victims Of Crime*. Pamphlet. Karachi CPLC.

Coffey, A. (1999) *The Ethnographic Self: Fieldwork and The Representation of Identity*. London. Sage.

Cohen, S. (1972) *Folk Devils and Moral Panics: the Creation of Mods and Rockers*. London. Paladin.

Cohen, S.P. (1971) The *Indian Army: It's Contribution To The Development Of A Nation*. University of California Press. Berkeley.

Colier, J. (1979) 'Visual Anthropology'. Chap 19 in Wagner, J. (ed) (1979) *Images of Information: Still Photography In The Social Sciences*. Beverley Hills. London. Sage.

Commission for Racial Equality (1979) *Brick Lane and Beyond: An Inquiry into Racial Strife and Violence in Tower Hamlets*, London. CRE.

Cook, D. and Hudson, B. (eds.) (1993) *Racism and Criminology*. London. Sage.

Cook, M. (2000) *The Koran: a very short introduction.* Oxford. Oxford University Press.

Corbey, R. (1995) 'Ethnographic Showcases, 1870-1930', Chap 4 in Pieterse, J. and Parekh, B. (eds.) (1995) *The Decolonization Of Imagination.* Zed Books.

Coulson, N.J. (1964) *The History of Islamic Law.* Edinburgh. Edinburgh University Press.

Crick, M. (1992) 'Ali and Me, An Essay In Street-corner Anthropology'. In Okely, Callaway, (1992) *Anthropology and Autobiography.* London. Routledge.

Crenshaw, K., Gotanda, N., Peller, G., Thomas, K., (eds.) (1995) *Critical Race Theory: The Key Writings That Formed The Movement.* New York. The New Press.

Crone, P. (1987) *Roman, Provincial and Islamic Law.* Cambridge. Cambridge University Press.

Crow, G. (2000) 'Developing Sociological Arguments Through Community Studies'. *Social Research Methodology*, 2000 Vol 3, No. 3, 173-187.

Crown, I., Cove, J. (1984) 'Ethnic Minorities and The Courts'. *Criminal Law Review.* 1984, July 413-417.

Cruise, S., Dunnachie, N. (1994) *Haslingden Perspectives: Top of the Town.* Rossendale Borough Council. Lancashire. England. UK.

Davis, K. (1951) *The Population Of India And Pakistan.* Princeton. Princeton University Press.

Dahya, B. (1974) 'The Nature of Pakistani Ethnicity in Industrial Cities in Britain' pp.77-117 in Cohen, A. (ed) (1974) *Urban Ethnicity.* London. Tavistock.

Delgado, R. (1995) 'The Imperial Scholar: Reflections on a Review of Civil Rights Literature' in Crenshaw, K., Gotanda, N., Peller, G., Thomas, K., (eds.) (1995) *Critical Race Theory: The Key Writings That Formed The Movement.* New York. The New Press.

Delgado, R., Stefanic, J. (eds.) (2000) *Critical Race Theory: The Cutting Edge*, Philadelphia. Temple University Press.

Delgado, R., Stefancic, J. (2001) *Critical Race Theory: An Introduction.* New York & London, New York University Press.

Demspey, K. (1992) *A Man's Town: inequality between women and men in rural Australia.* Oxford. Oxford University Press.

Desai, P. (1998) 'Spaces of Identity, Cultures of Conflict: The Development of New British Asian Identities', Ph.D. dissertation, Goldsmiths' College, University of London.

Doi, A.R. (1984) Sharī'ah: The Islamic Law. London. Ta-Ha Publications.

Durkheim, Emile (1858-1917) Suicide: a study in sociology. Translated by John A. Spaulding and George. London: Routledge and Kegan Paul 1952.

Dutt, R.P. (1949) *India Today.* Bombay. Peoples Publishing House Ltd.

Dutt, R.C. (1906) *The Economic History Of India.* 2 Vols. London. Kegan Paul.

Elias, N., Scotson, J. (1965) *The Established and The Outsiders.* London: Frank Cass.

Erikson, E. (1980) 'Identity and the Life Cycle' London: W.W. Norton, pp.20-21 in Gilliat-Ray, S. (1998) 'Multiculturalism and Identity: Their Relationship for British Muslims'. *Journal of Muslim Minority Affairs.* Vol 18 No. 2 1998, pp.347-354).

ESRC (2000) *Award Holders Handbook.* Economic and Social Research Council. London. ESRC.

EUMC (2001) *Anti-Islamic reactions within the European Union after the recent acts of terror against the USA: A collection of the EUMC country reports from RAXEN National Focus Points.* European Union Monitoring Centre on Racism & Xenophobia. Vienna, 3 October 2001.

Eze, E. (1997) *Race and the Enlightenment: A Reader.* Oxford. Blackwell.

Fernandes, N. and Fernandes, K. (1994) *Volunteer Contributions To Social Integration At The Grassroots: An Urban or Pavement Dimension.* Urban Resource Center

Karachi, United Nations Volunteer Programme, United Nations Research Institute For Social Development (UNRISD).

FitzGerald, M. (1993) 'Racism: Establishing The Phenomena', Chap 3 in Cook, D. and Hudson, B. (eds.) (1993) *Racism and Criminology*. London. Sage.

FitzGerald, M. (1997) 'Minorities, Crime and Criminal Justice in Britain.' Chapter 2 in Marshall, I. (ed.) (1997) *Minorities, Migrants and Crime- Diversity and Similarity Across Europe and the United States*. Thousand Oaks California. London. Sage.

Flick, V. (1998) *An Introduction To Qualitative Research*. London. Sage.

Frykenburg, R.E. (1999) 'India To 1858', Chap 11 in Winks, R. (ed.) 'The Oxford History Of The British Empire'. Vol. v. Histiography. Oxford. Oxford University Press.

Gardner, K., Shakur, A. (1994) 'I'm Bengali, I'm Asian and I'm Living Here' in Ballard, R. et al. (1994) *Desh Pradesh: The South Asian Presence In Britain*. London. Hurst and Co.

Gelsthorpe, L., Tarling, R., Wall, D. (1999) 'The British Society Of Criminology: Code of Ethics' in Aizlewood, A. and Tarling, R. (1999) *The British Directory of Criminology*. London: ISTD and BSC.

Giarchi, G. (1984) *Between McAlpine and Polaris*. London Routledge and Kegan Paul.

Gilliat-Ray, S. (1998) 'Multiculturalism and Identity: Their Relationship for British Muslims'. *Journal of Muslim Minority Affairs*. Vol 18 No. 2 1998, pp.347-354).

Glass, R. (1966/1989) 'Conflict In Cities' reprinted in *Cliches of Urban Doom and Other Essays*, Oxford. Basil Blackwell.

Goldman, S. (1985) 'Wild In Europe' in Mahmud, T. (1997) 'Migration, Identity and the Colonial Encounter', *Oregan Law Review*, Vol. 76, No. 3, 633-690.

Guardian Newspaper (8/9/99) 'Prison Service Gets First Muslim Adviser', p. 12.

Guardian Newspaper (11/12/99) 'Pakistani Men Three Times As Likely To Be Unemployed', Working Week, p. 21.

Guessous, F., Hooper, N., Moorthy, U. (2001) *Religion in Prison 1999 and 2000*. Home Office National Statistics, London, Crown.

Haddad, Y., Esposito, J. (eds.) (2000) *Muslims on the Americanization Path?* Oxford. Oxford University Press.

Hall, S., Critcher, C., Jefferson, T., Clarke, J., Roberts, B. (eds.) (1978) *Policing the Crisis: Mugging, The State and Law and Order*. London. Macmillan.

Halliday, F. (1992) *Arabs in Exile, Yemeni Migrants in Urban Britain*. London. Tauris.

Halliday, F. (1999) 'Islamophobia Reconsidered'. *Ethnic and Racial Studies* Volume 22 No. 5 September 1999 pp. 892-902.

Hanmer, J., Radford, J. and Stanko, E. (1989) *Women, Policing and Male Violence*. London. Routledge.

Haskey, J. (1990) 'The Ethnic Minority Populations of Great Britain: estimates by ethnic group and country of birth'. *Population Trends*, 60 (Summer): 35-38.

Hesse, B., Rai, D.K., Bennet, C., McGilchrist, P. (1992) *Beneath the Surface: Racial Harassment*. Aldershot: Avebury.

Home Office (1981) *Racial Attacks*, London: HMSO.

Home Office (1991) *Census*. Small Area Statistics: Haslingden Wards. Rossendale Collection: HMSO.

Home Office (1999a) *Prison Statistics England and Wales 1998*. London: HMSO.

Home Office (1999b) *Statistics on Race and the Criminal Justice System*. London: HMSO.

Hood, R. (1992) *Race and Sentencing: A Study in the Crown Court*. Oxford: Clarendon Press.

Heathcote, T.A. (1974) *The Indian Army: The Garrison Of British Imperial India, 1822-1922*. Newton Abbot. David and Charles.

Hesse, B., Rai, D.K., Bennet, C., Gilchrist, P. (1992) *Beneath the Surface: Racial Harassment*. Aldershot. Avebury.

Hirschi, T. (1979) *Causes of Delinquency, California*: Berkeley. London. University of California Press.

Home Office (1991) 'Census 1991: Small Area Statistics, Greenfield Ward'. Rossendale Collection. London, Crown.

Home Office (1999) *Prison Statistics, England and Wales 1998*. London. Crown.

Home Office (2001) *Review of the Criminal Courts of England and Wales*. Lord Justice Auld. London. Crown.

Home Office (2004) *2003 Home Office Citizenship Survey: People, Families & Communities*. Home Office Research Study 289. London, Crown.

Home Office (2005) *2001 Census of England and Wales*. London. Crown

Human Rights Commission of Pakistan (1997) 'Annual Human Rights Report'. Karachi. HRCP. Pakistan.

Humphreys, R.S. (1991) *Islamic History*. Princeton University Press. I.B. Tauris.

Humphries, L. (1970) *Tea Room Trade*. Chicago, Ill. Aldine.

Husbands, C. (1983) *Racial Exclusionism and the City: The Urban Support for the National Front*. London. Allen & Unwin.

Hussain, A. (1996) 'The Karachi Riots of December 1986: Crisis of State and Civil Society in Pakistan', chapter 7 in Das, V. (ed) (1996) *Mirrors of Violence: Communities, Riots and Survivors in South Asia*, Delhi, Oxford University Press.

Hussinat, M.M. (1997) *Leisure and Crime*. New Delhi. Rawat Publications.

Independent, The (2000, June 27), The Tuesday Review 'Meet Britain's Richest Family' page 7.

Institute of Race Relations (1979) 'Police Against Black People': Evidence Submitted to the Royal Commission on Criminal Procedure. London: IRR.

Institute of Race Relations (1987) *Policing Against Black People*. London: IRR.

Institute of Race Relations (2001) 'Counting the Cost: Racial Violence since Macpherson'. London. IRR/ London Borough Grants.

Islamic Human Rights Commission (2001) *The Oldham Riots: Discrimination, Deprivation and Communal Tension in the United Kingdom*. London. IHRC.

James, L. (1995) *The Rise and Fall of the British Empire*. London. Abacas. Little Brown.

Jefferson, T. (1991) 'Discrimination, disadvantage and police-work.' In Cashmore, E., McLaughlin, E. (eds.) *Out of Order? Policing Black People*. London. Routledge.

Joly, D. (1995) *Britannia's Crescent*. Aldershot. Avebury.

Jones, T., (1993) *Britain's Ethnic Minorities*. Policy Studies Institute. London.

Jupp, V. (1989) *Methods of Criminological Research*. Contemporary Social Research: 19. London. Unwin Hyman.

Jupp, V., Davies, P., Francis P. (eds.) (2000) *Doing Criminological Research*. London. Sage.

Juynboll, G.H.A. (1983) *Muslim Tradition: Studies In Chronology, Provenance and Authorship of Early Hadīth*. Cambridge. Cambridge University Press.

Kanwar, M. (1989) *Murder and Homicide In Pakistan*. Vanguard. Lahore.

Keith, M. (2004) 'Identity and the Spaces of Authenticity' chap 35 in Back. L., Solomos, J. (eds.) (2004) *Theories of Race and Racism*. London. Routledge.

Khan, R.A.R, Aoulakh, A.M.A, Ajmal, K.M. (1995) *Crime and Criminology: A Comparative Study In The Islamic Republic of Pakistan*. The Frontier Publications. Lahore.

Khan, S.A. (1999) *Principles of Criminal Law*. Umer Khurram Printers. Lahore.

Knowles, L.C.A. (1924) *The Economic Development Of The British Overseas Empire*. 2 Vols. London. Routledge and Sons.

Kool, M., Verboom D., Linden, J. (1988) *Squatter Settlements In Pakistan.* Karachi. Vanguard.

Kopf, D. (1980) 'Hermeneutics versus History'. JAS XXXIX 3 May 1980, pp.495-505.

Lancashire County Council (1993) 'Local Area Department Statistics'. Rawtenstall Library Archive.

Lavie, S. and Swedenburg, T. (eds.) (1996) *Displacement, Diaspora and Geographies of Identity.* Durham. London. Duke University Press.

Lawrence, B. (2000) 'Mixed-Race Urban Native Identity: Surviving A Legacy Of Genocide'. *Kinesis, Native Women's Issue,* Dec/Jan 2000, 15, 18.

Lings, M. (1983) 'Muhammed: His Life Based On The Earliest Sources' 81-84 in Mahmud, T. (1997) '*Migration, Identity and the Colonial Encounter',* Oregan Law Review, Vol. 76, No. 3, 633-690.

Lee, R.M., Renzetti, C. (1990) 'The Problems of Researching Sensitive Topics: An Overview and Introduction'. American Behavioral Scientist, 33: 510-28.

Lee, R.M. (1999) *Doing Research On Sensitive Topics.* London. Sage.

Lewis, P. (1994) *Islamic Britain: Religion, Politics and Identity among British Muslims.* London. I.B. Tauris.

Lofland, J., Lofland, L.H. (1995) *Analysing Social Settings: A guide to Qualitative Observation and Analysis.* 3rd Ed. California. Wadsworth.

Lombroso, C. (1876) *L'Uomo Delinquente,* first published (1876) 5th and Final edition (1897). Torino. Bocca.

Macey, M. (1999) 'Class, Gender and Religious Influences On Changing Patterns of Pakistani Muslim Male Violence in Bradford'. *Ethnic & Racial Studies,* 22, 5, September, 845-66.

Macpherson, W. (1999) *The Stephen Lawrence Inquiry.* Report of an Inquiry by Sir William Macpherson of Cluny. Advised by Tom Cook, the Right Reverend Dr John Sentamu and Dr Richard Stone. Cm 4262-1. London: Home Office.

Mahmud, T. (1997) 'Migration, Identity and the Colonial Encounter', Oregan Law Review, Vol. 76, No. 3, 633-690.

Mahmud, T. (1999) 'Colonialism and Modern Constructions Of Race: A Preliminary Enquiry', University of Miami Law Review 53:4, pp.1219-1246. University of Miami.

Mair, G. (1986) 'Ethnic Minorities, Probation And The Magistrates Court', *British Journal Of Criminology,* Vol 26, No. 2, April 1986, 147-155.

Mannheim, I., Winter, D. (eds.) (1996) *Pakistan Handbook.* Trade and Travel Publications. Bath. Footprint.

Marshall, I. (ed.) (1997) *Minorities, Migrants and Crime - Diversity and Similarity Across Europe and the United States.* Thousand Oaks California. London. Sage.

Mason, P. (1974) 'A Matter of Honour: An Account of the Indian Army, Its Officers and Men, p.1232 in Mahmud, T. (1999) 'Colonialism and Modern Construction', *University of Miami Law Review,* Vol. 23, Jul 1999, pp.1219-1296.

Massey, D. (1998) ' The Spatial Construction of Youth Subcultures' chap 7 in Skelton, T., Valentine, G. (eds.) (1998) *Cool Places: Geographies of Youth Culture.* London: Routledge.

Mawby, B., Batta, L. (1980) *Asians and Crime: The Bradford Experience.* Scope Communications. Middlesex.

Mehdi, R. (1994) *The Islamization Of The Law in Pakistan.* Richmond. Curzon.

Merton, R.K. (1957) *Social Theory and Social Structure.* New York. Free Press of Glencoe; London. Collier-Macmillan.

Metcalf, B.D. (1995) 'Deoband' in J. Esposito (ed.) *Oxford Encyclopedia of the Modern Islamic World.* New York. Oxford University Press.

McConville, M., Baldwin, J. (1982) 'The Influence of Race on Sentencing'. Criminal Law Review. October 1982, 652-658.

Mills, C.W. (1956/1959) *The Power Elite*, London: Unwin Hyman.

Modood, T. (1990) 'British Asian Muslims and the Salman Rushdie Affair'. *Political Quarterly*. 61(2) 143-160.

Modood, T. (1992) 'The End of Hegemony: The Concept of 'Black' and British Asians'. Centre for Research In Ethnic Relations Annual Conference. University of Warwick, 3-5 April.

Modood, T. (1996) *Not Easy Being British: Colour, Culture and Citizenship*. London: Runnymede Trust/Trentham.

Modood, T., Berthoud, R. (eds.) (1997) *Ethnic Minorities In Britain: Diversity and Disadvantages*. London. Policy Studies Institute.

Mol, H. (1976) *Identity and the Sacred*. Oxford. Blackwell.

Montoya, M.E. (2000) 'Silence and Silencing: Their Centripetal and Centrifugal Forces in Legal Communication, Pedagogy and Discourse', *33 MICH. J. L. REFORM 263 (2000) and 5 MICH. J. RACE & L. 847 (2000)*.

Moore, R. (1982) *The Social Impact of Oil*. London. Routledge and Kegan Paul.

Moorhouse, G. (1983) *India Britannica*. London. Paladin.

Murphy, D. (1987) *Tales from Two Cities: Travel of Another Sort*. London. Murray.

NACRO (2000) *Race and Prisons: A Snapshot Survey*. May 2000. NACRO. London.

Naoroji, D. (1901) *Poverty and Un-British Rule In India*. London. S.n.

NCCL (1980) Southall 23 April 1979, London: NCCL.

Nielsen, J. (1992) *Muslims in Western Europe*. Edinburgh. Edinburgh University Press.

Nigosian, S. (1987) *Islam The Way of Submission*. Crucible Publishing UK.

Nelken, D. (ed.) (1997) *Issues in Comparative Criminology*. Aldershot. Ashgate/Dartmouth.

Nelken, D. (1997) 'Whom Can You Trust? The Future of Comparative Criminology' Chapter 20 in: Nelken, D. (ed.) (1997) *Issues in Comparative Criminology*. Aldershot. Ashgate/Dartmouth.

Norris, C. (1993) 'Some Ethical Considerations on Fieldwork With the Police' in Hobbs, D., May, T. (eds.) (1993) *Interpreting the Field: Accounts of Ethnography. Clarendon Press*: Oxford.

Omissi, D. (1994) *The Sepoy and The Raj*. Basingstoke. Macmillan with King's College London.

Pakes, F. (2004) *Comparative Criminal Justice*. Cullompton, Devon, Willan.

Peach, C. (1994) 'Current Estimates of the Muslim Population of Great Britain', paper given to the seminar on Statistics and the UK Religious Communities at Derby University in May 1994 in Lewis, P. (1994) Islamic Britain: religion, politics and identity among British Muslims. London. I.B. Tauris.

Peach, C. (ed.) (1996) *Ethnicity in the 1991 Census: the ethnic minority populations of Great Britain*. London. HMSO.

Pieterse, J., Parekh, B. (eds.) (1995) *The Decolonization Of Imagination*. London. Zed Books.

Powers, D.S. (1986) *Studies In Qur'ān and Hadīth: The Formation of The Islamic Law Of Inheritance*. Berkeley. London. University of California.

Presdee, M. (2000) *Cultural criminology and the carnival of crime*. London. Routledge.

Punch, M. (1979) *Policing The Inner City*. London. Macmillan.

Q-News (1996) 'Poverty and Islamophobia and British Muslims' 19 April-9 May, page 3.

Quraishi, M. (2002a) 'A Comparative Study: Muslim Prisoners In France and England' paper to Conference: Muslim Prisoners In Europe. Stockholm. Swedish Islamic Council and IQRA Trust. 14 January 2002.

Quraishi, M. (2002b) *Muslims In Prison: A European Challenge* unpublished field notes, ESRC project, applicants Beckford and Joly, Department of Sociology and CRER, University of Warwick, project completion: 2003.

Quraishi, M. (2003) 'Muslims and Crime: A Comparative Criminological Study of South Asian Muslims in Britain & Pakistan'. Ph.D. Thesis. Centre for Comparative Criminology & Criminal Justice, University of Wales, Bangor.

Quraishi, M. (2005a) 'Muslims in Prison: A Barometer for British Ethnic Relations and Race Relations?' paper to Conference: Ethics, Religion and Prisons' Faculty of Theology, University of Aarhus, Denmark, 19-21 May, 2005.

Quraishi, M. (2005b) 'No-Go Zones: Racially Constructed Urban Spaces in Britain and Pakistan' paper to Conference: British Society of Criminology' Re-Awakening the Criminological Imagination', University of Leeds Law School, 12-14 July, 2005.

Ragin, J., Hein, J. (1993) 'The Comparative Study of Ethnicity: Methodological and Conceptual Issues' in Stanfield, J., Dennis, R. (eds.) (1993) *Race and Ethnicity In Research Methods.* Newbury Park California. London. Sage.

Ramesh. R. (1998) 'Police blame racist attacks on Asians'. October 3rd, page 14, *The Guardian.*

Ray, L., Smith, D., Wastell, L. (2004) 'Shame, Rage and Racist Violence'. *British Journal of Criminology*, May 2004; 44: 350-368.

Raychaudhuri, T. (1999) 'India, 1858 to the 1930s', Chap 12 in Winks, R. (ed.) 'The Oxford History Of The British Empire'. Vol. v. Histiography Oxford. Oxford University Press.

Rayside, D. (1991) *A Small Town in Modern Times.* Montreal and Kingston: McGill-Queen's University Press.

Reiner, R. (1985) *The Politics Of The Police.* Brighton: Wheatsheaf.

Rex, J., Moore, R. (1967) *Race, Community and Conflict.* London. Institute of Race Relations. Oxford University Press.

Ritzer, G. (1994) *The McDonaldization of Society.* Thousand Oaks: Pine Forge Press.

Robinson, F. (1999) 'The British Empire and The Muslim World', Chap 17 in Winks, R. (ed.) 'The Oxford History Of The British Empire'. Vol. v. Histiography Oxford University Press.

Rossendale Free Press, 'New help for Asians to topple barrier' 14/01/78.

Rossendale Free Press, 'Overtime rush - for lessons in English' 18/03/78.

Rossendale Free Press, 'Help sought to fell language barrier' 28/04/79.

Rossendale Free Press, 'Boss in fight for 'illegal' migrant: 'I would stake my life on him' 9/02/80.

Rossendale Free Press, 'Leaflets make life easier for immigrants' 26/01/85.

Roshier, B. (1989) *Controlling Crime. The Classical Perspective In Criminology.* Milton Keynes. Open University Press.

Runnymede Trust (1997) 'Report On British Muslims And Islamophobia' *The Runnymede Trust Commission* Professor Gordon Conway, Chair, Runnymede Trust.

Ruthven, M. (2000) *Islam.* Oxford. Oxford University Press.

Said, E.W. (1978) *Orientalism.* New York. Pantheon Books.

Said, E.W. (1993) *Culture and Imperialism.* London. Chatto and Windus.

Salahi, A. (ed.) (1994) *Our Dialogue Plus.* Arab News. Jeddah.

Sandhu, H.J. (1983) 'India' chapter 16 in Johnson, E.H. (ed) (1983) *International Handbook of Contemporary Developments in Criminology.* Westport. Connecticut, Greenwood Press.

Sartre, J-P (2001) *Colonialism and Neocolonialism.* Routledge. London & New York.

Savitz, L. (1982) *Official Statistics.* New York. John Wiley.

Sayyid, S. (2002) 'Muslims in Britain: Towards a Political Agenda'. Page 87 in Seddon, M.S., Hussain, D., Malik, N. (2002) *British Muslims: Loyalty and Belonging*. The Islamic Foundation, (UK) & The Citizen Organising Foundation.

Schacht, J. (1950) *The Origins of Muhammedan Jurisprudence*. Oxford. Clarendon Press.

Schacht, J. (1964) *An Introduction To Islamic Law. Oxford*. Clarendon Press.

Shaheed, F. (1996) 'The Pathan-Muhajir Conflicts, 1985-6: A National Perspective', chapter 8 in Das, V. (ed) (1996) *Mirrors of Violence: Communities, Riots and Survivors in South Asia*, Delhi, Oxford University Press.

Sibley, D. (1995) *Geographies of Exclusion. Society and Difference In The West*. London. Routledge.

Sieber, J.E., Stanley, B. (1988) 'Ethical and Professional Dimensions of Socially Sensitive Research'. *American Psychologist* 43: 45-49.

Silverman, D. (ed.) (1997) *Qualitative Research*. London: Sage.

Singha, R. (1993) 'Providential Circumstances: The Thuggee Campaign of the 1830s and Legal Innovation', 27 *Modern Asia Studies* 83.

Shamsi, S. (1998) 'Illegal Arms In Profusion' *Dawn Newspaper*, 27 Feb, Karachi, Pakistan.

Shaw, C., McKay, H. (1942) *Juvenile Delinquency and Urban Areas*. Chicago. University of Chicago Press.

Skogan, W. (1990) *The Police and Public in England and Wales*. Home Office Research Study no. 117. London: HMSO.

Small, S. (2004) 'Researching 'mixed race' experience under slavery', chapter five in Bulmer, M., Solomos, J. (2004) *Researching Race and Racism*. London, Routledge.

Smart, B. (ed) (1999) *Resisting McDonaldization*. London: Sage.

Smith, D.J., Gray, J. (1983) 'The Police In Action, Police and Black People in London', vol.iv, London: Policy Studies Institute, p. 332 in Cashmore, E., McLaughlin, E. (eds.) (1991) *Out Of Order? Policing Black People*. London. Routledge.

Smith, D.J. (1987) 'Policing and Urban Unrest' in Benyon, J., Solomos, J. (eds.) *The Roots of Urban Unrest*. London. Pergamon.

Smith, S.J. (1989) *The Politics of 'Race' and Residence: Citizenship, Segregation and White Supremacy in Britain*. Cambridge. Polity.

Smith, V.A. (1998) *The Oxford History of India*. Oxford. Oxford University Press. 4th ed, 5th impression.

Spalek, B. (2002) *Islam, Crime and Criminal Justice*. London, Willan.

Spalek, B. (2004) 'Muslims in the UK and the Criminal Justice System', Chapter 4 in Open Society Institute (2004) *Muslims in the UK: Policies for Engaged Citizens*. OSI/ EU Monitoring Programme Hungary, Budapest & New York.

Stallybrass, P., White, A. (1997) 'From Carnival To Transgression [1986]' in Gelder, K., Thornton, S. (eds.) (1997) *The Subcultures Reader*. Routledge.

Stevens, P, Willis, C. (1979) *Race, Crime and Arrests*. Home Office Research Study no.58. London. HMSO.

Stokes, E. (1959) *The English Utilitarians and India*. Oxford. Clarendon Press.

van Swaaningen, R. (1997) *Visions From Europe*. Sage.

Sztompka, P. (1990) 'Conceptual Frameworks In Comparative Enquiry: Divergent or Convergent' in: Albrow, M., King, E. (eds.) (1990) *Globalisation, Knowledge and Society*. London. Sage.

Tayob, A. (1999) *Islam: A Short Introduction*. Oxford. Oneworld.

Urban Resource Centre (2005) http://www.urckarachi.org/home.htm, 28/2/05.

Virdee, S. (1995) *Racial Violence and Harassment*. London. Policy Studies Institute.

Wagner, J. (ed) (1979) *Images of Information: Still Photography In The Social Sciences*. Beverley Hills. London. Sage.

Walker, M., Jefferson, T., Senevirate, M. (1989) 'Race and criminal justice in a provincial city' unpublished paper presented to British Criminology Conference, Bristol Polytechnic, July, in Cashmore, E., McLaughlin, E. (eds.) (1991) *Out Of Order? Policing Black People*. London. Routledge.

Wardak, A. (2000) *Social Control and Deviance: A South Asian Community In Scotland*. Aldershot. Ashgate.

Waters, R. (1990) *Ethnic Minorities and the Criminal Justice System*. Aldershot. Avebury.

Webster, C. (1994) *Youth Crime, Victimization and Harassment. The Keighley Crime Survey*. A Paper In Community Studies no. 7. Centre for Research. Department of Applied and Community Studies, Bradford and Ilkley Community College.

Webster, C. (1997) 'The Construction Of British Asian Criminality'. International Journal Of The Sociology Of Law, Vol 25, pp.65-86.

Webster, C. (2001) 'Representing Race and Crime', *Criminal Justice Matters*, No 43, Spring, 16-17.

West, C. (1995) foreword in Crenshaw, K., Gotanda, N., Peller, G., Thomas, K. (eds.) (1995) *Critical Race Theory: The Key Writings That Formed The Movement*. The New Press, New York.

Williams, G. (1991) *The Welsh In Patagonia*. Cardiff. University of Wales Press.

Wilmott, P. (1986) *Social Networks, Informal Care and Public Policy*. London. Policy Studies Institute.

Wilson, D. (1999) 'Muslims In Prison' in El-Hassan, S. (ed.) (1999) *Practising Islam in Prison*. London. The IQRA Trust.

Wilson, D. (2000) *Prison Imams - An ethno-graphic study*. London. The IQRA Trust.

Winks, R. (ed.) *The Oxford History Of The British Empire*. Vol. v. Histiography Oxford. Oxford University Press.

Yancey, W.L., Rainwater, L. (1970) 'Problems in the ethnography of the urban underclasses' in Habenstein, R.W. (ed.) (1970) *Pathways to Data*. Chicago. Aldine.

Yang, A.A. (ed.) (1985) 'Crime and Criminality in British India' in Mahmud, T. (1999) 'Colonialism and Modern Construction', University of Miami Law Review, Vol 23, Jul 1999, pp.1219-1296.

Zafar, M.D. (1999) *Islamic Education*. Aziz. Lahore.

Zahur-Ud-Din, Z. (1997) *New Islamic laws 1979*. Umer Khuraam Printers. Lahore.

Zuni Cruz, C. (2000) '*Whose Law Is It Anyway? The Future of Tribal Law and Programs: [Re] Incorporating Tribal Customs and Traditions into Tribal Law*,' paper presented to Federal Bar Association Indian Law Conference April 6 2000.

Index